Published with the
financial support of the
Scottish Arts Council

DAVID HUME

DAVID HUME

BICENTENARY PAPERS

edited by G. P. Morice

UNIVERSITY OF TEXAS PRESS

AUSTIN

International Standard Book Number 0–292–71515–3
Library of Congress Catalog Card Number 77–81915

Copyright © 1977 by Edinburgh University Press

Printed in Great Britain by
W. & J. Mackay Limited
Chatham

Preface

FROM THE 9th to the 14th August, 1976, the University of Edinburgh, in conjunction with its Institute for Advanced Studies in the Humanities, sponsored a conference in Edinburgh to commemorate the bicentenary of the death of David Hume. It was attended by some 200 scholars from Europe, North America, Asia and Australasia, and is remembered by many as a very happy occasion, prompting the speculation that some portion of the great philosopher's 'good nature and good humour' and 'gaiety of temper' descends upon those who devote themselves to the study of his works.

There are printed here, in the order in which they were delivered to the conference, seven of the eight invited plenary session addresses. The eighth paper was withdrawn at the author's request. There follows a selection from those seminar papers that have not been printed elsewhere, grouped according to topic. A number of the papers have been revised for publication, and some of the seminar papers have been expanded from the very severe limits that were imposed upon them by the exigencies of the conference time-table.

I wish to thank Professor W. H. Walsh, chairman of the Hume Conference Organising Committee, for help and advice concerning the publication of the book. I am particularly indebted to Mr Walter Cairns, of the Edinburgh University Press, for his assistance in preparing the papers for publication.

G.P.M. *Edinburgh, March* 1977

o

Contents

Abbreviations

Treatise   *A Treatise of Human Nature*, ed. L. A. Selby-Bigge,
Oxford 1888

Enquiries   *Enquiries Concerning the Human Understanding and
Concerning the Principles of Morals*,
ed. L. A. Selby-Bigge, 3rd edition with text revised
by P. H. Nidditch, Oxford 1975

Dialogues   *Dialogues Concerning Natural Religion*,
ed. Norman Kemp Smith, 2nd edition, Edinburgh 1947

Letters   *The Letters of David Hume*, ed. J. Y. T. Greig,
2 vols, Oxford 1932

Hume and the Legacy of the Dialogues

THE *Dialogues concerning Natural Religion*,[1] David Hume's posthumous work, like the *Treatise of Human Nature*, his first work, has
belatedly come into its own during our lifetime. The prime mover of
both of these achievements was Professor Norman Kemp Smith of the
University of Edinburgh. These two works are now generally regarded
as Hume's philosophical masterpieces, and Hume himself is more and
more frequently being called the greatest of British philosophers.
Although there is something remotely approaching a consensus regarding the teachings of the *Treatise*, there is little accord regarding
the teachings of the *Dialogues*. The basic reasons for this lack of agreement remain to be explored, and it is my intention to bring them out
into the open for study and explication.

The *Treatise* was the product of more than ten years of thinking and
composition of a young man, while the *Dialogues* was composed by a
middle-aged man and was still being revised twenty-five years later by
an elderly one, with publication always delayed. The delay was due to
the unanimous and repeated insistence of intimate and overly cautious
friends that the work be published only posthumously, or better, not at
all—and Hume himself, after much agonizing reappraisal, became
discreet enough to comply with the former alternative. It is mistaken,
however, to argue that the *Dialogues* was designed to be published
posthumously. Indeed, even during his terminal illness Hume momentarily harboured the thought of immediate publication but proved too
feeble for the effort. Finally, since neither his printer, William Strahan,
nor his best friend, Adam Smith, was willing to risk even posthumous
publication, that duty devolved upon his favourite and devoted nephew
David. The work appeared in 1779. (Adam Smith, I am inclined to
believe, had read the manuscript correctly and realized that it is far
more than the discussion of natural religion specified in the title.)

Even in the relatively tolerant intellectual society of eighteenth-
century Britain, prudence demanded that any attack on religion,
natural or revealed, especially natural *and* revealed as in the present
case, had better be written by indirection, that is, ironically; and the
philosophical dialogue provided an eminently suitable vehicle as well as
a sound classical precedent. Ever since the distant age of Plato, there
has been a close affinity between the philosophical dialogue and the
rhetorical device of irony, that is, 'a figure of speech wherein the real

meaning is concealed or contradicted by the words used'. In addition, Hume grew up during the heyday of satire and relished the writing of Swift, a master of ironic modes. It is not surprising, then, though virtually unnoticed, that irony is an indispensable factor of the *Dialogues* and holds, in truth, the key to its basic teachings.

Hume had been exposed to governmental and ecclesiastical menaces over the *Philosophical Essays concerning Human Understanding* (1748) and the *Four Dissertations* (1757).[2] Throughout life he had to endure social obloquy, above all, in his native hidebound Scotland. Quite naturally, therefore, and fully aware that he was living under the threat of external pressure, Hume made some prudential concessions to the accepted opinions of his time. It is in this light that one can understand Hume's resolution that Philo, the sceptic of the *Dialogues*, who would almost certainly be identified with the author, should not appear to win the debate, while Cleanthes, whose arguments and convictions were more closely aligned with those of Hume's public, should be named the victor. This prudential stratagem, which avoided an open rupture with popular prejudices, remains to this day a stumbling-block and a source of misunderstanding to those readers who have failed to recognize Hume's irony.

The *Dialogues concerning Natural Religion*, as an example of the philosophical dialogue, is beyond dispute the most brilliant in the English language, surpassing Berkeley's *Three Dialogues between Hylas and Philonous* (1713), the only serious contender. It has repeatedly been asked: If there is nothing fundamentally new in the *Dialogues* (which is the fact, with the exception of a new concept of *nature*), why was it written at all, and, after so much hindrance, published? This is surely an obtuse question. Religion, whether personal, philosophical, or as a social phenomenon, was one of the dominant interests of Hume throughout his life; and it may well be that the intense interest of the schoolboy in religion, as we learn from Boswell (p. 76) impelled the youth into the paths of philosophy. For is not speculative theism, as both Cleanthes and Philo remind us, 'only a branch of philosophy' (p. 138 & 223)? So the *Dialogues* was designed to be the fulfilment of Hume's thoughts on religion and to round out the presentations in Sections x and xi of the *Enquiry concerning Human Understanding* and in *The Natural History of Religion*, as well as in the two posthumous essays 'Of Suicide' and 'Of the Immortality of the Soul'.

The *Dialogues* is the final marriage of philosophy with art that had been Hume's ambition throughout a long career as man of letters. And it is this element of art that elevates the *Dialogues* from a strictly philosophical discourse that can be summarized to a literary discourse that cannot be summarized but that must be viewed in the totality of its presentation to be appreciated artistically as well as comprehended intellectually. The *Dialogues* is, if not original in the narrowest sense, Hume's most mature work on religion, in brief, his philosophical testament. Hume prized it, I believe, as the best thing he had ever written.[3] The dialogue form, which he had mastered through two previous experiments, provided him with the opportunity for an artistic display of the dialectic of ideas and images. As the interlocutors present their cases, or counter those of others, the pros and cons of the argument produce that state of ambivalence so congenial to the minds of sceptical thinkers such as Hume—whose propensity was to doubt rather than to believe.

The present essay is not designed to assess each argument of the three interlocutors and to pronounce it good or bad philosophy—that is the philosophical approach, which in its purest form is concerned only with the text, ideas and development, and is unconcerned with related historical information exclusive of other works by the same author. Rather, let us attempt what has not been attempted before, at least fully, consistently, and rigorously, that is, to approach the *Dialogues* from the biographical point of view, together with a survey of its artistic structure, and, inevitably, a modicum of philosophical analysis, seeking to determine whether a resolution may be found of the several disputed areas. At the very least, the biographical approach will have the merit of eliciting the author's intentions and other pertinent views insofar as they are available through external evidence.[4] At best, it may provide an altogether new reading of the *Dialogues*.

At the proper time, I shall present what, in my judgment, are the teachings of the *Dialogues*, including an interpretation of the peroration, which is Philo's version of the theistic argument and also of what I choose to call Philo's ironic 'prayer'. These conclusions are the rightful products of Hume's mitigated scepticism,[5] his fundamental philosophical position. At that final stage we shall have achieved, I trust, understanding of the 'legacy' itself, the ironic personal message of religious philosophy that Hume was determined to pass on to posterity.

To begin with the beginning: Hume's intentions, expressed and implicit. First of all, he has a fully articulated concept of what a dialogue should be. The 'spirit of dialogue', he declares, demands that 'a tolerable equality [be] maintained among the speakers'.[6] To be avoided is 'the appearance of *author* and *reader*', or even worse, of '*pedagogue* and *pupil*' (p. 127), and, above all, that 'vulgar Error...of putting nothing but Nonsense into the Mouth of the Adversary'.[7] (Incidentally, Berkeley's Hylas is generally regarded as a man of straw, a view that Hume presumably shared.)

The author is, quite naturally in Hume's opinion, one of the characters. In a letter written to a critic of his 'A Dialogue',[8] appended to the

Enquiry concerning the Principles of Morals (1751), where there are
two disputants, Hume complains: 'But you impute to me both the
Sentiments of the Sceptic, & the Sentiments of his Antagonist; which
I can never admit of. *In every Dialogue, no more than one Person can
be supposed to represent the Author*' (my italics). This last statement
has not, to the best of my recollection, been cited hitherto as material
to the reading of the *Dialogues*. Yet, one way or the other, it is of more
than passing consequence.

Who, then, represents Hume in the *Dialogues*? There really should
be no dispute on this question because the autobiographical evidence is
conclusive. Yet dispute there is and, oddly enough, not entirely confined to those readers who neglect the evidence. In a letter[9] of 10 March
1751 to his conservatively-minded friend, Gilbert Elliot of Minto,
Hume makes it positive that he himself is represented by Philo: 'I have
often thought, that the best way of composing a Dialogue, wou'd be for
two Persons that are of different Opinions about any Question of Importance, to write alternately the different Parts of the Discourse, &
reply to each other. By this Means, that vulgar Error would be avoided,
of putting nothing but Nonsense into the Mouth of the Adversary: And
at the same time, a Variety of Character & Genius being upheld, woud
make the whole look more natural & unaffected. Had it been my good
Fortune to live near you I shou'd have taken on me the Character of
Philo, in the Dialogue, which you'll own I coud have supported
naturally enough: And you woud not have been averse to that of
Cleanthes.'

Earlier in his letter Hume had provided his friend with an account of
the development of his scepticism, which became, of course, Philo's
scepticism: 'Doubts stole in, dissipated, return'd, were again dissipated,
return'd again; and it was a perpetual struggle of a restless Imagination
against Inclination, perhaps against Reason.' Quite obviously, Hume
did not need assistance 'to strengthen that Side of the Argument'. On
the contrary, he was soliciting Elliot's assistance in strengthening the
argument of Cleanthes, the 'Antagonist'.

In short, by his own testimony, Hume is Philo and Philo alone.[10]
That there are several passages of Cleanthes and even a couple of Demea
that are also Hume's own is beside the point. The views of the three interlocutors need not be mutually exclusive, any more than those would
be, in actual life, of three friends discussing religious philosophy from
three different points of view. To avoid 'putting Nothing but nonsense
into the Mouth of the Adversary' the interlocutors are left free, not
only to disagree with one another, but on occasion to agree with one
another. Therefore, by way of example, Hume ironically allows
Cleanthes, rather than Philo, to refute Demea's *a priori* proof of the

being on a God (p. 189). Furthermore, Cleanthes and Demea are used for artistic as well as ideational and logical effect in the structure of the *Dialogues*. Statements of both, for instance, are employed as plants to anticipate Philo's sceptical conclusions at the close of Part XII. Cleanthes, as early as Part I, remarks incredulously: 'You propose then, Philo,... to erect religious faith on philosophical scepticism' (p. 132); and Demea, attacking Cleanthes' empirical analogical argument in Part VI, cries in utter outrage: 'To all the purposes of life, the theory of religion becomes altogether useless...' (p. 170).

The *Dialogues*, it must be remembered, is imaginary philosophical conversation and, therefore, does not pretend to have the logical completeness of a philosophical treatise. In consequence, a ready but not entirely satisfactory answer can be made to a vexing question frequently asked by modern philosophers: If Hume is truly represented by Philo but has also placed several of his views in the mouths of Cleanthes and Demea, how can we recognize his personal convictions on religion? The answer is plainly that we cannot—certainly not without considerable effort on our part and even then not definitively. The conclusions of a sceptic—even a mitigated sceptic—cannot be summarized in a one-two-three pattern or creed if for no other reason than that a sceptic, unlike other types of philosophers, is not altogether stable in his thinking, is perpetually rethinking his principles. Scepticism, first and last, is a frame of mind, neither a collection nor a system of doctrines, and it frequently ends with suspense-of-judgment. The best we can do is to familiarize ourselves with the mind of the philosopher and also with his personality. Then, and only then, can we be be reasonably sure that we fully understand him in any given context. Adding to the difficulties of the reader is the fact that Hume is not only a sceptic but an ironist as well.

To proceed to Hume's implied or covert intentions, for which, fortunately, he has put us on the alert. On 15 August 1776, just ten days before his death, he wrote to Adam Smith concerning the *Dialogues*: '...I find that nothing can be more cautiously and more artfully written'.[11] Here, then, is the necessary clue to Hume's covert intentions: caution and artfulness.

Hume's basic prudential strategy in the *Dialogues* may now be formulated: Philo, who as Hume's spokesman for mitigated scepticism will perforce be the victor in the philosophical debate, will nevertheless be artfully depicted as being vanquished by the 'Antagonist', Cleanthes. To achieve these two ends Philo will be granted full scope to develop his arguments and to refute those of the others, and Cleanthes will forthwith be declared victor. The first of these ends is easily met: Philo is allotted more space than the other two put together: Demea, twelve per cent; Cleanthes, twenty-one per cent; and Philo, sixty-seven per cent. To put it dramatically, Philo requires more than three times the space of Cleanthes, the alleged hero of the *Dialogues*. Most importantly, Philo dominates Parts XI and XII, above all, the highly enigmatic peroration.

Having provided Philo with sufficient (or, some would say, more than sufficient) opportunity to win the debate philosophically, Hume now proclaims Cleanthes the victor. He began this dissimulation mischievously in the letter of 1751 to Gilbert Elliot, which opens: 'You wou'd perceive by the Sample I have given you, that I make Cleanthes the Hero of the Dialogue. Whatever you can think of, to strengthen that side of the Argument, will be most acceptable to me.'[12] And in a letter of 1776 to his printer,[13] Hume unashamedly compounds the dissimulation by assuring him that 'I . . . introduce [into the *Dialogues*] a Sceptic, who is indeed refuted, and at last gives up the Argument, nay confesses that he was only amusing himself by all his Cavils . . .'. Philo, it need hardly be emphasized, is far from being refuted, never gives up the argument, and is certainly in deadly earnest in his ironic position at the close.

The stratagem of ostensibly substituting Cleanthes for Philo as philosophical hero in the text of the *Dialogues* is carried out largely through the medium of Pamphilus. Now Pamphilus is a student under the tutorship of Cleanthes; he is variously described as a 'youth', as a 'pupil', as 'your adopted son', and as 'so young a man'. He takes no part in the discussion—'My youth rendered me a mere auditor of their disputes' (pp. 128–9)—and appears only as the narrator of the *Dialogues* in a letter designed for the edification of his friend, Hermippus. Paradoxically, it is this student, seemingly so insignificant in the conduct of the debate, who is actually Hume's ironical masterstroke of deception.

Pamphilus participates only at the opening and at the close, and in five brief asides (pp. 132, 150, 155, 166, 213) during the course of the discussion, superficially inconsequential but subtly belittling Philo's philosophical position and building up the case for him as the 'careless' sceptic. The sole function of Pamphilus is to provide cover for the dissimulation. Everything he says, therefore, is properly suspect as potentially exhibiting caution and artfulness. To be specific: Pamphilus' two substantive statements in the prologue are both dissembled. The first is the restriction of the topic for debate to the attributes of a God, to the exclusion of the being of a God: 'What truth so obvious, so certain, as the *being* of a God. . . . But in treating of this obvious and important truth; what obscure questions occur, concerning the *nature* of that divine Being; his attributes, his decrees, his plan of providence?'

(p. 128) As will be shown later, the discussion is devoted nearly equally to the being and to the attributes of a God.

The second dissimulation of Pamphilus in the prologue is his characterizations of the three speakers: 'the accurate philosophical turn of Cleanthes', 'the careless scepticism of Philo', and 'the rigid inflexible orthodoxy of Demea (p. 128). These characterizations are ironically offered at face value and are always, as far as I know, accepted at face value. Yet, just as soon as they are approached with the cautionary scepticism due to every statement of Pamphilus, they stand disclosed as deceptive. The purpose is, as usual, to play down the role of Philo and to play up that of Cleanthes. (Poor Demea is always condescended to by the others.) But to return to the characterizations. As a sheer matter of fact they are all designedly misconceived. For Cleanthes' 'philosophical turn' is not *accurate* (it is *muddled*); Philo's 'scepticism' is not *careless* (it is *disciplined*); Demea's 'orthodoxy' is not *rigid inflexible* (it is *politic expedient*).

Finally, there is the pupil's ironic verdict in favour of the master: '. . . so I confess, that, upon a serious review of the whole, I cannot but think, that Philo's principles are more probable than Demea's; but that those of Cleanthes approach still nearer to the truth' (p. 228). That Pamphilus has yet another reason to come to this implausible conclusion will appear in a moment. The already shaky thesis that Cleanthes is the philosophical hero is given the *coup de grâce* by recognition of Hume's deception through Pamphilus; but it is that very deception that makes Cleanthes Hume's artistic, or had I not better say, artful hero?

Irony is the most vital of Hume's rhetorical devices to foster caution and artfulness, and will be examined more fully in due course.

Another matter for consideration, meantime, is that Hume's *Dialogues concerning Natural Religion* is modelled upon Cicero's *De Natura Deorum*. This is of no paramount importance, but the general parallelism of characters and structure, as well as the significant divergences, tell us something about Hume's art. In *De Natura Deorum* Cicero, who is regarded by Hume[14] as 'one of the finest gentlemen of his age', but who is sometimes not sufficiently polite to the 'Antagonist' in his dialogues, appears in person at the beginning and the close, whereas Hume has employed Pamphilus, a Platonist mentioned by Cicero in passing. This device affords a prime example of Hume's subtly ironic mockery: to engage a fledgling Platonist, that is to say a rationalist, an anti-Humean, to pass judgment on the outcome of the learned discussion and thus seemingly to award the palm to Cleanthes. Were it not for Hume's artful manipulation of Pamphilus, what reader would be so naive as to deem Cleanthes the philosophical hero, the victor of the debate?

Cicero's disputants are Balbus the Stoic, Velleius the Epicurean, and Cotta the Sceptic, of whom the last is of some consequence to Hume in the portrayal of Philo. The final sentence in Hume's *Dialogues* made by Pamphilus, to which we have just referred, is a delicious ironical imitation[15] of Cicero's final sentence in *De Natura Deorum*: 'Velleius thought Cotta's view the truer; while I, on the contrary, thought that Balbus' views came nearer to what appeared to be the truth.'

De Natura Deorum was not the only model available to Hume for the structuring of his own dialogue. Galileo has been consistently overlooked by commentators on Hume in this rhetorical connection.[16] For Galileo's problem with his hero is exactly analogous to Hume's with his. Lauded by Philo as 'that great genius, one of the sublimest that ever existed' (p. 151), Galileo had published in 1632 the celebrated *Dialogue concerning the Two Chief World Systems*, wherein the merits of the Copernican and the Aristotelian-Ptolemaic hypotheses are discussed in a witty and altogether brilliant exchange of views. Sad to say, the rhetoric of irony proved unavailing, and the Inquisition, in its collective wisdom, judged that Galileo was advocating, rather than speculating about, the heliocentric hypothesis. The divine authority of Genesis was being impugned. So Galileo was constrained to abjure his heresy and to submit to punishment.

To turn now to the question of the identity of Hume's three speakers. Philo, and Philo alone, is Hume's spokesman, as he himself has made perfectly clear. The reader is thus placed under an artistic, as well as a historical and ideational, obligation to attempt to identify Philo's two 'Antagonists'. Who, then, can Cleanthes and Demea be supposed to be? I have long believed (since I wrote, forty years ago, my first essay on the *Dialogues*) that they were Bishop Joseph Butler and Dr Samuel Clarke respectively.[17] But this is a point I do not wish to insist on because it is not of the greatest consequence. Without troubling to review here all the evidence concerning these identifications, suffice it to say that Butler was Britain's outstanding empirical theologican of the eighteenth century while Clarke was the outstanding rationalist theologian —and Hume was well acquainted with the work of both, respecting the one and contemning the other. Demea, it may be observed, turns out to be a schizophrene, at once a metaphysician and a pious obscurantist, and this split in personality is what makes his identification as Clarke (or as anyone else, for that matter) less secure than that of Cleanthes as Butler.

The philosophical function of Demea in the debate is to present three theses: The being of a God can be proved *a priori* (pp. 188–9); the attributes of a God are incomprehensible (pp. 141–2, 156–7); and mankind is utterly miserable in this life, which is the 'porch' to a future life where inequities are rectified for those who have proved themselves morally (p. 199). Philo accepts and amplifies the second and the third of these theses (with his own mental reservations, to be sure, on the latter part of the third) and, ironically, is made to surrender to Cleanthes the privilege of refuting the first, which is Hume's own logical refutation of the metaphysical in the realm of matter of fact: '. . . there is an evident absurdity in pretending to demonstrate a matter of fact, or to prove it by any arguments *a priori*. . . . Whatever we conceive as existent, we can also conceive as non-existent . . .' (p. 189).[18]

Demea's orthodox expediency, his clerical smugness, and his concocting of theological mares' nests draw the scathing rebuke of Cleanthes: 'No! . . . No! These arbitrary suppositions can never be admitted, contrary to matter of fact, visible and uncontroverted. Whence can any cause be known but from its known effects? Whence can any hypothesis be proved but from the apparent phenomena? To establish one hypothesis upon another is building entirely in the air; and the utmost we ever attain, by these conjectures and fictions, is to ascertain the bare possibility of our opinion; but never can we, upon such terms, establish its reality' (pp. 199–200). In the dramatic sense, the gullible Demea acts as the unwitting ally of Philo in attacking the philosophical basis of Cleanthes' argument from analogy; and his presence has the tonic effect of making the *Dialogues* 'look more natural & unaffected'. This artistic touch is heightened by Demea's petulant withdrawal at the close of Part XI when the guile of Philo has belatedly become apparent to him.

The philosophical function of Cleanthes is likewise threefold: To refute Demea's *a priori* proof of the being of a God (p. 180); to explicate 'the proper office of religion',[19] which is relegated to the status of handmaiden to morality (p. 220); and, most importantly, to present the *a posteriori* argument of the being and the attributes of a God, specifically the argument from design in its eighteenth-century analogical scientific form (pp. 143–5 *et passim*). Cleanthes is convinced that this argument is the one and only: 'By this argument *a posteriori*, and by this argument alone, do we prove at once the existence of a Deity, and his similarity to human mind, and intelligence' (p. 143). In this conviction, Cleanthes is echoing the position taken by Bishop Butler, leading apologist of the Establishment: '. . . to an unprejudiced mind ten thousand thousand instances of design cannot but prove a designer'.[20] Cleanthes remains unperturbed by the fact that his argument is intrinsically anthropomorphic, as is pointed out by both Demea (p. 158) and Philo (p. 160).

In the dramatic sense, as befits his role as artful hero, Cleanthes is given more scope than his views justly deserve. He is, for instance, permitted to repeat arguments that have already been refuted by Philo, and the first two of the preceding arguments are Hume's own. At one point, Cleanthes is driven by Philo into the strangely muddled and certainly untenable philosophical position that 'Religion, however corrupted, is still better than no religion at all' (p. 219). Cleanthes might also have been taken to task for his deplorable habit of begging the question. Nevertheless, Cleanthes, artistically speaking, remains a rather engaging figure of a respectable theologian striving to maintain his composure and his argument in the face of a more imaginative and a more philosophical wit than his own.

The design argument, the sole argument that Philo acknowledges to have merit, becomes the target of a long series of refutations and counterproposals, both logical and imaginative, which display his amazing virtuosity of intellect and of tongue. Witness his sardonic gibe: 'What peculiar privilege has this little agitation of the brain which we call thought, that we must thus make it the model of the whole universe?' (p. 148) Who can forbear to smile at and to delight in the audacity of invention of Philo's treatment of the Brahminic myth of the 'infinite spider' that spun the world from 'his bowels'? 'Why an orderly system may not be spun from the belly as well as from the brain', observes Philo wryly, 'it will be difficult for him [that is, Cleanthes in presenting his analogical arguments] to give a satisfactory reason' (pp. 180–1). This passage illustrates Philo's *reductio ad absurdum* technique of displaying how the most outrageous analogy can be made to seem as plausible—and as implausible—as Cleanthes' generally more conventional analogies. Philo further points out that reason is not the only principle of order observable in the world, that there are also instinct, generation, and vegetation (p. 178), and that some variety of imperfect analogy can be drawn from each of these principles.

After Philo has teamed with Demea to press the argument of the misery of man, Cleanthes is driven to concede: 'If you can make out the present point, and prove mankind to be unhappy or corrupted, there is an end at once of all religion. For to what purpose establish the natural attributes of the Deity, while the moral are still doubtful and uncertain?' (p. 199). Philo then challenges Cleanthes 'to tug the labouring oar' (p. 202) in support of the analogical argument for the moral attributes of a God. And when Cleanthes tugs that oar all too feebly, Philo responds with a devastating picture of *nature*: 'Look round this universe. What an immense profusion of beings, animated and organized, sensible and active! You admire this prodigious variety and fecundity. But inspect a little more narrowly these living existences, the only beings worth regarding. How hostile and destructive to each other! How insufficient all of them for their own happiness! How contemptible or odious to the spectator! The whole presents nothing but the idea of a blind nature impregnated by a great vivifying principle, and pouring forth from her lap without discernment or parental care, her maimed and abortive children' (p. 211).

Nature here takes on a new and disquieting meaning that is not to be found in any of Hume's earlier writings and is far removed from his normally benign, life-enhancing view.[21] This new conception of nature, post-Darwinian as it were, comes as the culmination of the depiction of the evils inherent in nature that Philo had been pursuing with remorseless reiteration in the previous passage (pp. 205–11), and was to sum up in the succeeding passage (p. 212) as follows: 'The true conclusion is, that the original source of all things is entirely indifferent to all these principles, and has no more regard to good above ill than to heat above cold, or to drought above moisture, or to light above heavy.' The same argument, Philo proceeds, will apply to moral evil as well as to natural evil '. . . with little or no variation; and we have no more reason to infer, that the rectitude of the supreme Being resembles human rectitude than that his benevolence resembles the human.'

The 'blind nature' passage of Philo is both a shattering artistic parody and a shattering philosophical rebuttal of Cleanthes' prototype of the analogical argument: 'Look round the world: Contemplate the whole and every part of it: You will find it to be nothing but one great machine, subdivided into an infinite number of lesser machines, which again admit of subdivisions, to a degree beyond what human senses and faculties can trace and explain' (p. 143). Yet Philo's most shattering rebuttal of Cleanthes' analogical arguments, to my mind, is that concerning the very nature of analogy itself. For while it is a valid analogical argument to infer an architect when we see a building, that is solely because we have had many experimences of a like nature. But it is not valid to infer a world-maker from a world because we have had no experience of world-making. The argument from a unique effect (the world) to a unique cause (a God) is invalid (pp. 149–50).

(It is well known that Kant was so impressed with Hume's refutation of the argument from design in the *Dialogues* that he introduced it into his own *Critique of Pure Reason*.)

From the artistic point of view once again, I suggest that Philo, whether deliberately or not, was created in Hume's own image. For Philo resembles his creator to a remarkable degree: his inventiveness, his provocativeness, his dry humour. As with Hume himself, there is always an air of simple sanity about Philo.

To sum up our findings to the present. In general, it has been established that the *Dialogues* is far more complex in art, in structure, and in argument than meets the eye at the initial reading. This ironic complexity, together with its accompanying purposeful ambiguity, is caused primarily by Hume's prudential intent to play down the role of Philo, the sceptic and his spokesman, and to play up the role of Cleanthes, the 'Antagonist' and the advocate of 'experimental theism' (p. 165).

Specifically, the following five salient points have been established: (1) Philo and Philo alone is Hume's spokesman, in accordance with his dictum that *'In every Dialogue, no more than one Person can be supposed to represent the Author'*. In addition, Philo embraces several of Hume's views that had been artfully assigned to the 'Antagonists'. (2) Pamphilus is Hume's hitherto unsuspected masterstroke of ironic deception. Consequently his every statement is to be viewed with caution and scepticism. The results of this turnabout are far-reaching: the mind of the reader is subtly prepared beforehand to accept false evaluations of the philosophical tempers of the speakers and, in the event, is further prepared to accept a false statement of the outcome of the discussion. (Pamphilus will reappear in yet another variety of irony.) (3) Cleanthes may be taken as Butler and Demea as Clarke; but this, while fitting artistically, historically, and ideationally, is not mandatory. (4) Philo is the philosophical hero, the winner of the debate, but Cleanthes is the artful hero. (5) A new concept of nature has been introduced, one that is far removed from Hume's hitherto benign view. This new nature is amoral and indifferent to man. The first four of these findings supply bases for the better understanding of the major controversial areas. As such, they are instrumental, the means to the end, not the end itself. The fifth finding, that on nature, will play a significant role in the conclusion to this essay.

We are now in a position to see how irony, the most vital of Hume's rhetorical devices for fostering caution and artfulness, holds the key to the ultimate teachings of the *Dialogues*. Already noticed, a dozen or more times, in passing but not yet studied, irony, it may be recalled, has been identified as 'a figure of speech wherein the real meaning is concealed or contradicted by the words used'. It is time to call attention to the fact that Hume's term 'artfulness' is synonymous with my term 'irony'. It is also time to delve more deeply into a select few of the principal uses that Hume makes of irony.[22]

Recognition of irony is essential to the understanding of Hume in all his writings, but particularly in the *Dialogues*. Here the guidance of the biographer may prove helpful to the general reader and conceivably also to the philosopher. For irony to be recognized there is required intimate knowledge of the mind of the author, as seen through *all* his publications, and of his character, his personality, as further seen through his correspondence, his autobiography, his unpublished papers,

and possibly his biography. A word of caution: although Hume is a con-
summate ironist, one has to learn not to be overzealous and to see irony
lurking around every corner. Conversely and more importantly, when
we have truly recognized irony in accordance with the above criteria, it is
imperative that we do not hesitate to accept it no matter how radical
and venturesome the conclusion may seem to be in the first instance.

The form of irony most familiar to the modern philosopher is doubtless the Socratic. (The 'ironical' Socrates[23] is Hume's epithet on one of
the infrequent occasions that he uses the word.) Commonly understood
as 'pretended ignorance or willingness to learn from others assumed for
the sake of making their errors conspicuous by means of adroit questioning', Socratic irony generally holds the 'Antagonist' up to ridicule
or contempt. Hume takes pains to dissociate his own dialogue technique
and irony from the Socratic by 'preserving a proper balance among the
speakers', by avoiding 'the image of *pedagogue* and *pupil*', and by providing an atmosphere that 'woud make the whole look more natural &
unaffected'. The Humean dialogue technique and irony are more
subtle, more urbane, more naturalistic than the Socratic, and en-
gender a more refined and humane variety of humour. For Hume,
irony is pervasive, virtually a way of life.[24] Predictably, his irony is
most pronounced when he is treating of religion.

While the creation of the reporter Pamphilus is Hume's first masterstroke of irony, the speeches of Philo are, understandably, Hume's chief
ironic vehicle. So if there is in Philo's otherwise disciplined presentation
apparent inconsistency or manifest confusion or downright contradiction, it is meet to look for irony. Although 'a foolish consistency is the
hobgoblin of little minds', the philosopher stands apart from the rest of
mankind as being uniquely required to think in a clear and orderly
manner.

The vein of irony, which, as we have seen, runs piecemeal throughout the *Dialogues*, is opened decisively in the concluding Part XII.
Philo's ostensible confession of faith at the outset, a passage at which
many a commentator has boggled, sets the tone. Is there anything
disingenuous, anything contradictory, in brief, anything ironical here?
Yes, the professed fervour or zeal: '. . . no one', avers Philo with
duplicity, 'has a deeper sense of religion impressed on his mind, or pays
more profound adoration to the divine Being as he discovers himself to
reason, in the inexplicable contrivance and artifice of nature' (p. 214).
Deeper sense of religion? Profound adoration to the divine Being? No.
These pious feelings, or rather passions, are totally alien to the man
David Hume. They derive solely from faith, and by his own avowal
David Hume ever since youth was devoid of religious faith.[25] They are
ironically presented here only as precautionary accommodation to the

conventions of the times, in accordance with the philosopher's standard practice when writing on religion, and are fully, though still ironically, nullified at the close.

Pamphilus, that youthful herald of irony, had taken for granted in the prologue to the *Dialogues* that the being of a God is a truth 'so obvious, so certain' (p. 128), as to require no proof. This limitation of the debate to the attributes of a God is accepted without question by the three debaters at the same time as it is ignored by them in practice. Thus the wary reader, who has schooled himself to be sceptical of every utterance of Pamphilus, is quite prepared to learn that in reality the argument to the being of a God is brought to the fore nearly equally with that to the attributes of a God: if my count is correct, by Demea, four times; by Cleanthes, seven times; and by Philo, ten times.[26] The indisputable fact is that the being of a God, Pamphilus to the contrary notwithstanding, is a major, if not *the* major, issue of the *Dialogues*. The cumulative effect of arguing this issue so frequently is to take on the ironical implication that the being of a God not only is not a self-evident truth but on the contrary is not rationally provable. This in-stance of reverse-psychology is substantiated by Philo on the empirical level (pp. 144–50 *et passim*), and demonstrated by Cleanthes (p. 189) on the metaphysical level. The outcome, when the veil of ambiguity is lifted, is unmistakable: the being of a God is susceptible neither of rational proof nor of rational disproof. Hence it follows that no room is left to the sceptical philosopher for either dogmatic (or blind) theism or dogmatic (or blind) atheism. To him the part of wisdom is suspense-of-judgment.

What is more, in a work professedly restricted to natural religion and peopled with characters bearing Ciceronian names, it seems incon-gruous that the terms Christian, Christianity, and Christendom should appear no fewer than seven times (pp. 138, 141, 160, 228), not to men-tion such minor incongruities as 'reverend gentlemen', 'orthodox divines and doctors', 'pious divines and preachers', 'revealed theology', etc. Morover, Demea is condescended to throughout as a not overly bright clergyman who is wont to lapse into the cant of the preacher; and Philo repeats, from the notorious footnote to the essay 'Of National Characters', the charge that the clergy from the very nature of their profession are driven into hypocrisy (p. 222). Again, if my identification of Cleanthes and Demea as Christian divines is acceptable, we have further indication of what may be taken as deliberate incongruity: the plentiful and uncalled-for infusion of Christian nomenclature into a discussion of natural religion.[27]

More direct and more cogent than the foregoing, indeed a clear giveaway, is the last sentence, the ironic 'amen' to Philo's ironic 'prayer': *To be a philosophical sceptic is, in a man of letters, the first and most essential step towards being a sound, believing Christian . . .*' (p. 228, my italics). (To Hume, it is well to bear in mind, 'man of letters', in this context, means one of the enlightened minority.) These final words of Philo in the 'prayer' are followed only by Pamphilus' ingenuous and already discredited assessment of the outcome of the debate. The evidence presented so far, mainly circumstantial, begins to afford a presumption that the *Dialogues concerning Natural Religion* is, in fact, overtly directed against natural religion and covertly directed against revealed religion, Christianity and Christianity's God.

Hume's lifelong study of human nature, 'the science of man', embraces the conviction that all forms of 'popular' or 'vulgar' revealed religion (in effect, Christianity as commonly practised) as opposed to 'philosophical and rational' religion (p. 220) tend to oscillate between the polarities of superstition and enthusiasm (p. 222). As early as 1741 Hume had published an essay, 'Of Superstition and Enthusiasm,' both of which passions in their extremities are stigmatized as the 'corruptions of true religion'.[28] The evidence adduced is largely drawn from the religious turmoils in Christian states during the seventeenth century.

Hume had long since forsworn Christianity, belief in which he had stipulated in 'Of Miracles' requires a 'continued miracle'.[29] With the publication of that essay in 1748 after its excision from the *Treatise* a decade earlier, Hume recognized that he had passed the point of no return in the public disclosure of his religious thinking, and was entirely willing to own the 'character of an infidel'.[30] This resolution was humorously detailed in 1757: 'I believe I shall write no more History; but proceed directly to attack the Lord's Prayer & the ten Commandments & the single Cat[echism]; and to recommend Suicide & Adultery; and so persist, till it shall please the Lord to take me to himself.'[31] From Paris, a few years later, he exclaimed irritably: 'Some [Englishmen] hate me because I am not a Tory, some because I am not a Whig, some because I am not a Christian, and all because I am a Scotsman.' Also from Paris he castigated the English nation as 'relapsing fast into the deepest Stupidity, Christianity & Ignorance'. In 1766 he remarked about his protégé Rousseau: 'He has a hankering after the Bible, and is indeed little better than a Christian in a way of his own.'[32]

On 7 July 1776 the dying philosopher was subjected to a searching probe of his religious convictions by James Boswell. According to that busybody, Hume 'said flatly that the Morality of every Religion was bad, and, I really thought, was not jocular when he said "that when he heard a man was religious, he concluded he was a rascal, though he had known some instances of very good men being religious". . . . I asked him if the thought of Annihilation never gave him uneasiness. He said not the least; no more than the thought that he had never been, as Lucretius observes' (pp. 76–7). Hume's indictment of Christianity continued on his death-bed, when he assured his physician, not without a touch of ironic humour, that 'he had been very busily employed in making his countrymen wiser and particularly in delivering them from the Christian superstition, but that he had not yet compleated that great work'.[33] 'That great work' was carried one step further in the posthumous *Dialogues* and constitutes a component of its 'legacy'.

Hume's aversion—I choose the word advisedly—to Christianity was deep-rooted and informed his entire career as philosopher, from *Treatise* to *Dialogues*. This is not to say, however, that Hume was in any sense a Scottish Voltaire flourishing the banner of *Ecrasez l'infâme* —that would have been unthinkable, simply out of character. Nevertheless, it is abundantly clear that irony in the *Dialogues concerning Natural Religion* starts with the title. (Adam Smith, I rest assured, had indeed read the manuscript correctly and recognized it for what it is: an open attack on natural religion and a disguised attack on all 'popular' religions, in particular, Christianity. Smith, no doubt, felt it improper to attack Christianity in public.)[35]

The peroration of the *Dialogues* was composed during the last months of his life when Hume was fully aware that death was imminent. In the first half (p. 227), Philo, assuming the part of advocate, presents Hume's summary theistic position: 'natural theology' is resolved into 'one simple, though somewhat ambiguous, at least undefined proposition, *that the cause or causes of order in the universe probably bear some remote analogy to human intelligence*'. Moreover, this proposition can 'afford no inference that affects human life . . .' and 'the analogy, imperfect as it is, . . . can be carried no farther than to the human intelligence; and cannot be transferred, with any appearance of probability, to the other qualities of the mind . . .', namely, the moral.

Some readers of the *Dialogues* no doubt remain perfectly content to be able to detect in Philo's 'simple . . . somewhat ambiguous . . . undefined' proposition a residual nominal theism. So be it. Other readers, perhaps more perceptive, perhaps more sceptical, perhaps more realistic, might be inclined to protest: that a God without recognizable moral attributes can provide no solace for errant mankind;[36] that such an impoverished God bears little or no resemblance to the personal God of Christianity; that Philo's highly qualified and watered-down proposition, in effect, borders on suspense-of-judgment; that the 'religious hypothesis' (p. 216), the supernatural, for all practical purposes so far as mankind is concerned, has been phased out.

In the second half of the peroration Philo offers an artfully couched prayer' invoking divine revelation to meliorate the ignorance of man concerning the human condition. The plaintive tone gives way to the hortative. Christianity is the target: 'But believe me, Cleanthes, the most natural sentiment, which a well-disposed mind will feel on this occasion, is a longing desire and expectation, that Heaven would be pleased to dissipate, at least alleviate, this profound ignorance, by affording some more particular revelation to mankind, and making discoveries of the nature, attributes, and operations of the divine object of our Faith. A person, seasoned with a just sense of the imperfections of natural reason, will fly to *revealed truth* with the greatest avidity: While the haughty dogmatist, persuaded that he can erect a complete system of theology by the mere help of philosophy, disdains any farther aid, and rejects this adventitious instructor. *To be a philosophical sceptic is, in a man of letters, the first and most essential step towards being a sound, believing Christian . . .*' (pp. 227–8, my italics).

The incredulous prediction of Cleanthes back in Part I that Philo proposed 'to erect religious faith on philosophical scepticism' (p. 132) has at long last come to pass—but not without having undergone a sea-change. For this final sentence of Philo in the 'prayer', the 'amen', may now be viewed in proper perspective and stand revealed as the climactic and supreme irony of the *Dialogues concerning Natural Religion*. (In the nineteenth century the religious faith of a Kierkegaard, who liked to think of himself as a 'Master of irony,' was to find no deception in Hume's position but a genuine source of strength to ensure the 'Christian Leap.')

I shall now proceed to the consequences of penetrating through the mask of Philo's ironical 'prayer' and of speculating what Hume might have said had he felt free, in the religious and social climate of his day, to be entirely frank and outspoken. Another way of putting the problem is: *after the philosophical exorcism of the supernatural from religion, what remains?*

The answer to this crucial question calls for an inquiry into the bed-rock teachings of the *Dialogues*, which compose the personal message of religious philosophy that Hume was ironically bequeathing to posterity. Three propositions cover the ground. The first deals with natural religion, the second, with revealed religion, Christianity, and both are negative in purport; the third is positive, dealing with man alone in an indifferent nature. All in all, and at the risk of over-simplifying, these three propositions constitute, in my judgment, the core of Hume's thinking on mitigated scepticism as a way of life. This enlightened, Humean way of life is free of the supernatural, free of theology, free of revelation, free of a God—in fine, in the words of Philo, a 'philosophical and rational' religion (p. 220), to which I shall only add (surely gratuitously) one that is wholly secular and humanistic, man-made for man. This enlightened, Humean way of life may appropriately, albeit ironically, be named the *religion of man*.

First proposition. The *a priori* proof of the being of a God is refuted by an unimpeachable demonstration.[37] The *a posteriori* argument from design proves only that the being of a God is faintly analogous to human intelligence and this analogy, faint as it is, cannot be transferred to the moral attributes of a God. So the conduct of human life remains unaffected. The 'religious hypothesis' is impotent. There is no natural religion.

Second proposition. Revealed religion, Christianity, fares the same as natural religion philosophically. It is sanctioned only by faith, which is itself a standing miracle and, consequently, unphilosophical. Christianity as commonly practised tends to fall into corruption, its clergy, into hypocrisy. The Christian dispensation is left empty.[38]

Third proposition. The implied response to the crucial question, *After the philosophical exorcism of the supernatural from religion, what remains?*, is short and simple: the *religion of man*. Put more explicitly it reads: *man, intrepid and enlightened man, stands starkly alone to fend for himself in an indifferent nature.*

Let us now consider how these three teachings, the two negative and the one positive, develop, how the portrait of the philosopher as an enlightened and mitigated sceptic comes into focus on the humanistic level.

At this point, the fictional Philo, Hume's spokesman, is to be abandoned for the philosopher himself. In contrast to the ironic Hume of Philo's 'prayer', the candid Hume is intrepid. Stripped of the mask of ironic ambiguity, there emerges a Hume who is cautiously optimistic, sounding a note of quiet confidence. (This muted optimism is not to be confused with the so-called 'easy' optimism of the Enlightenment, the idea of necessary progress found in some of the *philosophes*, notably the *Physiocrates*.)

Hume's quiet confidence is strictly limited to the relatively few 'men of letters', the enlightened minority, the 'party of humanity'. He had long since concluded that the vulgar will always be seducible by one variety or other of corrupt religion. The 'vulgar, that is, indeed, all mankind, a few excepted, being ignorant and uninstructed' (as they are described in *The Natural History of Religion*)[39] are set apart from the select few who comprise the enlightened. These enlightened few, the 'learned and wise',[40] have the capacity and the courage and the will to live without the supernatural in religion, to remain undaunted when compelled by intellectual integrity to relinquish unresolved philosophical profundities for suspense-of-judgment, 'that very suspense or balance, which is the triumph of scepticism' (p. 136), as Philo puts it. Moral philosophy, which had antedated metaphysics in Hume's philosophical development, remains dominant at the close. It is truly the 'science of human nature', man's understanding, limited though it may be, of himself and of his role in an indifferent nature, in short, the *religion of man*. Once again Hume cautions: 'Be a philosopher; but, amidst all your philosophy, be still a man.'[41]

For better or for worse and bereft of divine guidance, as well as of the beneficence of nature, man, intrepid and enlightened man, remains free to keep his own counsel; and human nature is so framed as to make it feasible for him to live the good life, 'a manly, steady virtue, . . . calm sunshine of the mind'. When Hume wrote 'calm sunshine of the mind' some score of years earlier in 'The Natural History of Religion,'[42] was he consciously rendering into English Sextus Empiricus' mood of ataraxia? I do not know, and there is no means of knowing. But that he himself had achieved that blessed state of 'calm sunshine of the mind' is, I think, beyond dispute.

First to last, *Treatise* to *Dialogues*, Hume is ever the humanist, true to his own premise that 'Human Nature is the only science of man. . . '.[43] The two essential components of the *religion of man* are present in his final thinking: first, philosophical exorcism of the supernatural (the demise of religions, natural and revealed) and, second, implicit trust in enlightened man, the only hope for the future. For Hume's mitigated scepticism, in the end, is not wholly negative, neither is it deadening or apathetic. Rather, it is active, it is creative. Above all, it is a declaration of independence of the living spirit of man: *'Man and for ever!'*.[44] Call this creative scepticism and declaration of independence humanism, or naturalism, or neopaganism, or secularism, or positivism, or pragmatism, or agnosticism, or what you will, it is a serene and confident affirmation, in the most authentic voice of the Enlightenment, of the perennial theme of the dignity of man, his dignity in living and his dignity in dying. In the most profound sense, this ironic insight into the *religion of man* 'philosophical and rational' is the legacy out of the grave, as it were, of David Hume's *Dialogues concerning Natural Religion*.[45]

1. David Hume *Dialogues concerning Natural Religion*, ed. Norman Kemp Smith, 2nd ed. (Edinburgh and London 1947). All references to the *Dialogues* are to this edition; page numbers are given within parentheses in the body of the text.
2. See E. C. Mossner *The Life of David Hume* (Edinburgh and Austin 1954, reprinted Oxford 1970), especially chs. 22, 24, 38. Cited hereafter as *Life*. *Philosophical Essays concerning Human Understanding* (1748) became the familiar *Enquiry concerning Human Understanding* in 1758. The latter will be cited hereafter as *Enquiries*.

3. *Letters*, ii. 323: 'Some of my Friends flatter me, that it is the best thing
    I ever wrote.' See also n. 10, below. Most important is Hume's over-
    riding determination to publish.

4. Michael Morrisroe, Jr. in a series of articles explores the rhetorical
    approach to the *Dialogues concerning Natural Religion*. I list three items.
    (1) 'Hume's Rhetorical Strategy: A Solution to the Riddle of the *Dia-
    logues concerning Natural Religion*' *Texas Studies in Literature and
    Language* XI (1965) 963–74; (2) 'Characterization as Rhetorical Device
    in Hume's *Dialogues concerning Natural Religion*' *Enlightenment Essays*
    I (1970) 95–107; (3) 'Linguistic Analysis as Rhetorical Pattern in David
    Hume' in W. B. Todd (ed.) *Hume and the Enlightenment* (Edinburgh and
    Austin 1974) pp. 72–82. Giancarlo Carabelli in *Hume e la retorica dell'
    ideologia* 'Uno studio dei *Dialoghi sulla religione naturale*' (Firenze 1972)
    explores a number of different approaches.

5. The term 'mitigated' scepticism, which I shall be employing throughout,
    is discussed at length in *The Enquiry concerning Human Understanding*,
    sec. XII, pt. III. It is sharply differentiated from '*Pyrrhonism* or the ex-
    cessive principles of scepticism' (*Enquiries*, pp. 158–9). 'Mitigated' does
    not appear in the *Dialogues*; but Cleanthes (p. 154) provides a description
    of 'reasonable' scepticism: 'The declared profession of every reasonable
    sceptic is only to reject abstruse, remote and refined arguments; to ad-
    here to common sense and the plain instincts of nature; and to assent,
    wherever any reasons strike him with so full a force, that he cannot,
    without the greatest violence, prevent it.' 'Moderate' scepticism is men-
    tioned in *Treatise* I. iv. 3.

6. 'Of the Rise and Progress of the Arts and Sciences' in *The Philosophical
    Works of David Hume*, ed. T. H. Green and T. H. Grose (London 1874–5)
    vol. III, p. 189, n. 2. Cited hereafter as *Phil. Works*.

7. *Letters*, i. 154.

8. National Library of Scotland, MS 3582, f. 214; *Letters*, i. 173, from prin-
    ted source. My italics.

9. *Letters*, i. 154.

10. The anonymous writer of the 'Avertissement' to a French translation of
    the *Dialogues* in 1780 makes two interesting statements: (1) 'l'Auteur qui
    la regardait comme son chef-d'oeuvre' and (2) 'Il parait avoir voulu se
    peindre sous le personage de Philon'. This information was kindly
    brought to my attention by Professor Ian S. Ross of the University of
    British Columbia. I am also obliged to Professor David Raphael of the
    University of London for pointing out an error of inference.

11. *Letters*, ii. 334.

12. *Letters*, i. 153–4.

13. *Letters*, ii. 323.

14. 'Of the Rise and Progress of the Arts and Sciences' in *Phil. Works*, vol.
    III, pp. 188–9.

15. I owe this reference to Peter Gay *The Enlightenment: An Interpretation*
    (London 1967) vol. I, p. 415n. John V. Price also notes the parallelism:
    'Sceptics in Cicero and Hume' *Journal of the History of Ideas* XXV (1964)
    98.

16. Until enlightened by the historian, Priscilla Robertson, I was one of the
    delinquents.

17. Mossner 'The Enigma of Hume' in *Mind* XIV (1936) 334–49. Candidates

for the role of Demea are few, Clarke being the favourite. For Cleanthes
the competition is keen, though few candidates have merit. Perhaps the
most substantial, after Butler, is the Newtonian, Colin Maclaurin. See
Robert Hurlbutt *Hume, Newton, and the Design Argument* (Lincoln,
Nebraska 1965) pp. 103–4 and p. 103, n. 1. Passages from Maclaurin's *An
Account of Sir Isaac Newton's Philosophical Discoveries* (London 1748)
pp. 378–80, 381, are cited by Hurlbutt as parallel in argument and in language to some of Cleanthes. Parallels of Cleanthes with passages in the
Analogy of Religion (1736), however, are also numerous. Butler is in the
empirical tradition, a follower of the methods of the New Science. It is, to
be sure, not unlikely that Hume was deliberately following select passages of both Butler and Maclaurin. It should not be overlooked that at
least one commentator has said that 'Pamphilus is Hume'! See C. W. Hendel
Studies in the Philosophy of David Hume (Princeton 1925) p. 307.

18. cf. *Enquiries*, p. 164, and see also n. 37 below.
19. Taken from the MS of a suppressed preface to the second volume of the
history of the Stuarts. The suppressed preface contains an elaboration of
Hume's ironic view of the role of religion in history. See *Life*, pp. 306–7.
20. Joseph Butler *Analogy of Religion* (London 1736) pt. II, Conclusion.
21. See Norman Kemp Smith *The Philosophy of David Hume* (London 1941)
p. 564: 'Coming in the dramatic setting of the *Dialogues*, this view of
Nature may not, however, be taken to be Hume's own. No other passage
in any of his writings is on these lines.' But surely it is conceivable that
Hume, in the last resort, may have altered his earlier view when the
argument in the *Dialogues* demanded reassessment of *nature*. Philo: '. . .
that vague, indeterminate word, nature, to which the vulgar refer everything, is not at the bottom more inexplicable [than *reason*]' (p. 178).
22. I restrict myself to Part XII, and then only to the opening and the close.
23. 'A Dialogue' in *Phil. Works*, vol. IV, p. 293.
24. John V. Price *The Ironic Hume* (Austin 1965) is pre-eminently useful in
this context.
25. *Letters*, i. 154, and the Boswell interview (p. 76).
26. The count is necessarily arbitrary because the discussion can hardly avoid
the question of the being of a God; but the following references may be
regarded as minimal: *Demea*: pp. 141, 143, 145, 188–9; *Cleanthes*: pp.
143, 144–5, 163, 185, 189, 190, 216; *Philo*: pp. 142, 144, 161–2, 165–6,
168–9, 178, 180, 214–15, 216–17, 227.
27. Contrast Hume's 'plentiful infusion of Christian nomenclature' with
Butler's spare use in Pt. I, 'Of Natural Religion', of the *Analogy of
Religion*. In the text 'Christian' appears three times only, together with
five references to revealed religion. In the notes 'Christianity' appears
once only together with three references to revealed religion.
28. 'Of Superstition and Enthusiasm' in *Phil. Works*, vol. III, pp. 144–50.
29. *Enquiries*, p. 131.
30. *Letters*, i. 106.
31. *New Letters of David Hume*, ed. Klibansky and Mossner (Oxford 1954) p.
43. Cited hereafter as *New Letters*.
32. *Letters*, i. 470, 498. *Life*, p. 523.
33. *Life*, p. 601.
34. Hume in 1747 wrote 'the Church is my Aversion'; the occasion was a
review of the several professions available to him. *New Letters*, p. 26. 'Of

Miracles', in one form or another was originally a part of the *Treatise*. It was withdrawn out of deference to Butler.

35. Adam Smith explained to Strahan what his policy would have been had Hume left the publication of the *Dialogues* to his discretion: '. . . the manuscript should have been most carefully preserved and upon my decease restored to his family; but it never should have been published in my lifetime' *Letters*, ii. 453.

36. Had not the simple-minded Demea cautioned Cleanthes against this very outcome? (p. 170).

37. Cleanthes' demonstration (p. 189): 'Nothing is demonstrable, unless the contrary implies a contradiction. Nothing, that is distinctly conceivable, implies a contradiction. Whatever we conceive as existent, we can also conceive as non-existent. There is no Being, therefore, whose non-existence implies a contradiction. Consequently there is no Being, whose existence is demonstrable.'

38. With Hume's philosophical rejection of both natural and revealed religions, the question of atheism inevitably arises. Although to a Christian, an unbeliever may qualify as an atheist, a true sceptic on his own terms can never be an atheist because he abhors dogmas negative as well as dogmas positive. Unlike some philosophers and almost everyone else, Hume was content to remain in a total suspense-of-judgment position when this was demanded. This may be called agnosticism, if you please. From the biographical point of view, at least, it is certain that Hume did not regard himself as an atheist. Witness the confrontation in Paris with Baron d'Holbach and his atheistical club, the 'seiks in the Rue Royale'. Hume startled the Baron by observing that 'he did not believe in atheists, that he had never seen any' (see *Life*, p. 483). In the *Dialogues* (p. 218) Philo repeats the same opinion: 'I next turn to the atheist, who, I assert, is only nominally so, and can never possibly be in earnest . . .'. See also the *Enquiries*, p. 149. Some British theologians of the eighteenth century, e.g., Thomas Broughton and William Baxter, concur.

39. *Phil. Works*, vol. IV, p. 334.

40. *Enquiries*, p. 133.

41. *Enquiries*, p. 9.

42. *Phil. Works*, vol. IV, p. 360. Hume may have found his 'poetical inspiration' in one of his favourite poets. See Pope *Essay on Man* IV, l. 168: 'The soul's calm sunshine, and the heart-felt joy'; and *Eloisa to Abelard*, l. 209: 'Eternal sunshine of the spotless mind'.

43. *Treatise*, p. 273.

44. 'I allow the justness of the poet's exclamation on the endless projects of human race, *Man and for ever!*' in 'Idea of a perfect Commonwealth' in *Phil. Works*, vol. III, pp. 492–3. The poet is Pope *Satires*, 5, l. 252.

45. A new text of the *Dialogues* based entirely on the MSS in the Royal Society of Edinburgh was published on 2 December 1976 by the Clarendon Press. This new text, which is faithful to the intent of the author, is edited by John V. Price of Edinburgh University. I regret that it appeared too late to be available for my essay.

'The true old Humean philosophy'
and its Influence on Adam Smith

WHEN HUME WROTE, in his short autobiography, that the *Treatise* 'fell *dead-born from the press*', he was quoting poetry and so perhaps allowing himself to indulge in poetic licence. Ernest Mossner has told us of the reception of the *Treatise*, both in England and on the continent of Europe. There is no doubt that Hume was well aware of the reviews, and Professor Mossner takes the statement in *My Own Life* to mean that the book was misunderstood and unappreciated rather than unnoticed.[1]

One gets a different impression from the discussion of Hume's views, after mature reflection, by contemporary Scottish thinkers. The ablest of them was Reid, and although he was highly critical of Hume's philosophy, as expounded in the *Treatise*, he certainly appreciated its importance. So did an earlier critic, Henry Home, Lord Kames, who argued against Hume's account of belief, causation, self-identity, and justice in *Essays on Morality and Natural Religion* (1751). In the third edition of that work (p. 149), published in 1779 after Hume's death, Kames concluded a criticism of the *Enquiry concerning the Principles of Morals* with an apology, saying that Hume's earlier work had caused him to be 'justly esteemed the greatest philosopher of his time'.

Not all the Scottish philosophers shared that view. We must except 'that bigotted silly fellow, Beattie', whose understanding in these matters was not much better than that of his admirers, Dr Johnson and Fanny Burney. In her Diary for 1780,[2] Fanny Burney describes a conversation with a young lady who happened to let fall the remark that she did not believe in an afterlife. Fanny was deeply shocked.

'Where, for Heaven's sake,' I cried, 'where have you picked up such dreadful reasoning?'

'In Hume,' said she; 'I have read his *Essays* repeatedly.'

'I am sorry to find they have power to do so much mischief. You should not have read them, at least till a man equal to Hume in abilities had answered him. Have you read any more infidel writers?'

'Yes, Bolingbroke, the divinest of all writers.'

'And do you read nothing upon the right side?'

'Yes, the Bible, till I was sick to death of it, every Sunday evening to my mother.'

'Have you read Beattie on the Immutability of Truth?'
'No.'
'Give me leave then to recommend it to you. After Hume's
    Essays you ought to read it.'
But then that was a meeting of two young ladies in the drawing
rooms of London. There was more enlightenment in some quarters of
Scotland. Note the words of Kames's tribute to Hume in 1779: he 'was
justly esteemed the greatest philosopher of his time'. Kames is report-
ing not simply his own judgement but a general one which he endorses.
It seems to me likely that he is referring to the circle of 'literati' in
Edinburgh of which he was a prominent member. Adam Smith wrote,
with utter sincerity, in 1776 that he had always regarded Hume as
approaching perfection in wisdom (as well as in virtue);[3] so he clearly
was one of those who esteemed Hume 'the greatest philosopher of his
time'. There is no reason to doubt Kames's evidence that others thought
the same. Hume was not without honour in his own country as a
philosopher.

What sort of a philosopher, though? The published comments of
Kames and Reid suggest that they saw Hume simply as a sceptic. Reid
even said that Hume must have been joking when he wrote, in the
Introduction to the *Treatise*, of making the science of human nature
the foundation of a complete system of the sciences; this could not be
taken seriously, Reid thought, 'when the intention of the whole work
is to shew, that there is neither human nature nor science in the
world'.[4] This is a familiar picture. There is no appreciation of Hume's
positive contribution to epistemology, his alternative to a rationalist
account of our knowledge of the world and ourselves. It was different
when Reid came to discuss Hume's ethics. He knew that Hume had
positive views in this field of philosophy: moral judgement rests on
feeling, justice is an artificial virtue depending on utility. But Reid had
little awareness of the connection between Hume's ethics and his
epistemology.

Scholars have commonly supposed that this was the typical reaction
to Hume in the eighteenth as in the nineteenth century. Nowadays we
see more clearly what Hume was getting at when he talked of founding
a complete system of the sciences on the science of man or the principles
of human nature. For my part I have learned most about this topic
from H. H. Price and Kemp Smith.[5] Price showed us the crucial role of
the imagination in Hume's theory of knowledge. Kemp Smith stressed
the continuing influence, throughout Hume's philosophy, of Hutcheson's ethical theory, in which reason is subordinated to feeling. While I
find Kemp Smith's thesis persuasive, I think that it does not pay enough
attention to the *differences* between Hume's theory of ethics and

Hutcheson's. Much of the progress beyond Hutcheson that Hume made in ethics depends on adding the functions of the imagination to those of feeling. The addition is vital to the role of sympathy in ethics; it is needed, again, for the stability and impartiality of moral judgement; and it is implied in the formation of artificial virtue. The whole of Hume's constructive philosophy of human nature was unperceived by Reid and Beattie—and so by the later critics who took their cue from Reid and Beattie.

I want to suggest to you that not all of Hume's contemporaries in Scotland shared this blind spot. Let me begin with part of a letter sent by John Millar to David Douglas on 10 August 1790 after the death of Adam Smith. Douglas must have written to Millar about the manuscripts that Adam Smith insisted on having destroyed and about those that he had allowed to survive. On the latter Millar comments:

> I am glad to hear that a part of Mr. Smith's writings are likely to see the light—for I hope you and your privy council will use all the latitude you can upon that side of the question. Of the discourses which he intended upon the imitative arts, he read two to our Society at Glasgow, but the third was not then finished. I wish it may be finished now. Of all his writings, I have most curiosity about the metaphysical work you mention. I should like to see his powers of illustration employed upon the true old Humean philosophy.

Millar's words in the last sentence imply that Douglas had seen a connection between Smith's work and the philosophy of Hume. They do not necessarily imply that Douglas would have agreed with Millar in regarding Hume's philosophy (or the relevant part of Hume's philosophy) as 'true', but they do at least suggest that he would not think the judgement novel or bizarre.

The letter was printed by W. R. Scott, in his book *Adam Smith as Student and Professor* (1937), pp. 311–13. Scott was not sure whether 'the metaphysical work' of Adam Smith that is referred to could be identified. In a note on p. 313 he said there was no trace of the manuscript so described, but in an earlier part of the book (p. 115, note 3) he suggested that it might be either an unknown manuscript or the work entitled 'The Principles which lead and direct Philosophical Enquiries' that was printed in Smith's posthumous *Essays on Philosophical Subjects*. I have no doubt that this is what David Douglas was talking about. The work is in three parts, and the full title of the first part is 'The Principles which lead and direct Philosophical Enquiries; illustrated by the History of Astronomy'. The second and third parts carry the same title except for the final words: the second deals with the history of ancient physics, and the third with the history of ancient logic and metaphysics. The term 'illustrated by' appears in all three titles and is picked up in John Millar's phrase, 'I should like to see his powers of illustration employed . . .'. In fact the 'metaphysical' discussion, on Humean lines, occurs only at the beginning of the first and longest essay, the 'History of Astronomy', though it is intended to be a general introduction to the work as a whole. It is the introductory sections that David Douglas must have had in mind when he talked of a 'metaphysical work' in the spirit of Hume. I shall shortly quote one of the passages that will have led Douglas to speak of Hume's philosophy. Meanwhile, however, I shall add some confirmatory evidence that the work referred to in John Millar's letter is Smith's essay on the 'History of Astronomy'.

The paragraph that I have quoted from Millar's letter is about the manuscripts which Smith had allowed his executors to retain with a view to possible publication of any that they thought fit. Millar urges the executors to be liberal and to publish as much as they can. He assumes, from what he has been told by Douglas, that this will include three essays on the imitative arts and the metaphysical work illustrating the Humean philosophy. Earlier in his letter Millar says, evidently in response to a request, that he will be glad to furnish Dugald Stewart with information about Adam Smith's 'professorial talents' at Glasgow. Now Smith's literary executors published most of the surviving fragments in *Essays on Philosophical Subjects* (1795), introduced by Dugald Stewart's 'Account of the Life and Writings of Adam Smith'. The account included direct quotation of contributions from John Millar about Adam Smith's performances as Professor of Logic and then Professor of Moral Philosophy at Glasgow. Smith's own *Essays* in the volume begin with the three on the history of astronomy, of ancient physics, and of ancient logic and metaphysics. These are followed by an essay, in three parts, on the imitative arts. Since Millar writes of this in his letter, it is probable (quite apart from the reference to 'illustration' and Hume) that 'the metaphysical work' was also something that would be included in the *Essays on Philosophical Subjects*.

Another piece of evidence pointing in the same direction is contained in the next letter that Scott printed on p. 313 of his book. It is from Lord Loughborough (Alexander Wedderburn), is probably addressed to David Douglas, and is dated 14 August 1790. The contents make it almost certain that this letter, like that of John Millar, is in reply to one from David Douglas describing the destruction of most of Smith's papers, the survival of others, and the proposal to publish some or all of the latter group. On this matter Loughborough wrote:

> The disposition of his unprinted Works is exactly what I expected as he told me it was his determination to destroy the

greater part of them, and He particularly excepted the History of
Astronomy and the Treatise on the imitative Arts.
As I see it, Loughborough is referring to the same two essays as Millar,
and is no doubt picking up things that David Douglas had said about
the surviving manuscripts.

Well, what is Humean about Adam Smith's view of the history of
science and philosophy? Smith follows the dictum of Plato that philosophy begins in wonder, but he gives this a Humean twist. Wonder
arises when the smooth course of the imagination is disturbed by an unusual sequence of events. It is assuaged when philosophy (meaning
science) shows the unusual event to be part of a system, a customary
order, and so enables the imagination to resume an easy passage. Smith
describes the work of the imagination in words that recall the doctrine
of Hume's *Treatise*:

> When two objects, however unlike, have often been observed to
> follow each other, and have constantly presented themselves to the
> senses in that order, they come to be so connected together in the
> fancy, that the idea of the one seems, of its own accord, to call up
> and introduce that of the other. If the objects are still observed to
> succeed each other as before, this connection, or, as it has been
> called, this association of their ideas, becomes stricter and stricter,
> and the habit of the imagination to pass from the conception of the
> one to that of the other, grows more and more rivetted and con-
> firmed. . . . When objects succeed each other in the same train in
> which the ideas of the imagination have been accustomed to
> move, and in which, though not conducted by that chain of events
> presented to the senses, they have acquired a tendency to go on of
> their own accord, such objects appear all closely connected with
> one another, and the thought glides easily along them, with-
> out effort and without interruption. . . . There is no break, no stop,
> no gap, no interval. The ideas excited by so coherent a chain of
> things seem, as it were, to float through the mind of their own
> accord, without obliging it to exert itself, or to make any effort in
> order to pass from one of them to the other.
>
> But if this customary connection be interrupted, if one or more
> objects appear in an order quite different from that to which the
> imagination has been accustomed, and for which it is prepared, the
> contrary of all this happens. . . . The imagination no longer feels
> the usual facility of passing from the event which goes before to
> that which comes after. . . . The fancy is stopped and interrupted
> in that natural movement or career, according to which it was
> proceeding. Those two events seem to stand at a distance from
> each other; it endeavours to bring them together, but they refuse

to unite; and it feels, or imagines it feels, something like a gap or interval betwixt them. It . . . endeavours to find out something which may fill up the gap, which, like a bridge, may so far at least unite those seemingly distant objects, as to render the passage of the thought betwixt them smooth, and natural, and easy. The supposition of a chain of intermediate, though invisible, events which succeed each other in a train similar to that in which the imagination has been accustomed to move, and which link together those two disjointed appearances, is the only means by which the imagination can fill up this interval, is the only bridge which, if one may say so, can smooth its passage from the one object to the other.[6]

Smith is drawing here on Hume's account both of causation and of our belief in an external world. He writes not only of *constant* conjunction but also of *coherence* in our experience. When he describes the 'interruption' of customary connections and of the 'smooth passage' of the imagination (or 'the fancy' or 'the thought'), and when he proceeds to say that the imagination fills up the gap by supposing a chain of intermediate though invisible events, he is making use of Hume's doctrine in *Treatise* I.iv.2, the section entitled 'Of scepticism with regard to the senses'. Smith is not simply taking over Hume's theory, for Hume deals with our belief in the continued existence of material things while Smith talks about scientific theory. But Smith is adapting Hume's account of the imagination from the one subject to the other. Smith thinks that philosophy or science is an enlargement of common-sense belief as represented by Hume. Philosophy, 'the science of the connecting principles of nature . . . may be regarded as one of those arts which address themselves to the imagination'.[7] Of course Hume himself says that systems of philosophy are also a product of the imagination, but his description of the processes of the imagination in filling up gaps comes into his account of our ordinary belief in an external world, and that is what Adam Smith uses in his account of scientific theory.

When I first read this section of Adam Smith's 'History of Astronomy' I was immediately struck by its Humean character. (At the time I was not aware of John Millar's letter to David Douglas.) It seems that David Douglas had the same experience and that his conception of Hume's philosophy included the role of the imagination in building up our beliefs about the world. There can be little doubt that Adam Smith himself appreciated this side of Hume. Although his debt to Hume is not mentioned in the 'History of Astronomy', the phrases from the *Treatise* are unmistakable.

Smith takes seriously his conclusion that scientific theory is the work of the imagination. His history of astronomy leads up to a detailed account of the theory of Newton. While Smith writes in more than one place of the attractions of the Newtonian system to the imagination, his description of it very naturally uses at times the language of objective fact. So he ends by recognizing that a work of imagination can seem to be the discovery of truth.

> And even we, while we have been endeavouring to represent all philosophical systems as mere inventions of the imagination, to connect together the otherwise disjointed and discordant phaenomena of nature, have insensibly been drawn in, to make use of language expressing the connecting principles of this one, as if they were the real chains which Nature makes use of to bind together her several operations. Can we wonder then, that it should have gained the general and complete approbation of mankind, and that it should now be considered, not as an attempt to connect in the imagination the phaenomena of the Heavens, but as the greatest discovery that ever was made by man, the discovery of an immense chain of the most important and sublime truths, all closely connected together, by one capital fact, of the reality of which we have daily experience.[8]

Smith seems to be implying here that it is in fact a mistake, though a natural one, to think of Newton's system as the discovery of objective truths and to think of gravity as a 'real chain' that binds operations in nature. This belief is an 'illusion of the imagination', to use a Humean phrase that Smith borrows in *The Theory of Moral Sentiments* (1759),[9] composed a little later than the 'History of Astronomy'. The *Moral Sentiments* is much concerned with the role of the imagination in moral judgement, but there is one place where Smith also relates it to economics. This comes at the beginning of Part IV. Again Smith builds on a doctrine of Hume, whom he describes, without naming him, as 'an ingenious and agreeable philosopher, who joins the greatest depth of thought to the greatest elegance of expression, and possesses the singular and happy talent of treating the abstrusest subjects not only with the most perfect perspicuity, but with the most lively eloquence'.[10] Hume, he says, has explained the beauty of utility. The owner of a useful object receives aesthetic pleasure from it by being reminded of its convenience. A spectator receives similar pleasure by sympathy. We find 'the palaces of the great' beautiful because we imagine the satisfaction we would get if we owned and used them. Smith then adds his own contribution, that we often come to set a greater value on the convenient means than on the end which they were designed to promote. 'The poor man's son, whom heaven in its anger has visited with ambition,' goes beyond admiration of palaces to envy. He labours all his life to outdo his competitors, only to find in the end that the rich are no happier than the poor in the things that really matter. 'And it is well that nature imposes on us in this manner. It is this deception which rouses and keeps in continual motion the industry of mankind.' The individual does not reap for himself the full benefit of his exertions; there is a benefit to society at large, for the rich 'are led by an invisible hand' to distribute much of their substance among a circle of retainers and so, 'without intending it, without knowing it, advance the interest of the society, and afford means to the multiplication of the species'.[11]

Smith has an ambivalent attitude to this 'deception' by nature or the imagination. On the one hand, he says it is deception; the ambition of the poor man's son is unfortunate, a visitation of the anger of heaven, and is succeeded in the end by the discovery that power and riches afford little satisfaction and are dangerous. On the other hand, this realization of the truth is a 'splenetic philosophy', that comes to us only 'in the languor of disease and the weariness of old age'. In a normal healthy state we let our imagination run away with us, and this is just as well because the deception is useful to society and mankind. At any rate Smith is clear that it is a deception and that there is an alternative view which is true, though apparently less preferable.

Would he say quite the same of Newton's scientific theory? He does imply that we are deceived in thinking the theory to be a discovery of truth and not just an 'invention' of the imagination. But would he be ready to add that it is therefore *false* and that there is, or could be, an alternative theory which is true? Apparently not, for he puts all scientific theories in the same boat. Are there then no objective truths of astronomy to be discovered, or is the position rather that there are truths of nature but they cannot be discovered by man because he has to rely on his imagination?

In either event, why does astronomy differ from economics? For Adam Smith, economic theory is as much a part of 'philosophy' (or science) as is astronomy, and so any theoretical construction in economics too must be a product of the imagination. Perhaps he thinks that the economic truth which we discover in illness or old age is not a theoretical construction (despite his calling it a 'splenetic *philosophy*'), but is rather a datum of experience. If so, his claim is dubious. Even in this bicentennial year of 1976 we do not have to accept as holy writ everything that Adam Smith said on economics—especially if it is not contained within the holy book, *The Wealth of Nations*. It seems to me romantic fiction to say that the successful tycoon who began in poverty obtains no real addition to happiness from his riches and power, or that (to use Adam Smith's own words): 'In ease of body and peace of mind, all the different ranks of life are nearly upon a level, and the beggar, who suns himself by the side of the highway, possesses that security which kings are fighting for.'[12]

How does Smith's view of Newtonian astronomy compare with Hume's view of commonsense belief in an external world? Smith writes of an invention of the imagination, Hume of a fiction. Smith says, or implies, that we are mistaken to take Newton's theory as a statement of truth. Would Hume say this of belief in a continuing external world? It is hard to know. Hume first tells us it is 'in vain' to ask whether there be body or not, since 'we must take [it] for granted in all our reasonings'. Professor Price has considered, in *Hume's Theory of the External World*, how we should interpret this statement. Are we to understand 'in vain' as 'meaningless', the idea being that we cannot say the proposition 'Body exists' is either true or false, although we must act as if it were true? Or does Hume mean that the question is pointless because the answer to it has to be positive, that is, that the proposition 'Body exists' is undoubtedly true? Yet there is a passage later in this section of the *Treatise*[13] where Hume says firmly that the imagination's fiction of the continued existence of material objects is 'really false'.

There is one important difference between Hume's view of the problem of body and Adam Smith's view of Newtonian mechanics. Smith has endeavoured to answer the Humean question, 'What causes induce us to believe in the existence of gravity?' Smith would not, however, have added: 'But 'tis in vain to ask, Whether there be gravity or not? That is a point which we must take for granted in all our reasonings.' Earlier theories of astronomy did not include a belief in gravity; and if anyone had suggested to Smith that a later theory might abandon Newton's concept of gravity and explain the observed facts in a different way, Smith would have agreed that this was quite possible. So although he is following Hume in the type of explanation that he gives, there is an important difference in their conclusions. In Smith's time it was a bold thing to say that Newton's mechanics was an 'invention of the imagination' rather than a discovery of truth, but it was far less bold than Hume's theory that belief in a continuing material world is due to 'fiction' by the imagination. Since past systems of astronomy had done without gravity, one could conceive that future systems might dispense with it. There is no analogue in a history of different systems of ordering common experience. The belief in continuing material bodies has not been preceded by one or more different ways of interpreting sense experience, in consequence of which we could conceive of yet another interpretation becoming standard at some future time. There have of course been *philosophies* that have denied the existence of a material world and have given an alternative explanation of experience. We can ask of them, as we can ask of scientific theories, whether they should be described simply as 'inventions of the imagination' or whether they can properly aim at the discovery of truth. We cannot, however, say that the interpretation of experience in terms of an external world comes naturally to modern man but did not come naturally to the men of some other culture in the past and might not do so to the men of the future.

Perhaps this is too sweeping. Primitive animists and early systems of law attribute a kind of personality to phenomena that modern man treats as material. It is possible to suppose that some early human cultures had no conception of inanimate objects and interpreted all their experience in personalist terms. It is also possible to suppose that a human culture of the future may obliterate the distinction between the animate and the material by interpreting all experience within a framework of materialism. Some philosophers take happily enough to a thesis that identifies the mind with the brain, and quite a number of people who are uncontaminated by philosophy but imbued with natural science find it hard nowadays to distinguish mind and brain. One can envisage such an attitude becoming standard at some future time. Different ways of interpreting experience under the categories of mind and matter, mind and body, space and time, are not confined to philosophy but can be traced in the language of different cultures. For example, Biblical Hebrew has no word for 'matter'. The term for a thing is the same as the term for a word and is derived from the verb 'to speak'. Presumably the ancient Hebrews formed the concept of a thing from the idea of what was denoted by a word. So there have been cultures that did not use the modern concept of matter, and there might be a culture that would not use the present concept of mind.

All this, however, is not relevant to Hume's theory. Hume says that he is answering the question, 'What causes induce us to believe in the existence of *body?*' (meaning material things), but he does not intend to contrast a belief in the existence of material things with a belief in the existence of animated beings. His question, and his answer to it, could apply just as well to a society of universal animists who believed that everything in the world was animate. If they found themselves in Wonderland, they would not be surprised to see croquet being played with animals as implements (what else could one use?) but they would be as much astonished as Alice at the sight of the Cheshire cat's grin without the cat. Hume's problem is to account for our belief that what we perceive continues to exist beyond our transient perceptions. The problem is not affected by the question whether these objects of perception are material substances or something else. Hume in fact denies that they can be material substances in Locke's sense of that term and argues for a neutral monist theory which treats both mind and matter as having the same sort of component elements. It makes no difference whether we think that the man on the Clapham omnibus believes this theory, or Locke's, or Berkeley's, or the universal animist's, or something else. In any event he believes that the objects of perception persist beyond his perception of them, and it is to *this* belief that Hume addresses himself.

Hume distinguishes the commonsense belief in the existence of body from philosophical theories about the nature of body. He says that both are products of the imagination but of different 'principles' of that omnicompetent capacity. The peripatetic theories of matter, with their talk of substantial forms, occult qualities, sympathies and antipathies, and abhorrence of a vacuum, were 'guided by every trivial propensity of the imagination', like the fables of poets and the follies of children. We must distinguish the 'changeable, weak, and irregular' principles of the imagination that produce such ideas from 'the principles which are permanent, irresistable, and universal'.[14] The commonsense belief in continuing objects of perception is due to these, and so is itself permanent, irresistible, and universal. The theories of ancient philosophy, Hume continues, are not founded on these principles. 'The modern philosophy', with its distinction between perceptions and external things, 'pretends . . . to arise only from the solid, permanent, and consistent principles of the imagination',[15] but Hume takes himself to be refuting that claim in his criticism of the theory. He can suppose that he is doing so because he now describes the permanent principles of the imagination as 'solid' and 'consistent', so that they cannot support a theory which he shows to be inconsistent and resting on weak argument.

Is the 'vulgar' belief in body any better off in *this* respect? Unlike the theories of philosophy, whether ancient or modern, it is held universally and irresistibly. But is it consistent and based on a solid foundation? The imagination produces it in order to maintain coherence among our perceptions, but according to Hume there is inconsistency within the state of mind of the 'vulgar'. They '*suppose* their perceptions to be their only objects, and at the same time *believe* the continu'd existence of matter'. This is inconsistent because the supposition that our perceptions are our only objects implies that two perceptions separated by an interruption cannot be one persisting object. Hence the belief must be assigned to the imagination and not to reason.[16] Here Hume seems to think that the imagination can accommodate inconsistency, as reason cannot. If so, he has no business to say that the modern philosophy cannot be the product of the same operations of the imagination because it is not 'consistent' and 'solid'. In the paragraph where he describes the inconsistency of the 'vulgar' conception, Hume goes on to claim that his examination discloses 'a consistent system' in which each part 'is supported by the strongest proofs'.[17] The 'system' of which he speaks here, and at the beginning of the paragraph, is his own system of philosophy, not the notions of the 'vulgar'. He is entitled to claim that his philosophical theory is superior to 'the modern philosophy' because it is consistent and solidly based, the superiority being judged by criteria of reason, as is proper for the appraisal of philosophical theories. But if one of the differences between imagination and reason is that the imagination can ignore these criteria, then Hume is not entitled to dispute the supposed claim of the modern philosophy to arise, like the belief of the vulgar, from the 'permanent' principles of the imagination.

Hume's attribution of consistency to his favoured type of imagination is not, however, a groundless aberration. Even the kind of imagination employed by poets and novelists normally maintains a consistency within its own fictitious creations. Walt Whitman was deliberately outraging the customary norms even of poetry when he said

Do I contradict myself?

Very well then I contradict myself.

Consistency is a negative form of coherence, and when Hume's 'permanent principles' of the imagination pursue coherence among perceptions they follow a kind of logic. It is not surprising, therefore, that Hume should at times write of 'the imagination or understanding'[18] when he wants to distinguish this kind of imagination from the more flighty kind (even though at other times he contrasts imagination with understanding when he equates understanding with 'reason'[19]). The most important function of the imagination, as depicted in Hume's account, is not to form mental images (which is relatively infrequent anyway) but to provide a constructional framework, so to speak, into which impressions of sense are fitted as building blocks. Hume talks as if the main job of the imagination were to fill up the gaps between impressions with ideas that are images of impressions; but it seems to me that if we are looking for an accurate phenomenological description, the gaps are commonly left vacant: the important supplement to impressions of sense is their synthesis, the construction of a framework into which they are fitted. If we wish to describe this framework in terms of a Humean empiricism, we should do so, following Professor Price's lead, by saying that it is the postulation of a set of series of resembling sensibilia.

It seems reasonable enough to attribute this to the imagination, for it is the kind of synthetic function performed by the imagination in creating fictions proper. Hume's 'permanent principles' of the imagination differ from the imagination of fiction in confining the synthetic framework so as to accommodate sense impressions. The imagination of fiction is free from any such limitation. The former kind of imagination is universal and irresistible because it conforms to sense impressions which, taken by and large, are closely similar for most persons and which are themselves irresistible or independent of our will. And if we ask ourselves why sense impressions have these characteristics, we are naturally inclined to suppose it is because they are caused by external objects. An imaginative synthesis that is anchored to sense impressions is universal and irresistible because the sense impressions themselves are universal and irresistible. A fictional synthesis may be equally coherent, but it is fiction, not fact, because it is uninhibited by that universal and irresistible experience which we take to be objective fact.

Hume's method of distinguishing the stable imagination of belief from the more free imagination of fantasy and art is helpful but does not go far enough. He assimilates them too closely in saying that both produce fiction. It is typical of Hume to be so carried away by an important discovery as to exaggerate its consequences *pour épater le rationaliste*.

Adam Smith was a more cautious character, who had no wish to shock anybody. In saying that scientists have imagined inventions he does not say they have invented science fiction—or any other sort of fiction. But he does contrast an invention by the imagination with a discovery of truth, and so he implies that scientific theory cannot be true. The constructions of scientific theory are certainly closer to the constructions of perceptual belief than to those of fiction, for they too are intended to accommodate and render coherent the data of experience. But unlike the belief in persistent objects of perception, they are not permanent, universal, and irresistible. One theory is succeeded by another, and today we should be more ready than Adam Smith to think that the replacement of the currently favoured theory of physics or astronomy is not just possible but probable. The replacement of one theory by another is not always in order to accommodate new empirical facts. The new facts could often be accommodated within a revised, but more complicated, version of the old theory. The new theory may be preferred because it is simpler or because it can be connected more directly with the theory of a related branch of science. If so, the criteria for preference are quasi-logical and aesthetic, like the criteria that shape the course of the imagination in Hume's theory of the external world. Is it then proper to claim that the preferred theory is more *true* than its rival? In these days of relativity theory, physics itself seems to cast doubt on any idea of strictly objective truths in nature independent of observers at different points of space and time. Adam Smith's view of science appears more perceptive today than it will have done in the eighteenth century.

I have said that the criteria for preferring one scientific theory to another may be quasi-logical and aesthetic, which means that scientific theory has something in common with works of art. The similarity includes a measure of freedom in the construction of schemata. Science is less free than art because it has to accommodate itself to empirical facts, but it is more free than perceptual belief because the synthesis that it adopts is not irresistible. The reason for this is that the gaps between empirical data in the postulated series of sensibilia are vastly greater in scientific synthesis than in perceptual synthesis. In perception, although the experienced data are fragmentary, there are enough elements of the various series to bring the synthetic structure to mind without effort and inevitably. In science this is not so, and the imagination has to cast around for analogies and underlying resemblances; effort and initiative are needed to think of a synthesis that will do the job.

A clear example to illustrate this is evolutionary theory in biology. Actually observable instances of change in a species are rare, and so the similarities between different species do not readily suggest the possibility of change from one species to another. The gaps in the series of events postulated by evolution are enormous, and most of the data of common experience suggest instead that species are unchanging and so were 'special creations'. In working out an evolutionary hypothesis, Darwin's imagination was stimulated both by unusual evidence and by the analogy of Malthus's theory about human population. Even when Darwin had produced a convincing theory of natural selection to explain why certain varieties of a species survived, the gaps in the postulated series of events were still wide enough to leave uncertainty (and so room for alternative hypotheses) about the process of genetic mutation. Another clear example is provided, as Adam Smith saw, by the history of astronomy. Each of the theories postulates a system in which the actually observable phenomena form only a tiny part of all that would be observable by an omnipercipient being. The gaps are so great that the observed phenomena can be accommodated by several theories of very different character. The same thing holds good of present-day theories in astrophysics about black holes, antimatter, and other novel entities.

People familiar with scientific work often say that it needs imagination, and imply that in this respect it resembles art. We commonly think of the imagination as free (unlike sense-perception and deductive reasoning) and as requiring initiative. There is no surprise in the news that science is like this. The surprise is Hume's news that perceptual belief involves imagination, *despite* coming upon us irresistibly and without effort on our part. Hume's account is enlightening not only for showing us the relation between actual experience and the persisting world we take ourselves to perceive, but also for bringing out a leading feature of imaginative activity, the disposition to fill gaps in a schema, a feature that can be detected in perceptual belief and also, as Adam Smith saw, in science. Kant too was to write of the work of the imagination in perception and was to emphasize its character as synthesis. We should not simply say that Hume anticipated Kant. Each of them has drawn attention to different aspects of the imagination in contributing to our perception of the external world.

Hume's philosophy influenced Adam Smith even more deeply in ethics, but I suppose that this is commonly understood, in general outline at least. The influence here was not direct, so as to make Smith a follower of Hume, except in relatively minor matters. Instead it stimulated Smith to criticism and to the production of alternative views that surmounted the faults he found in Hume. Both Hume and Smith again had much to say that is enlightening about the work of the imagination in moral judgement, and on that particular topic Smith was, I think, even more perceptive than Hume. But all this is only marginally relevant to my subject today.

In speaking of 'the true old Humean philosophy' I have confined myself to certain sections of the *Treatise*, and this may seem perverse in the light of Hume's purported repudiation of that work in later life. There are three things that I would say in justification. First, Adam Smith was influenced far more by the *Treatise* than by the *Enquiries*, both in his theory of science and throughout his theory of ethics. On theoretical questions of philosophy the young Adam Smith was almost as much enraptured by parts of the *Treatise* as he was by the Stoics on issues of practical doctrine. Secondly, only the *Treatise* gives a detailed explanation of Hume's theory of our belief in a continuing external world. And finally, this bicentennial conference is a proper occasion for me to repeat what I have said elsewhere, that in my judgement Hume's *Treatise of Human Nature* is the greatest work of philosophy written in the English language.

1. E. C. Mossner *The Life of David Hume* (1954) ch. 10, especially pp. 131–2; also E. C. Mossner 'The Continental Reception of Hume's *Treatise*, 1739–1741' *Mind*, N.S. lvi (1947).
2. *Diary and Letters of Madame D'Arblay*, ed. Austin Dobson (1904–5) i. 398–9.
3. Letter to William Strahan, dated 9 November 1776.
4. Thomas Reid *Inquiry into the Human Mind* (1764) ch. 1, §5.
5. H. H. Price *Hume's Theory of the External World* (1940); Norman Kemp Smith *The Philosophy of David Hume* (1941), following upon his seminal articles 'The Naturalism of Hume' *Mind*, N.S. xiv (1905).

6. 'History of Astronomy', II, §§7–8.

7. §13.

8. IV, §76.

9. Hume *Treatise*, p. 267; cf. p. 200, and 'illusion of the fancy', pp. 314, 360: Smith *Theory of Moral Sentiments* (hereafter *TMS*), ed. D. D. Raphael and A. L. Macfie (Oxford: Clarendon Press 1976), III. 2.4; cf. I. iii. 2. 2, II. i. 5.11, IV. 1.9.

10. *TMS*, IV. 1.2.

11. *TMS*, IV. 1.8–10.

12. *TMS*, IV. 1.10.

13. *Treatise*, p. 209.

14. *Treatise*, pp. 224–5.

15. *Treatise*, p. 226.

16. *Treatise*, p. 209.

17. *Treatise*, p. 210.

18. 'The imagination or understanding, call it which you please', ibid., p. 440; 'the understanding or imagination', p. 104.

19. In two closely similar footnotes (pp. 117–18 and p. 371), Hume distinguishes a wider and a narrower sense of 'imagination'; the narrower sense is contrasted with 'reason' in the first of these notes, with 'the understanding' in the second.

Hume's Science of Politics

TOWARDS THE END of his contribution to the volume of essays presented to E. C. Mossner,[1] Professor Jessop says that a precondition of sound exegesis of Hume is to study him widely, and other writers have stressed the fact that a Hume caged in the English empirical tradition is an anaemic and attenuated Hume. No less attenuated and anaemic, and indeed seriously distorted, is a political Hume studied exclusively in the light of English politics and the English political tradition: one result has been the application to him of the unhelpful label 'Tory', the most conspicuous outward sign of the refusal to take seriously Hume's claim to be a philosopher above party. The view of Hume's philosophy as essentially critical, negative and destructive which held sway for so long, cast its shadow also over the interpretation of his political thought. As Vlachos said in one of the earliest attempts to study Hume's politics comprehensively: it is not an exaggeration to say that nowadays (1955) Hume is known almost exclusively, meaning, of course, as a political theorist, for his critique of contract theory.[2] This could easily be regarded as 'anti-Whig' and therefore 'Tory'. And I suppose the common view still is that Hume, a philosophical revolutionary, was timid and conservative, even reactionary, in his politics.

I would argue that Hume's science of politics, studied in its full extent and in its historical circumstances, was constructive, forward-looking, a programme of modernization, an education for backward-looking men. I use these terms neutrally. I am trying to see the thing as Hume saw it, and of course I am having to leave out a very great deal, Hume's historiography, for instance, and much else.

The obvious starting place for a study of Hume's science of politics might seem to be the famous essay with the challenging title: *That Politics may be reduced to a Science*. This essay, however, makes large claims on a comparatively narrow front which are notoriously not very impressively backed up by its contents, and puts forward a sort of political geometry that was neither typical of nor seminal for Scottish eighteenth-century social and political theory. Perhaps it is most fittingly interpreted, in the light of Hume's thought as a whole, as an example of political moderation in action, the application of scientific detachment to party politics in the context of the hounding of Walpole, the sting, or balm, of the essay being in its tail.

If one is to properly appreciate and understand Hume's science of politics, one must take one's bearings on the definition offered in the Introduction to the *Treatise*: 'politics consider men as united in society and dependent on each other'. This is broad enough to take one right across all Hume's writings from the *Treatise* to the *History*, a perilous journey, which philosophers, as such, are not called on to face. They can confine themselves to the *Treatise* and the *Enquiries*, or even just the former, and quarrel over meanings and interpretations without having to *use* this controversial material to interpret other aspects of Hume's thought. The trouble is that those who do have to go beyond the *Treatise* and *Enquiries* often proceed with a confidence in their portmanteau abridgements of the philosophy expounded in those works that scarcely seems justified to anyone who listens seriously and intensively to the debates of the professional philosophers as to how they are to be interpreted. Those who are not professional philosophers, the 'rabble without doors" apparently do *not* get the impression that 'all goes not well within'. If they did, they might be more strongly tempted to try other routes involving wider study and using 'philosophy' in its much more extended eighteenth-century sense.[3]

These other, more historical routes have their own difficulties and complexities, however. What is nowadays called the Scottish Enlightenment, for instance, is by no means such a homogeneous affair as the name, and the introductory literature, might suggest, nor, in some important respects, is Hume respresentative of it; in social science, particularly, he is neither as representative, nor was he such a seminal influence as his friend Adam Smith. To make this point properly calls for elaborate enquiry. In general, one can say that Smith aimed at a complete social science, of which *The Wealth of Nations* is one part only and *The Theory of Moral Sentiments* another, while his projected work on jurisprudence and government never saw the light of day, although there is enough evidence to give one some idea of what it would have been like, whereas Hume does not seem to have felt such a compelling need 'to be at home in the world when I know it', so that one can see why it was Smith, not Hume, who for John Millar was the 'Newton' of the history of civil society. Smith aimed at a science that would explain social change, the progress of society, in terms of human drives and propensities familiar to every one, and what was later called the law of heterogeneity of ends or unintended consequences, bridging the gap between the rationality and complexity of the result, that is, civilization, and—if one removed providential agency—the puny and not very rational means, namely, the mainly self-interested purposes and objectives of individuals. To bring out the difference between Hume and the wider objectives of Smith in the science of politics, one may employ a distinction between locating change and comprehending it. Smith was not content simply to describe the progress of society in Europe—commerce and manufactures giving rise to liberty and the rule of law—as he said Hume had been the first to do.

Smith agreed with Hume that the development of liberty was the result of historical circumstances peculiar to Europe. He agreed that it was a European, not an exclusively English phenomenon, because the representative or parliamentary institutions absent in the absolute monarchies were not the be-all and end-all of liberty; that was something more fundamental, namely, the independence and security of individuals guaranteed by the rule of law, and that, for all practical purposes, was found in the European monarchies. This reflects the Europocentric outlook of Hume's science of politics: the framework of his thinking on government, liberty, political civilization generally, being Europe, not just England. And this is one aspect of his 'sceptical' Whiggism, a Whiggism that appeared dubious to contemporaries because the science of politics involved was iconoclastic, destructive of favourite Whig idols and prejudices such as the unbridgeable gulf between English freedom and French slavery. In Hume one finds a comparative study of types of government that brings out the serious ingrained disadvantages, as well as the advantages, of the 'matchless' British constitution, and a theory of political obligation that has a legitimate place for the absolute monarchy of France, as Locke's has not, and which reduces Locke's theory of consent to a parochial absurdity. Hume's idea of political civilization included what he called the 'civilized monarchies' of Europe. There was no qualitative difference between them and the British form of government, as there was for those who, in Hume's eyes, excessively admired the latter: an attitude which rendered difficult, if not impossible, the sort of comparative study of the governments of Europe that is to be found in Hume's *Essays*. Thus, among other things, Hume's view of liberty as an achievement of modern European civilization, a perspective in which, as in Sir James Steuart's *Principles of Political Economy*, the Revolution did not mean 1688, but the transition from a feudal / military to a commercial Europe, which was a surer guarantee of liberty than any revolution or particular type of government. Such a view of liberty made nonsense of orthodox Whig historiography and broke down the insular prejudice that blocked the road to a science of comparative politics.

A Whiggism or establishment philosophy that involved such a slaughter of holy cows must have seemed equivalent to Toryism or worse in the eyes of orthodox Whigs, but it was the result of the same attitude of detached and impartial observation that one finds in Smith.

But Smith widened the horizon of the science of politics still further, in that for him, the progress of commerce and liberty in Europe was an example of and, in some important respects, an exception to a general principle or law of social evolution as such. Hume was not a 'philosophical' historian in that wider sense.

I HAVE SAID that the Scottish Enlightenment is a complex affair, and generalization about it is liable to be dangerous. Perhaps as a single peg on which to hang the interpretation of its social and political theory, one may usefully employ Burke's maxim: we must all obey the great law of change. There were special circumstances in eighteenth-century Scotland that brought the fact of change home to men's minds in specially compelling ways, and further, brought home to their minds the need for change and the fate of those who are unwilling or unable to adapt to change. This is a recurring theme in the Waverley novels, where Scott shows us a whole gallery of figures who in their various ways, tragic or comic, are left in psychological rigidity on the sandbanks of time. 'We must all obey the great law of change' implies not merely the detached observation that for Smith is the task of the philosopher, par excellence: it is a recommendation and a warning, it implies resistance and defence mechanisms and the consequent need for programme, propaganda and rhetoric. Smith, it is worth remembering, had begun his career as an expert in the science of rhetoric, and the *Wealth of Nations* is propaganda as well as science: the science is *ipso facto* programme and propaganda. Likewise, studying Hume widely surely involves examining his philosophy in the light of the science of rhetoric and its history.

Be that as it may, whatever else Hume's scepticism may mean, it does not mean lack of political programme and commitment. Obeying the law of change meant modernizing, and Hume's science of politics seen in the light of the mood and needs and opportunities and challenges of eighteenth-century Scotland was essentially a programme of modernization. Even the promotion of moderation in party politics, usually regarded as Hume's main political objective, can be viewed in the light of the need for modernization: the party politics Hume objected to were not party politics as such—because in a mixed government such as the British, a division of parties was inevitable, given human nature and that type of government—but the backward-looking party politics of Whigs and Tories based on the dynastic question. His aim was to modernize the political thinking of a post-revolutionary establishment, to bring it up-to-date.

Hume's republicanism—and Rousseau wrote in his *Confessions* of Hume's *'âme républicaine'*—though purely academic, because the republican form of government, although ideally the best, was unrealizable in modern Britain, may be seen as an example of the nostalgia that necessarily accompanies realization of the need to obey the great law of change and is the other side of that medal. Not for nothing did sentimental nostalgia become a characteristic Scottish product and export. Obeying the law of change has nothing to do with the idea of progress, which none of the leading Scottish social theorists subscribed to, however ardently they believed in 'improvement' and the need for 'improvement', but on the contrary suggests a harsh necessity to adapt more or less painfully to something objective and coldly observed. Obedience to the great law of change was Hume's teaching for not only Tories, but Whigs also, whose fixation on 1688 and 1714, the establishing of the establishment, was backward-looking and inhibiting; their political theories were both out-of-date, not only divine right and passive obedience, but also the 'fashionable system' of contract, the latter because among other things it induced a trigger-happiness about the right of resistance, which post-1688 was inept and uncalled for. Hume's object was to get men, both Whigs and Tories, to turn round and face the present and the future; a new secular, scientific age of economic challenge and opportunity especially. Seen in this context, his definition, already quoted, of the science of politics has a ring of modernity about it, society being seen as a rationally comprehensible system of mutual needs and services, Hegel's *System der Bedürfnisse*, not an arena for aggressive display and contention over outmoded dynastic and religious loyalties and dogmas.

It sounds modern. But one has to remember that the fact of men united in society and dependent on each other was the official and, so they claimed, empirical and, so they also claimed, classical starting point of the 'modern' school of Natural Law, Grotius, Pufendorf and their numerous followers, including Hutcheson. Failure to appreciate this, which may be due to tangling too exclusively with Hobbes and Locke—the sort of selectivity and looking down the wrong end of the telescope that so seriously distorts the history of ideas—has led to a great deal of misunderstanding and confusion, with respect to both Smith and Hume. For example, one finds admirers of Smith, anxious to make out that the ground of the teaching of *The Wealth of Nations* is empirical, that his economic doctrines were not deduced *a priori* from some natural system of liberty reflecting the cosmic optimism of fashionable eighteenth-century Deism, and so forth, charging in to rescue him from Natural Law, as though Newtonian empiricism and Natural Law were totally incompatible. This sort of abridgement to the point of distortion of Natural Law is what lies behind the description of Hume's science of politics as involving the destruction of the 'metaphysical', 'rationalistic' and 'individualistic' foundations of Natural

Law. From Hume's point of view, what had happened was that the old foundations were becoming less tenable and secure in an increasingly secular age; the opinion on which all government rests had moved and was moving in a secular direction (and this after all was the constant cry of the clergy, including notable thinkers like Berkeley), while the foundations of Natural Law, in spite of the great show of experimental method, of starting from the fact of human nature as given to observation, were, in the final analysis, theological, and for Hume, at any rate, not truly empirical. Hume's approach to Natural Law, therefore, was an example of the need to obey the great law of change: the theoretical foundations of modern society and government needed to be secularized. It was the first part of Hume's campaign to bring the political thinking of the establishment up to date: to give the regime philosophically respectable and secure intellectual foundations. From this point of view, what looks like critical destruction may be regarded as an attempt to salvage Natural Law, the alternative being Hobbism and the anti-social 'selfish system'.

But the danger of this sort of operation is that one is liable to be accused of undermining and destroying the very thing that one wants to save by adapting it to the needs and spirit of the age.

This was, for example, the fate of Hume's ecclesiastical friends, the progressive party in the Church of Scotland, the so-called Moderates, whose attempt to save religion and the authority of the Kirk by obeying the great law of change as they understood it—the alternative being ineffective isolation on a sand-bank of outmoded theology in a sea of godlessness—appeared to their opponents as selling the fort to the spirit of the age and the powers that be.

And similarly Adam Smith's ingenious use of sympathy and the impartial spectator to accommodate the economic opportunism of modern commercial society in a moral theory that avoided the offensive paradoxes of the *Fable of the Bees*, was seen by his contemporaries as a sell-out on the ethical front. A theory so adjustable could accommodate a gang of murderers; in effect, it meant turning ethics into social psychology, and so on. Similarly, Hume was accused of the very thing he was trying to save Natural Law from: Hobbism or quasi-Hobbism and the destruction of the natural foundations of justice. And of all the various responses to the needs of the age and the great law of change, Hume's attempt to give Natural Law a more truly empirical foundation was perhaps the most avant-garde and dangerous. It meant, among other things, the exclusion of the 'religious hypothesis' from the science of politics. So that the modernity of Hume's science of politics in this respect must not be taken for granted: it was an achievement, a defiance of Newtonian empiricism as that was understood by contemporaries, because that included the existence of a Deity with a purpose for his creatures.

Otherwise, there is far more continuity between Hume and Natural Law theory than is usually allowed for; the range of agreement has been obscured by oversimplified readings of such things as the state of nature and the social contract, and especially by the common misunderstanding of Natural Law already referred to. Proper exegesis by studying Hume widely should include the literature of natural jurisprudence; the teaching of that was just as important in the Scottish universities as the teaching of Newton, which has long been a commonplace of Hume interpretation. But the natural jurispurdence, which was just as much in the air Hume breathed as Newtonian science, has been comparatively neglected and its nature misunderstood.

An example of such misunderstanding was seen recently when a distinguished authority on the ethical philosophy of the period, in an elaborate and closely argued account of Hume's critique of ethical rationalism, equated the latter with Natural Law in such a way as to imply that the demolition of ethical rationalism entailed the demolition of Natural Law.[4] This is to take the wrong turning at the very start of a journey that leads not only to Hume's science of politics, but, as has been seen, to Adam Smith's; misunderstanding of the Natural Law known to Smith was a prime cause of the cluster of misconceptions that surrounded the classical idea of Smith's laissez-faire liberalism, and crucially the failure to appreciate the empirical social emphasis and framework of *The Wealth of Nations*, which is the *legacy* of Natural Law. Commentators have gone to work on Hume with the same abridged and misleading notion of Natural Law as *a priori*, rationalistic and individualistic. Hume is then said, by Meinecke, for instance, to have rejected Natural Law or destroyed its rational foundations, only to remain under the spell of *naturrechtlich* thinking (for example, in his idea of the uniformity of human nature, an idea which has traditionally been oversimplified to the point of caricature), whereas it is nearer the truth to say that as far as his thinking is sociologically orientated, it is precisely because he *was* under the influence of Natural Law. The starting point of the natural jurisprudence taught by Hutcheson and the authorities he recommended—Grotius, Pufendorf, Cumberland, and others—was man's social nature and the facts of his social life as given to observation and 'experiment', or what was called man's 'social constitution'. Hume's science of politics, of men united in society and dependent on each other, can be seen as a more intensive cultivation of the same field, applying a more genuinely empirical, more deeply researched science of man, and Smith's still more so, since Smith, for example, more consistently than

Hume, substituted moral consensus for utility, and carried research into men's material and psychological interdependence much further, so much further, in fact, that Smith described natural jurisprudence as the most important, but least cultivated, of all the sciences. One has the impression that Smith thought that so much had to be done as to constitute virtually a new departure—and Hume no doubt experienced the same peak-in-Darien feeling when he first discovered his key to all the sciences of humanity. Nevertheless, the ground theme of the project of a science of jurisprudence and politics was provided, in both cases, by the theorists of Natural Law: the social emphasis and comprehensiveness of the science of politics of Hume and Smith is their legacy.

And in Hume's account of political obligation in *Treatise* III, much of the apparatus of old-style Natural Law is still there. There is a place in Hume, in fact if not in name, for the state of nature, that is, a social state preceding the establishment of regular government or 'civil society'; a state which, as Hume pointed out, is more of a genuinely social state than, for example, Locke's, governed by rules of justice, which Hume is prepared to call 'natural laws' in so far as they are common to the species, universal in that sense, a justice that is prior to government and which government is instituted to maintain and enforce. Nor was there anything new in Hume's *use* of the idea of a wholly non-social or absolute state of nature as a fiction or methodological device, which is all it can be if men have always been social; in asserting that, Hume is merely aligning himself with Natural Law orthodoxy, against Epicurean and neo-Epicurean extravagance and 'mere' or useless hypothesis. Much of what has appeared to commentators so striking in Hume's account of government and justice in *Treatise* III can be found in Cumberland, Pufendorf and other natural law writers. I have given details elsewhere.[5] And Hume himself was anxious to make the point that only inconsistency in Grotius and Pufendorf, due to the spirit of system, separated his account of justice derived from social utility from theirs—basically, he claimed, they were in agreement.

But this is ingenuous. It conceals what really does strain the continuity between Hume and the jusnaturalists, namely, the secularization involved in Hume's application of what he regarded, and his contemporaries did not, as a more truly empirical method.

It is in the light of this attempt at a more truly empirical and therefor secular version of Natural Law, or the ground of Natural Law, that one can approach the famous so-called is/ought passage in the *Treatise*; over which it seems, to a historian at least, that a great deal of philosophical ingenuity and effort has been spent to little purpose. Because if one is asking the question: what did he mean? that is a historical question and demands knowledge of the somewhat complex back-ground, and if one is doing logic, then why drag in Hume, who wasn't a logician, at least not in the twentieth century sense of the word?

What Hume says in the is/ought passage applies not only to the rarified position of the ethical rationalists, who are outwardly the main and already, by Hutcheson and others, much battered target in *Treatise* III, the official opposition, but also to the systems of morality described towards the end of the is/ought paragraph as 'vulgar' (and by that Hume could not possibly have meant the ethical rationalists), which are not to be overthrown and got out of the way, but, as with the beliefs of the vulgar consciousness in general, are to be methodized and corrected: the systems of the classical moralists, the jusnaturalists, Butler, Hutcheson, that claimed in more or less sophisticated ways to be grounded on the facts of human nature as given to experience and familiar to everyone. What worries Hume about these 'vulgar' systems of morality is not the attempt to deduce 'ought' from 'is'—he proceeds to do it himself shortly afterwards—but the failure to do it properly. As Hume says, the 'ought' is suddenly and imperceptibly there; how it comes to be there is neither 'observed', nor 'explained'. And why it was not done properly in Hume's eyes is a fairly long story, which bears out very nicely Professor Jessop's point about wide study being the pre-condition of sound exegesis.

What is involved, in the final analysis, is Hume's eccentricity with respect to the whole background of Newtonian empiricism, owing to his crisis of religious belief as a young man, which made impossible for him any continuance of the alliance between theology and natural science.

The reader of, say, Hutcheson, Cumberland or Pufendorf, says Hume, in effect, in the very elliptical 'is/ought' passage, starts with the familiar basic facts, man's sociableness, the law of self-preservation, the sexual impulse and so on, only to find that these fundamental facts about mankind are also duties, the change being 'imperceptible'. We are endowed with the passion or propensity in order to be able to carry out the duty of propagating and preserving the species. The 'is' in fact is derived from the 'ought', unless one can establish empirically the existence of the ultimate 'is' and his laws and purpose for his creation. But the jusnaturalists and vulgar moralists took it for granted that philosophers had done that. The reader of the vulgar systems of morality finds that in spite of the great show of Newtonian method and renuncia-tion of 'mere' hypotheses, the facts of human nature are taken not as they come but as arranged prior to experience in a value system with reason, superior to the feelings, at the apex. The 'is' of human nature constitutes a reason-governed 'system' that is an 'ought', which in turn presupposes a God-governed system of all rational beings who recognize their obligation as moral agents. The reader finds that behind the fact of men united in society and dependent on each other is a prior 'society' of rational agents, which is not accounted for; man's 'social constitution' is seen to have two dimensions and one of them, the prior superior one, the locus of the origin of duty, obligation and justice, which have ultimately a divine source and sanction, has no truly empirical title. This was the point brought out by the fiction of an 'absolute' state of nature as used, for example, by Pufendorf: in a totally non-social state such as could never actually have existed, in which men are conceived as wholly independent of each other, men would still be morally bound by recognition of their rational humanity; they would still acknowledge the duty of giving every one his due, which is Justice in the superior sense; such a state would not be a state of war but a society. That society in Locke is not just a fact but a prior obligation is a point made by Polin, for instance.[6]

If, however, a true empiricism demands, as Hume wrote, in effect, to Hutcheson, that one bracket off the religious hypothesis and final causes, and if piety is not a primary feeling, as Hume argued in the *Natural History of Religion*, then in an imaginary absolute state of nature men entirely independent of one another would be entirely self-enclosed; there would be no justice, no obligation—indeed perhaps one can go so far as to say that the human psyche would cease to *be* altogether: 'the minds of men are mirrors to one another'. With the closing of the empirical route to God and the Great Society of Stoic provenance, man's 'social constitution' becomes one-dimensional, and the idea of society is given a wholly secular meaning and importance: *all* the social bonds are forged in the only sort of society we can know, that is society in what for the jusnaturalists and the vulgar systems of morality was the 'lower' sense.

Secularity and godlessness were traditionally connected with the 'selfish system', Epicureanism, neo-Epicureanism, Hobbism. What is new in Hume is the combination of secularity, the bracketting off of the religious hypothesis, with the intensely social thinking that is the legacy of Natural Law—a combination that intensifies the sociality. This daring application of the Newtonian principle of economy against the contemporary Newtonians is Hume's apparently unacknowledged contribution to social theory.

And because Hume's critique of contract theory is separate from his examination of the 'religious hypothesis', which had to be heavily camouflaged, it has not been generally noticed that the former is incomplete without the latter. The 'fashionable system' had a theological ground no less than had the passive obedience of the Tories. The promise remained the ultimate ground of political obligation, because it carried the divine sanction, which the mere institution of government in the interest of society did not: the two things were qualitatively different. Those who were not driven to question this would not have found Hume's reasoning impressive: his appeal to common experience, his massing of arguments on that front, was of relatively secondary importance.

On that front, the most telling contractarian reply would be to ask why the common experience that Hume appeals to does not include contract and consent as one of those beliefs of the vulgar consciousness which the ordinary man can only assert, or which are presupposed by what he says and does—the philosopher's task being to methodize and correct them. Hume says: ask the man in the street if he has consented to obey the government and he will think it a crazy question. But he thinks it a no less crazy question if you ask him why he believes that the sun will rise tomorrow. What, therefore, outside *Treatise* I does constitute a belief of the vulgar consciousness? The decision to regard the contract theory as a local philosophical aberration and not a non-rational assumption of all political, or at least truly human or civilized, political discourse, seems wholly arbitrary, and rests on a dubious knowledge of the history and ancestry of the theory, which Hume appears to regard as recent.

As Coleridge said in his essay *On the Constitution of Church and State*, the labourer discussing the injustice of the present rate of wages in an alehouse is fully possessed by the idea of an ever-originating social contract. He is not conscious of it, but, as St Augustine said about Time, he knows it well enough when you do not ask him.[7] That is not Hume, but is it not Humean?

But criticism of Hume's science of politics opens lengthy vistas. One might ask, as, for instance, Arnold Brecht does in his book *Political Theory*, whether bracketting off the religious hypothesis has not closed a possible source of fruitful ideas and damaged political science. And Silvana Castignone's demonstration that Hume's theory of justice and political obligation is internally self-contradictory seems to me difficult to answer.

My point, however, has been to show how studying Hume's science of politics widely against the historical background, for instance the related and overlapping Scottish and European backgrounds, and the context of Hume's political intentions and the needs and opportunities of the age as he understood them, shows us a Hume rather different from that of the conventional interpretation and perhaps even academic consensus. It shows us a constructive, forward-looking Hume, whose conservatism, if one must use the word, was like that of his friends, and other leading social theorists of the Scottish Enlightenment, the conservatism of realism, not complacency or fear, eternally suspicious of the quick solution and the political short-cut because insistent on the need for detached observation, and best understood as embodying Burke's maxim: we must all obey the great law of change. In Hume's case this led to the paradox of a post-revolutionary, establishment political philosophy, which in some respects was too avant-garde for his contemporaries.

1. W. B. Todd (ed.) *Hume and the Enlightenment* (Edinburgh and Austin 1974).
2. G. Vlachos *Essai sur la Politique de Hume* (Paris 1955) p. 16.
3. This is the multiple and more or less well-defined sense in which I used it in *Hume's Philosophical Politics* (Cambridge 1975).
4. D. D. Raphael 'Hume's Critique of Ethical Rationalism' in *Hume and the Enlightenment*: p. 15 'ethical rationalism, the contemporary form of natural law theory'; p. 19 'Now ethical rationalism went along with natural law theory'.
5. In Part One of *Hume's Philosophical Politics*.
6. R. Polin *La Politique Morale de John Locke* (Paris 1960) p. 135.
7. Samuel Taylor Coleridge *On the Constitution of Church and State*, ed. J. Barrell (London 1972) pp. 7–8.

Convention and Value

IT IS UNWISE to assume, when the first third of a work has been read, that that part can be fully understood without the need to pay attention to the remainder. Hume conceived the *Treatise of Human Nature* as a unity, and it is, therefore, not surprising that one may have to wait until one has read the third book, *Of Morals*, before one can be certain of having understood the first book.

The relation between the three books of the *Treatise* has been much discussed. Norman Kemp Smith argued that the second book throws great light upon the first book, and that it precedes the first book in date of composition.[1] I have myself tried to show that the reading of Book II is essential for the understanding of Book III.[2] I have now concluded that aspects of Book III contain a clue to the understanding of certain features of Book I. Thus Hume's account of the nature of virtue enables us to see what kind of justification can be given for believing in a continuously and independently existing external world, and also for believing that it is in some sense reasonable to rely on past experiences in the planning of our future actions. Tendencies to hold these beliefs are virtues, although their truth cannot be established by reason. The concept of virtue is thus fundamental to Hume's epistemology. But these are not virtues I propose to discuss in this lecture, since I have discussed them elsewhere.[3]

However, I shall here be concerned to advocate that an aspect of Book I of *The Treatise* is intelligible only in the light of the account of virtue in Book III. In coming to the end of a good detective story one understands some of the strange happenings at the beginning of it. Things fall into place. I believe this to be true of Hume's *Treatise* also.

THE IMPORTANCE of the concept of artificial virtue in Hume's moral theory can hardly be disputed. Respect for property rights, chastity, faithfulness to promises and allegiance to government are such virtues. Although these are the only artificial virtues Hume discusses, he nowhere suggests that there are not other such virtues. All artificial virtues are intelligible only in the light of certain conventions entered into by members of a society, and their value depends upon general continuance of behaviour conformable to the conventions adopted. What has not been appreciated is that the concept of artificial virtue is crucial for the understanding of aspects of Hume's philosophy other than his moral and political theory as normally understood. I shall be particularly concerned to show that Hume's account of the place of language in human life cannot be understood unless due weight is given to his discussion of artificial virtues, and in particular to the special concept of convention that plays a crucial role in the explanation of such virtues.

In the first part of this essay, I shall criticize what has been called Hume's 'official view' about the meanings of words, according to which view the meanings of words are mental images. If the meanings of words are such images their essentially private nature entails the impossibility of communication. It is, of course, possible that Hume thought that the meanings of words are ideas, and that some or all ideas are private, although they are not images. This is a possibility I shall not discuss. Nor shall I consider the possibility that ideas are neither images nor necessarily private. In this essay I want to be taken neither to accept nor to reject these possibilities. In my criticism of the so-called 'official view', I shall simply allow to go unchallenged the contention that at least most ideas are, in Hume's view, private images. It is the claim that ideas, conceived as images, are meanings, that I shall challenge.

Although I shall refuse to attribute to Hume the view that words mean ideas, I shall not ask, 'What do words mean if they do not mean ideas?', for I am not at all inclined to believe that Hume had a theory of meaning of the kind that such a question seems to presuppose.

However, Hume does, in different parts of his work, discuss issues that concern the place of language in human life. It is my contention that when attention is paid to these discussions a picture of Hume different from the one often drawn will emerge. I hope at least to show that he can no longer be seen as committed to a life of splendid isolation within his own private world of incommunicable ideas.

I T   I S   W I D E L Y believed that Hume had little interest in language, and that what little he did say on this topic is not only inadequate but also singularly wrong-headed. It is difficult to disagree with this assessment if one accepts Antony Flew's interpretation. Flew writes:

> The first thing to appreciate is that in Hume's official view ideas always just are mental images. Furthermore the meanings of words are ideas, ideas again being identified with mental images. From time to time not surprisingly he says things which are hard or impossible to square with this official position. Nevertheless there is no doubt that this is his opinion when he is on guard. In the *Treatise* ideas are identified explicitly with mental images on page one: *impressions* are to include 'all our sensations, passions and emotions'; while *ideas* are 'the faint images of these in thinking and reasoning'.[4]

Although Flew is primarily concerned with the first *Enquiry*, the reference he here makes to the *Treatise* strongly suggests that Hume held the same view when he wrote that work.

Hume may of course have had an 'official' and an unofficial view, and his unofficial view may have represented his considered opinion. But this is not a possible interpretation of Flew's words, for he aims all his criticisms against what he calls Hume's 'official view'. If then the view that meanings are private mental images represents Hume's considered opinion, as is suggested by the claim that it is his 'official view', then Hume's doctrine is easily refuted, for it entails that communication by the use of language is impossible. Words used by me can mean only my ideas or images, and your words can mean only your ideas or images. Since my ideas are inaccessible to you, the meaning of my words would always be out of your reach. No more needs to be said about such a doctrine to show its total inadequacy. But, as Flew notes, Hume says things incompatible with his allegedly 'official' doctrine. I shall attempt to show that some of Hume's so-called careless lapses are nothing of the sort, but are suggestive of a view about the place of language in human life which is vastly more complex and interesting than the 'official' view.

Jonathan Bennett seems in general agreement with Flew when he writes: 'Hume's view of meaning is essentially Locke's: to understand a word is to associate it with a kind of "idea", and "ideas" are quasi-sensory states.'[5] And a little later we are told that it is well known that 'Hume . . . took over all the main elements of Locke's meaning-empiricism, except for the part about abstract ideas . . . '.[6] This is hardly a minor difference between Hume and Locke, for a theory of meaning would surely be more concerned with the meaning of general terms than with proper names, and it is commonly thought that Locke's theory of abstract ideas was meant to explain how general terms have meaning. In one respect Bennett's view seems to differ from Flew's, for Bennett says that to understand a word is to *associate* it with an idea. Thus he may not want to say that meanings are ideas. But the difference between the two commentators is only apparent, for at the end of the chapter from which I have been quoting, Bennett indicates that Hume should have been forced to admit ' . . . that his equation of meaning with ideas is hopelessly wrong'.[7] Thus, if Bennett's somewhat obscure expression 'quasi-sensory state' means the same as 'image', and this does not seem unlikely, then the two interpretations are identical. Flew and Bennett are among the most influential commentators on Hume's philosophy. If their interpretation is questionable, it is important to question it.

Hume, Flew claims, had an inverted approach to language, and hence to philosophy, for he approaches language from 'the logically private realm of one man's experience'.[8] The doctrine, we are told, is clearly stated by Locke, but it is tacitly presupposed by Hume, who would no doubt have stated it if he had been at all interested in language and semantic considerations. I do not propose to take issue directly with this attempt to discover Hume's thought in Locke's writing. The dangers of this approach are obvious and fully granted by Bennett and Flew, the latter wisely, if somewhat truistically, stressing that 'Hume is and always must be the supreme authority on Hume'.[9] The views I shall attribute to Hume will be based entirely on Hume's own writings.

I SHALL NOW argue that Hume, in the chapter 'Of Abstract Ideas' in the *Treatise*, clearly rejects the view that the meanings of words are private mental images. The fact that he does not in this chapter discuss the social context of the use of language goes no way towards showing that he considered words to stand for private ideas in the speaker's mind, as Locke sometimes appears to have thought. For Hume, in this part of the *Treatise*, is simply not concerned with the problem of communication and the social significance of language. It is the possibility of general or abstract thoughts that he here wants to explain, and thinking is clearly an activity we can engage in on our own. Perhaps all but the most rudimentary kind of thinking requires language. But there is no reason to believe that Hume would want to deny this, for in this part of the *Treatise* Hume is not discussing how language may be acquired. He takes the existence of language for granted.

Hume stresses at the beginning of the discussion that all ideas are particular and that 'general ideas' are no more than ' . . . particular ones, annexed to a certain term, which gives them a more extensive signification, and makes them recall upon occasion other individuals, which are similar to them' (p. 17).

It may seem obvious that if ideas are images then they are particular, for any possession of an image, or the conjuring up of one, is a datable occurrence. Thus, I now form an image of my car standing in front of my house, and this is a different image from the image I may form, a few minutes from now, of the same car, standing in front of the same house. But this is not what Hume is seeking to establish. For, even if it were possible to form an abstract idea of man, this would clearly be a particular occurrence, in this respect exactly like the occurrence of forming a particular idea. Hume is not trying to show, what is in any case obvious, that all ideas, or images, are themselves particular, conceived of as mental occurrences. He is rather making the much more contentious claim that all ideas are *of particulars*. 'The image in the mind is *only that of a particular object*, tho' the application of it in our reasoning be the same, as if it were universal' (p. 20, my italics).

Abstract ideas, he thinks, are impossible because they would be of something that could not have separate existence. I do not particularly want to deny that images may, in some circumstances, be thought of as having determinate characteristics. Perhaps the image of a line may have determinate length. Thus I may project an image upon a wall and it could perhaps be said that the image is the length of the width of the wall, or half the width of the wall, as the case may be. But Hume is clearly wrong to claim that our images or lines not only may, but *must* have determinate lengths. Thus, if we consider the image we may form of such an object as a house, we may form an image of a large or a small house without either the image itself or the imaged house having a determinate size. Any existing house will, of course, have a a determinate size, but one seems to be able to form images, of indeterminate size, of houses the sizes of which are not conceived of as determinate either. If impressions do not differ from ideas in kind, they ought likewise to admit of possible indeterminacy. Yet Hume insists that ' . . . no impression can become present to the mind, without being determin'd in its degrees both of quantity and quality' (p. 19). Impressions, it is true, may be 'faint and unsteady', and this may lead to confusion, but the mind cannot ' . . . receive any impression, which in its *real existence* has no particular degree nor proportion' (p. 19, my italics). Here it seems that 'impression' refers not only to a mental phenomenon, but to a *real objective existence*. Hume then claims that whatever is true of an impression must be true of the idea which copies it. He adds the final contention that ' . . . to form an idea of an object, and to form an idea simply' (p. 20) is the same thing. If, therefore, one attributes determinate qualities to an object one has an impression of, one must attribute the same determinateness to one's idea.

What is significant here is that Hume argues from what he takes to be known qualities of objects to the characteristics we must attribute to ideas. He appeals to ' . . . a principle generally receiv'd in philosophy, that everything in nature is individual . . . ' (p. 19). 'If this . . . be absurd in *fact and reality*, it must also be absurd *in idea*; since nothing of which we can form a clear and distinct idea is absurd and impossible . . . ' (pp. 19, 20). A publicly accessible world is presupposed, and it is not at all stressed that the ideas we derive from the impressions of this world are essentially private. They rather take on, in Hume's mind, some of the characteristics of the public world such as determinateness of quality and quantity. His error is not that of attributing to the real world characteristics of private images. He seems, on the contrary, wrongly to credit ideas or images with characteristics known to belong to an idependently existing world of objects.

Hume's reasoning may have been as follows: he notes that existence is not a special characteristic of what exists. It is, he thinks, 'an established maxim in metaphysics, *That whatever the mind clearly conceives includes the idea of possible existence . . .* ' (p.52). Any possible existence we can think of may be an actual existence. The actual and the possible thus must, in a sense, have the same characteristics. Since the actual is always determinate, any possible existence one may think of must be determinate. If not, what turns out to exist, for example, the golden mountain, will be different from the possibly existing mountain.

Strictly speaking there are no ideas of anything abstract or general or indeterminate. What happens is that, after noting a resemblance between a number of objects, we use the same term to cover them all, in spite of some differences between them. When a customary association between the term and these objects has been established, the hearing of the term conjures up an idea of one of the objects covered by the term, together with a readiness to call up ideas of other particulars to which the term applies. Not all of these can actually be surveyed on each occurrence of the term's use. In most cases their number is, indeed, undetermined. They are there 'in power', as Hume puts it. It is clear that the idea called to mind is not to be equated with the meaning of the term. It is the actual idea, and not those existing in power only, that can be described as an image. Hence the meaning of no general term can be an image. Indeed, what Hume gives us here is an account of how he believes we do manage to use general terms in our thinking, although all ideas are of particulars. It is, he thinks, simply a fact about human beings that images have the place he ascribes to them in our thinking. In this he almost certainly is mistaken, if he intends to deny the possibility of thinking entirely in words, as opposed to images, which Price calls quasi-instantiative instances. Words rarely resemble what they stand for, whereas images of objects are like the objects imaged. We manage to use general terms in our thinking because we acquire a certain capacity to check ourselves if we are tempted to misuse the term. On different occasions of the use of the term a different particular may be actualized or imaged as opposed to remaining in our minds in power only. This does not mean that a different meaning is attached to the term whenever a different image comes to mind. General terms do not have ideas or images as their meanings. Ideas or images come in, only as part of the contingent psychological description of the way in which we do think. It is the nature of the *habit* associated with the occurrent idea that determines the meaning we

attribute to the term. Thus the same image, for example, that of a
Scottish terrier, may be used in thinking of a Scottish terrier, a dog and
an animal. If the meaning of a word were an image, it is hard to see
how one could distinguish between thinking of colour and thinking of a
particular colour, such as red, between the thought of an animal and
the thought of a particular kind of animal, such as a dog, for an image
must, according to Hume, be of a particular colour and of a particular
dog. It is the habit of linguistic usage and what exists in power only
that determine the meaning attached to a term in our thinking, and an
image that exists in power only is no image at all.

Hume stresses not only that the same image may be used in the
thinking of two different thoughts, but also that the limitations of our
powers of imagining are not limitations of our powers of thinking.
Thus, one cannot distinguish the image of a figure with 999 sides from
the image of another with 1,000 sides. In spite of this, the natures of
the two figures can be distinguished. This shows that understanding
the natures of these figures is not essentially dependent upon our
ability to form images of them.

The account Hume gives of our ability to have the most sublime and
compounded ideas, such as the idea of God, can hardly be thought of as
an aberration. This topic was of such importance to him that he must
have given it serious consideration. He writes in the *Enquiry concerning Human Understanding*: 'The idea of God, as meaning an infinitely intelligent, wise, and good Being, arises from reflecting on the
operations of our own mind, and augmenting, without limit, those
qualities of goodness and wisdom.'[10] We clearly cannot form an image
of a being of this nature any more than of a chiliagon, but our capacity
to understand the concept of progressive enlargement enables our
understanding to reach beyond the limits of imaging in these cases, as
well as in that of large numbers such as 1,000. We can have an image
of a pair and add to it, and that of a square and increase the number of
sides.

In addition to what has been said so far, we may remind ourselves
that all distinctions of reason involve coming to understand the meaning of something that cannot be imaged. No independent images can
be formed of the shape and the colour of a globe. Yet we may distinguish them in our thought.

With respect to the possibility of thinking without non-verbal images,
it may be noted that Hume stresses

> . . . that in talking of *government, church, negotiation, conquest,*
> we seldom spread out in our minds all the simple ideas, of which
> these complex ones are compos'd. 'Tis however observable, that
> notwithstanding this imperfection we may avoid talking nonsense

on these subjects, and may perceive any repugnance among the ideas, as well as if we had a full comprehension of them. Thus if instead of saying, *that in war the weaker have always recourse to negotiation*, we shou'd say, *that they have always recourse to conquest*, the custom, which we have acquir'd of attributing certain relations to ideas, still follows the words, and makes us immediately perceive the absurdity of that proposition; in the same manner as one particular idea may serve us in reasoning concerning other ideas, however different from it in several circumstances. (*Treatise*, p. 23)

It is, of course, highly questionable whether one can make good sense of the notion that the ideas or conquest, negotiation, government, church, are composed of simple ideas, particularly if ideas are thought of as images. In any case, if I am right, Hume has denied that there is any one idea or image for which these terms stand. However, this passage makes it clear that talking or thinking, in such as way as to avoid nonsense, does not necessarily depend upon having non-verbal images. Such images as may be typically associated with the words can be dispensed with and the words by themselves strike us as absurd. One need not use quasi-instantiative particulars in one's thinking, but in such cases there are at least, according to Hume, ideas or impressions of words. To be conscious is to have perceptions and these are either impressions or ideas. The following quotation may serve to illustrate this. He says: "'Tis evident, that the idea, or rather impression of ourselves is always intimately present with us, and that our consciousness gives us so lively a conception of our own person, that 'tis not possible to imagine, that any thing can in this particular go beyond it' (ibid., p. 317). Hume's hesitation in deciding whether the perception of ourselves is an impression or an idea may be due to the fact that, when we are deep in thought, we may be so faintly aware of the impressions of our body and surroundings that they are almost like ideas.

Although Hume is primarily concerned with thinking in his discussion of abstract ideas, he does, in the long passage I have quoted, refer to the way in which, when we have learned a language, we can avoid talking nonsense without the aid of non-verbal images or ideas. But the reader is not told how language is acquired and communication achieved. To understand what Hume thought about the place of language in the social setting of human communication, one needs to look at certain discussions in Book III of the *Treatise*. The absence from Book I of a discussion of language as a public phenomenon and a means of communication should not be taken to indicate that he thought of words as having private meanings in the form of mental images. He says far too many things incompatible with this view for these to be attributed to mere carelessness. Indeed, I have already tried to show that Hume rejects the 'official view' in the chapter 'Of Abstract Ideas'. Let us now explore what his discussion of artificial virtues can teach us about his real view.

HUME STRESSES that, compared with other animals, man seems ill-endowed by nature to satisfy his many needs. Although society tends to increase these needs, the power and security co-operation provides leave man ' . . . in every respect more satisfied and happy, than 'tis possible for him, in his savage and solitary condition, ever to become' (ibid., p. 485). The artificial virtues are essential if man is to achieve the benefits of society.

In discussing these virtues Hume distinguishes the question of their origin from the reasons why we approve of people who possess them. Let us begin by considering the question of origin. He tells us that ' . . . the sense of justice and injustice is not deriv'd from nature, but arises artificially, tho' necessarily from education, and human conventions' (ibid., p. 483).

In looking for the origin of justice Hume is not pursuing history in any ordinary sense. He wants to show that without postulating a special innate or God-given faculty of justice it is wholly intelligible, and not the least bit surprising, that man in society should have established conventional rules governing the possession and use of material goods. So far is the origin of property from being surprising that the known motives of self-interest and confined benevolence can be seen to lead naturally to the establishing of the rules governing property, independently of moral considerations. Of course, the rules governing property may vary from one society to another, but human nature is such that some such rules are bound to be developed in any society, given the scarcity of material goods. That such rules will be established can thus be thought of as a law of nature. Similarly, languages may vary, but no human society will be found without some language, for human nature is such that men will necessarily come to have language, and the usefulness of the conventions that give rise to language will not escape man in society, seeking to augment his power to satisfy his own and society's desires and needs. Hume, in discussing how the comparative weakness of man as an individual can be overcome by social co-operation, stresses that communication is indispensable for the success of this enterprise.

The 'artificial convention' that gives rise to justice is not to be understood as a promise, for promises themselves are made possible only by a similar human convention. These conventions are 'a general sense of common interest', expressed by all the menbers of society to each other.

Each individual sees it to be in his own interest, and in the interest of those for whom he is naturally concerned, to follow certain rules of behaviour with regard to transferable goods. People are left to possess and enjoy certain goods on the understanding that others will follow the same rules in their conduct. This, he says, ' . . . may properly enough be call'd a convention or agreement betwixt us, tho' without the interposition of a promise; since the actions of each of us have a reference to those of the other, and are perform'd upon the supposition, that something is to be perform'd on the other part' (ibid., p. 490). The example is given of two men rowing a boat in harmony without having given a promise to each other. The regularity of behaviour in accordance with rules of justice arises gradually. People discover how deviations from the regularity are disadvantageous, and confidence in the continuation of the regularity is gradually built up. The sense of common interest will make it reasonable for us to base our conduct on the assumption that others will follow the rules as well. Let Hume speak for himself:

> Nor is the rule concerning the stability of possession the less deriv'd from human conventions, that it arises gradually, and acquires force by a slow progression, and by our repeated experience of the inconveniences of transgressing it. On the contrary, this experience assures us still more, that the sense of interest has become common to all our fellows, and gives us a confidence of the future regularity of their conduct: and 'tis only on the expectation of this, that our moderation and abstinence are founded. In like manner are languages gradually establish'd by human conventions without any promise. (ibid., p. 490)

And in Appendix III of the *Enquiry concerning the Principles of Morals* Hume again says that ' . . . speech and words and language are fixed by human convention and agreement'.[11] He also asserts in Appendix III that 'convention' usually means 'promise' and that, in this sense of the word 'convention', it is absurd to suggest that justice and, as we shall see, language as well, arise from human conventions. For Hume claims that 'observance of promises' is an important part of justice and that it would therefore be viciously circular to argue that we ought to keep our promises because we promised to do so. This leaves unexplained the reason why we ought to keep that original promise. And languages cannot be based upon a promise since they are possible only if we already have language. The position Hume attacks is not to be confused with the view that the nature of a promise is such that it ought to be kept, for this latter view does not lean on a promise to keep promises in order to explain why promises ought to be kept.

We have seen that Hume, in the *Treatise*, argues that promises are

intelligible only if a human convention is presupposed. But the sense in
which 'convention' is used in that account differs in important respects
from convention as promise, or mutual explicit agreement. Not only
Hume, but Bertrand Russell and William Alston have taken 'convention' to naturally mean 'explicit agreement' or 'mutal promise' and
both these deny, with considerable justification, that language can have
had such an origin. Alston writes: 'By the nature of the case, making
agreements and conventions presupposes that people already have a
language in which to carry on these activities.'[12] And Russell writes:
'We can hardly suppose a parliament of hitherto speechless elders meeting together and agreeing to call a cow a cow and a wolf a wolf. The
association of words with their meanings must have grown up by some
natural process, though at present the nature of the process is unknown.'[13] Hume would wholeheartedly agree, for the convention that
accounts for the origin of promises is not a promise and can therefore be
appealed to without circularity. In the same way the conventions that
give rise to a natural language do not presuppose linguistic behaviour
and, therefore, can also be appealed to without circularity. For when
Hume says that the artificial virtues, and language, have their origin
in human conventions, he means by this a perfectly natural process. It
consists in ' . . . a sense of common interest; which sense each man feels
in his own breast, which he remarks in his fellows, and which carries
him, in concurrence with others, into a general plan or system of
actions, which tends to public utility. . . .'[14]

It is important to remind ourselves that Hume is not saying that the
conventions he refers to are necessary to secure for people the enjoy-
ment of their property, or to make people keep their promises or use
language successfully. He is making the more radical claim that without the conventions there would be no property, no promises and no
language.

It matters not at all whether Hume's sense of 'conventions' is the
ordinary sense or a special sense. It is, for example, perfectly true that
we often talk of conventions that may or may not be adopted. Thus
there are several different conventions people can adopt for bidding in
bridge. The conventions exist whether or not they are adopted. To give
rise to property we must actually adopt a convention, behave in a particular way. It may also be noted that agreeing upon a convention, and
thus adopting it, is not usually thought of as involving promises. When,
in playing bridge, one bids 3 no trumps when the convention agreed
upon, or adopted, demands a bid of 4 spades, one's partner has no right
to complain that a promise to him has been broken. A guarantee in the
form of a promise would normally be demanded only if there is in one
partner doubt about the reliability of the other. It would be something

over and above the adoption of the convention. But Hume's sense of convention is not only not a promise, it does not involve an explicit agreement, or at least not necessarily so. The concept of 'adopting' may too strongly suggest an explicit, deliberately decided upon and temporally datable action, whereas Hume's convention normally is established by the gradual coming into being of an actual pattern of behaviour involving tacit understanding only.

Consider now the case of the oarsmen that Hume uses in explaining the sense of convention we are concerned with. Firstly, there is no need to presume that the two oarsmen, rowing in unison, are seeking a common end, that end being to get both safely to their destination. The important point is that each has his own aim, which can be achieved only on the understanding that the other will behave in a certain way. The boat will go in a circle if one rows and the other does not. The same result will follow if one consistently rows more strongly than the other. If they are erratic in this regard they will follow a course that is less efficient in achieving the result sought by each of them. The co-ordinated endeavour of the two oarsmen presupposes that each can understand and recognize intentional activity. Each must be able to modify his conduct on the assumption that the other will see it as reflecting awareness of what he is trying to do. If languages come into existence by a similar convention, it is therefore understood that those becoming party to the conventions that give rise to language already understand intentional activity of a non-linguistic kind and can recognize it in themselves and in others. In this case the rowers' aim happens to be the same: each wants to get safely ashore. We have here a situation close to what has been called a perfect co-ordination equilibrium.[15] Each is better off than he would be if either were to behave differently. Hume sometimes seems to think that justice is like this. 'And even every individual person', he says, 'must find himself a gainer, on balancing the account; since, without justice, society must immediately dissolve, and everyone must fall into that savage and solitary condition, which is infinitely worse than the worst situation that can possibly be suppos'd in society' (*Treatise*, p. 497). Usually, however, Hume realistically grants that in individual cases behaviour contrary to justice may benefit an individual or even the general public. A perfect equilibrium need not exist. But a general adherence to the pattern of behaviour is a necessary condition for there being any convention at all.

Knowledge of, or at least belief in, the other oarsman's performance, is a necessary condition for the reasonableness of your performance, just as his actual performance is a necessary condition for the success of your own.

A co-ordination equilibrium may exist without a convention. One may drive always on the same side of the road and this may benefit everyone, because everyone else drives on that side as well. But, until there is a general awareness that the practice is followed by others, no convention can be said to exist. Your awareness of the practice others follow, and your realization that each is aware of the practice followed by all and sees his actions as dependent upon this practice, strengthens your reliance upon the dependability of others. This reliance is, of course, reasonable if one presumes that people in general seek to realise their aims.

Thus the individual will know that others are going to depend upon his performance, and that deviations are likely to lead people astray in their plans and anticipations. He will not be able to escape observing the disadvantages of the deviations in his own case and will appreciate that others are similarly affected, because of what Hume calls 'the general sense of common interest'. Thus the establishing of the convention creates a standard of behaviour, which must be conformed to if one is to derive the benefit the convention confers.

Hume gives an example of the way in which a linguistic convention comes to be woven into social life. The reason why 'I promise' and similar expressions come to be used in making promises is that people see it to be to their mutual advantage to have agreed ways of committing themselves to future behaviour by laying their dependability upon the line. I will help you if you promise to help me later. If you do promise, but do not help me, you incur the risk of not being able to secure help by promising in the future. But, although you are using language irresponsibly if you make false promises the temptations to do so are many. It is obvious that people often get away with making false promises or unjustifiably not doing what they promised to do. Taken in isolation, each individual act of justice, fidelity to promises, or adherence to the truthful use of language, may seem to benefit neither the individual nor the society at large. It is the whole system of conventional behaviour that is beneficial. Those who see the general utility of the artificial virtues will not want to do anything that will tend to erode them. They will, through sympathy with the interests of the general public, come to approve of those who stick to the rules even when sorely tempted to break them in order to achieve short term gain. Hume, as we have seen, sometimes seemed to think that the long term interests of each individual would be best served if he stuck rigidly to the rules of justice. However, people can hardly be presumed to be always sufficiently perceptive to see this. This is why it is most important to inculcate in people feelings of obligation to stick to the rules even in cases when the advantages of breaking them seem greater. Parents and other educators, and politicians, are most active in the attempt to instill in people the sense of obligation to be just in respecting property rights and responsible in the use of language. The concept of a responsible language-user is strictly analogous to the concept of a just man. He will neither make irresponsible promises nor say things about the world that will arouse false expectations and therefore disappoint. The motive of duty will, through education, be added to the already existing motives of self-interest and confined benevolence that led to the convention being adopted in the first place. This in turn will increase the regularity of behaviour that constitutes the convention and thus strengthen adherence to the convention among reasonable people. There may still, of course, be occasional exceptions to the desirability of strictly sticking to the convention. Thus one may have to swerve to the wrong side of the road to avoid an accident, tell a lie to a would-be murderer or make an insincere promise to a robber. One can, of course, say that these are not so much exceptions to the conventions as refinements of them, for it is not in his private capacity that the person is granted the exception but rather as a party to the convention. Anyone else in the same situation could have done the same with impunity.

The responsible language user has to learn objectivity. We must '. . . fix on some *steady* and *general* points of view; and always, in our thoughts, place ourselves in them, whatever may be our present situation (ibid.,pp. 581 – 2). Without this capacity to adopt standpoints shared with others no communication about the world is possible and no value judgments are possible. Hume says:

> Experience soon teaches us this method of correcting our sentiments, or at least, of correcting our language, where the sentiments are more stubborn and inalterable. Our servant, if diligent and faithful, may excite stronger sentiments of love and kindness than *Marcus Brutus*, as represented in history; but we say not upon that account, that the former character is more laudable than the latter. We know, that were we to approach equally near to that renown'd patriot, he wou'd command a much higher degree of affection and admiration. Such corrections are common with regard to all the senses; and indeed 'twere impossible *we cou'd ever make use of language, or communicate our sentiments to one another*, did we not correct the momentary appearances of things, and overlook our present situation. (ibid., p. 582, my italics)

Language presupposes a shared world where people check their linguistic utterances by reference to public criteria. This, Hume seems to be saying, is a presupposition of all use of language and communication. Thus the understanding of expressions of likes and dislikes, that you may not share, presupposes the overlooking of your present situation. You have to learn what kinds of situations license the use of 'I like x' as well as those that entitle you to say 'x is good'. Indeed, the development of the convention that gives rise to this distinction is entirely parallel to the artificial virtues, so that it is part of the virtue of a responsible language-user not to say 'x is good' when he is only entitled to say 'I like x'. To adhere to the conventions of language in general, and not only moral language, is to possess a special kind of artificial virtue. All the users of the language have a right to assume that a speaker is intending to communicate what the convention lays down. Knowing what his intention will be taken to be, the speaker has a duty not to mislead, not to disappoint. The development of language thus gives rise to certain rights and duties, and the value of the whole system of linguistic performances is based upon utility. The system could break down not only if deliberate lying became general but also if people became so sloppy in their use of language that they failed to communicate effectively, thus ensuring that the social ends served by language could not be achieved. Some linguistic practices, such as those involved in baptism and holy orders, are to be condemned because, unlike promises, these practices serve no human needs.

As we have seen, language arises in a social context to satisfy human needs. It is within this context of an already existing language that philosophical speculation arises. We all need to rely for successful living on our general beliefs about an independent world of relatively stable objects and regular events. But some of us will pursue philosophy some of the time. 'Those who have a propensity to philosophy, will still continue their researches; because they reflect, that, besides the immediate pleasure, attending such an occupation, philosophical decisions are nothing but the reflections of common life, methodized and corrected.'[16] The continuous existence of an independent world of objects such as hats, shoes and stones, must be taken for granted in all our reasoning. Of these we have impressions. Indeed, seen from certain points of view, they *are* impressions and the most obvious way in which we could convince someone of their existence is to point them out. To produce an impression to show that our words are meaningful is nothing more than to draw attention to the conditions under which the relevant observations can be made and the relevant experiences obtained. If we are dealing with a simple characteristic we produce the impression. 'To give a child an idea of scarlet or orange, of sweet or bitter, I present the objects, or in other words, convey to him these impressions; but proceed not so absurdly, as to endeavour to produce the impressions by exciting the ideas' (*Treatise*, p. 5).

Anyone can, of course, be irresponsible in the use of language, can deliberately lie or take insufficient care not to mislead by what he says. The value of language as a means of communication depends upon such practices not becoming too general. If they did, then just as property would disappear from the scene if property rights were generally neglected, and promises could not be made if no-one were careful to keep them, so all use of language, based as it is upon a comparable convention, would fail in its communicative function. The very existence of a language depends upon general adherence to the conventions by those using it. One may likewise observe that just as there is no property in addition to objects owned, there are also no meanings in addition to the sounds, visible marks and ideas that we use in thinking and communicating by the use of language. But philosophers have been prone to use words in such a way as to populate the world with mythical objects and powers. The challenge to produce the impression from which an idea is derived is not of course the demand for an impression in the past to be dragged up. This is for all time lost, as Hume himself rightly stresses. It is, he says, '. . . impossible to recall the past impressions, in order to compare them with our present ideas . . .' (ibid. p. 85).

Hume, as is well known, maintains that a person who has not had the opportunity to become acquainted with certain simple impressions will not know the meaning of the terms referring to these. Thus a man born blind will not know what we mean by colour words. He can, to be sure, come to use these words correctly if he has experiences which are systematically related to colours. He may of course also have colour images, although it is doubtful whether he can recognize them as such. If he says that by 'red' he means the colour of pillar-boxes and phone booths, he will not be able to tell whether the image he calls 'red' is an image of the same colour. The challenge to philosophers whom one suspects of using words without meaning does not consist merely in the claim that they cannot have acquired an idea because they cannot have had an impression. It is rather being demanded of them that they give a description of a state of affairs that will entitle them to say what they say. It is easy to be misled if one thinks that Hume, in hunting for impressions, is looking for meanings. Where is the vice in murder? In the mind of the judge who contemplates the action. Where is the necessity in causal relations? In the mind of the person making causal inferences. But this does not seem to make sense. The reason is that we have here a description of the situations in which we come to understand why murder is called a vice and why causal relations are necessary. It is not that the feelings of disapproval in the case of murder and psychological constraint in the case of causal inference always need to be felt when we make a moral judgment or a causal inference; our verbal pronouncements come to be governed by rules so that we are carried by habit straight into the making of the verdict: murder, we say, is clearly wrong, and fire causes warmth. But if we reflect we find we are constrained to think this; it causes us too much pain to think otherwise. The charge that philosophers and others sometimes use words without any idea or meaning is not based upon the contention that they do not have a certain image in mind when they use the word. What they must be able to do, to meet the charge, is to point out the circumstances in which the use of the expression can be learned. To use language without seeing this as a reasonable challenge is to be an irresponsible participant in the most important of all conventions for social life, the conventions of language.

1. Norman Kemp Smith *The Philosophy of David Hume* (London: Macmillan & Co. 1941).
2. Páll S. Árdal *Passion and Value in Hume's Treatise* (Edinburgh University Press 1966).
3. Páll S. Árdal 'Some Implications of the Virtue of Reasonableness in Hume's Treatise, in *Hume: A Re-Evaluation* (New York: Fordham University Press 1976).
4. Antony Flew *Hume's Philosophy of Belief* (London: Routledge and Kegan Paul 1961) p. 22.
5. Jonathan Bennett *Locke, Berkeley, Hume* (Oxford: Clarendon Press 1971) p. 222.
6. Bennett, p. 223.
7. Bennett, p. 234.
8. Flew, p. 39.
9. Flew, p. 37.
10. *Enquiries*, p. 19.
11. *Enquiries*, p. 306.
12. William Alston *Philosophy of Language* (New York: Prentice Hall 1964) p. 57.
13. Bertrand Russell *The Analysis of Mind* (London: George Allen and Unwin 1921) p. 190.
14. *Enquiries*, p. 306.
15. David Lewis defines a co-ordination equilibrium as ' . . . a combination in which no one would have been better off had *any one* agent alone acted otherwise, either himself or someone else', *Convention* (Cambridge: Harvard University Press 1969) p. 14. Hume, however, sometimes suggests that everyone would be *better off* if no-one acts contrary to the convention that gives rise to an artificial virtue.

    Lewis acknowledges indebtedness to Hume for the sense of convention he develops in his theory of language. (*Convention*, pp. 3–4) I do not, of course, wish to suggest that Hume anticipated Lewis' sophisticated theory. My sole aim is to show that the comparison Hume draws between the origins of justice on the one hand and language on the other is suggestive of a view about language which is quite different from the theory of meaning often attributed to him. Whether it is possible to find in Hume a coherent theory of meaning at all still remains to be shown. I can certainly not claim to have done so.

16. *Enquiries,* p. 162.

I am much indebted to Queen's University at Kingston for giving me the Sabbatical leave during which I wrote this paper, The Institute for Advanced Studies in the Humanities at the University of Edinburgh for excellent facilities for work, and The Canada Council for generous financial help in the form of a Leave Fellowship.

The errors and other imperfections of this paper would have been more numerous by far, if it had not been for the many valuable discussions I had with Dr J. J. Bricke at The Institute for Advanced Studies in Edinburgh during the winter of 1975–1976.

Edmund Husserl and
'the as yet, in its most important respect,
unrecognised greatness of Hume'

DAVID HUME'S QUALITY of concealing under the deceptively placid, apparently limpid, surface of his philosophy, the passionate ratiocination of an insatiable thought that keeps on springing surprises and shocks, was already being commented upon, in his own time and his own country, as a fact all too liable to be overlooked, a century and a half before Edmund Husserl, writing in 1929 for a Continental audience, made his striking remark about Hume's real greatness as being still unrecognized in its most important aspect. It was very much this same paradox of the toughly cerebral core behind the bland façade that Adam Smith had in view, when, in the very emphatic language of his obituary letter, he warns us not to be put off by all that easy sociality and good nature into regarding Hume as, in A.E. Taylor's words, not a great philosopher but only a very clever man. 'That constant pleasantry', that 'gaiety of temper', which is 'so agreeable in society, but which is so often accompanied with frivolous and superficial qualities, was in him certainly attended with the most severe application, the most extensive learning, [and] the greatest depth of thought'.[1] But the point both Adam Smith and Edmund Husserl are trying to put, that, if we want to get the most out of Hume, we must remember we are dealing with a man who to some extent hides his light, who, intellectually speaking, keeps much more in reserve and under the counter than he puts on public display—this point is perhaps most candidly and clearly expressed by his chief opponent Thomas Reid. One must always bear in mind, Reid was fond of telling his students, that in consolidating his literary reputation before the world 'Mr Hume appears to have forgot his metaphysics'. Anyone desirous of fathoming the full depth of what Hume has to teach us must go back behind the *Enquiries* to the difficult pages of the youthful work which its author disowned and which in consequence was being left unread.

However, it is not only that the leading figures of the Scottish Enlightenment coincided in this general way with Husserl in pointing out that the real nature of Hume's genius tended to be missed by his professed admirers, especially those of the empiricist camp. What is still more remarkable, Adam Smith, Thomas Reid and Edmund Husserl are also relatively close to one another in their more particular estimate that the greatness of Hume lay in the originality of his work in pin-pointing the intellectual weakness of our civilization and in thus opening the way to a new stage in the development of human culture. When, for instance, Adam Smith, in *The Wealth of Nations*, speaks of his friend as 'by far the most illustrious philosopher and historian of the present age',[2] he wasn't thinking merely of the point explicitly before his mind—Hume's originality in seeing, long before any one else, the intimate connection between the spread of the market economy on the one hand and the establishment of liberty under law on the other. He was also acknowledging his indebtedness to Hume for drawing attention, as nobody else at the time was doing, to the deep and daunting problem of the relation of our advancing economies to the science on which they depend, both in respect of the considerable danger, discussed in Smith's *History of Astronomy*, of subordinating the speculative, unverifiable non-utilitarian side of science—the creative side (what Hume calls the imagination)—to the practical, bread-and-butter side, and also in respect of the equally real danger, highlighted in *The Wealth of Nations*, of the insidious growth, under a highly complex advanced civilisation, of an intellectual atomisation in which the learned and the conversable, as Hume calls them (that is to say, the polite part of society), get out of contact with one another, losing in the process the sobering sense of the common origin of their respective modes of culture in what Hume refers to as the animality of the vulgar.

Moreover, Adam Smith's estimate of Hume from the standpoint of ethical and social philosophy coincides very largely with those of Reid and Husserl from the stand-points of their respective epistemologies. As seen by Reid, the great achievement of the deep-wrought, sceptical arguments of *Treatise* I was to have brought into the open the fundamental flaw that had entered into the intellectual structure of our civilization at the time of its birth in Greece and that had not been exposed and eliminated by the great Cartesian reform—namely, an excess of technical bias, which had, from the first, cut philosophy off from the plain man by divorcing it from the realist standpoint of common sense. Exposing for the first time the real nature of this built-in contradiction, the author of the *Treatise*, amid all the confusions of his impressions and ideas and without exactly knowing what he was doing, had prepared the way for what Reid called the 'third age of humanity'—the Age of Common Sense—which, advancing beyond the previous two ages, the Aristotelian and the Cartesian, would at last bring to an end the fatal division between the learned and the vulgar, by bringing to light a new *a priori* of first principles less simplified than the Cartesian, less complex and animistic than the Aristotelian. Sharing

Reid's epistemological standpoint but more favourable than he to the constructive side of *Treatise* I, Husserl seems to be claiming, in a manner very similar to Reid's, that Hume's significance as a key-thinker lies in his showing the way to our bringing to a triumphant ful-filment the programme for a pre-suppositionless philosophy, which had been inaugurated, but not carried through, by Descartes at the begin-ning of the scientific era. Properly developed along phenomenological lines, Hume's much-questioned impressions and ideas provided a clue for evolving a new sort of material *a priori* capable of closing the gap, so disastrous for Descartes' dream, between the teachings of nature on the one hand and the light of nature on the other. Thus, just as for Reid, the metaphysical passages in *Treatise* I, which Hume preferred to forget about in the *Enquiries*, or, for Smith, the analysis of the rela-tions of the learned professions with polite society, which Hume was later to exclude from his essays,[3] possessed the special significance of opening the way for a philosophy capable of coping with the modern version of the intellectual atomisation, which had been in part res-ponsibe for the ruin of classical civilization, so in a somewhat similar way for Husserl, 'the as yet, in its most important respect, unrecognized greatness of Hume' would seem to have consisted in Hume's vital role in discovering an intellectual method that would bring into being the critical inwardness requisite to offset the over-extrovert science of our time without stifling its great qualities.

If we are to understand aright the general sense of Husserl's high claims as to the hidden depths of the Humean philosophy, we must, I believe, take him to be re-asserting in twentieth-century terms very much the same thing as Reid was trying to make explicit for his scho-larly auditors and as Adam Smith was trying to put over for the serious public at large: that Hume's rather sceptical attitude to the Baconian schemes for modern civilization, far from simply spotlighting the merely practical difficulties of realizing the radical version of the scientific dream, in reality is concerned with bringing to light certain fundamental difficulties of principle, epistemological as well as ethical, which if not removed would seem to make nonsense of the whole ex-perimentalist programme of modern civilization. Looking back to Hume from the standpoint of our century, Husserl thus, in some measure, re-captures insights originally won by Adam Smith and Reid and lost again by Bentham and the Mills—namely, that, while David Hume certainly accepts as his starting point the post-renaissance scheme for a science-based renewal of civilization in which material advance was to proceed side by side with intellectual advance, he differed very sharply from the other standard-bearers of the Enlightenment, French as well as English, in respect of the question of the relative importance of the theoretical elements in the programme as opposed to the practical, refusing to regard the theoretical problem as a simple and secondary one that already, in principle, had been solved, and uncovering the scandal of the basic epistemological contradictions that made nonsense of all the high claims about the Age of Reason. Thus, whereas adherents to the experimental philosophy, whether the 'philosophers' and associationists of the eighteenth century or the logical positivists and linguistic philosophers of the present age, tend to be of the opinion that the application of science for the practical end of providing a sufficient quantity of goods and shelter for all was modern civilization's primary practical task, by comparison with which the merely theoretical issues of founding science on experience or diffusing its spirit through the society were of very secondary importance, presenting no great difficulties of principle and safely left to solve themselves by laissez-faire, the uniqueness of David Hume, glimpsed by Husserl as well as by Reid and Adam Smith, consisted in his seeing that the purely intellectual side of the problems of civilization was not only as difficult as the practical side but even in some sense constituted the key to the latter.

IT WAS ONLY at the very end of Husserl's career that he gave to the world *The Crisis of the European Sciences*, which, far more than any of his other books, begins to make explicit his developing affinity with Reid and the Scottish philosophers, not only in respect of its drawing attention, as they do, to the hidden significance of the overlooked paradoxes of the *Treatise* for the future of humanity, but even in respect of its locating the roots of Europe's scientific crisis precisely where the Scottish school had located them—namely, in the reductive, atomising procedures fatefully introduced by Descartes' arithmetization of geometry. Already, some fifty or sixty years before the appearance of the *Krisis* in 1936, certain traces of common-ground with the classical philosophy of Scotland, as developed in and through the tension between David Hume and the Scottish geometers, would seem to have been present at the very start of what was to become the phenomenological movement—in Franz Brentano's lectures on the *Treatise of Human Nature*, which Husserl would have heard in his student days. Thus in the very decade—the seventies of the last century—when, amid the final decadence and disruption of the presbyterian polity, the intellectual pre-eminence of Edinburgh as a centre of philosophy and science was overtaken and overthrown by the rising prestige of the cultural contribution of South Britain, some of the leading ideas of the Scottish school—especially those centring in its tradition of Hume-scholarship but also some of those connected with its tradition of a holistic mathematics as reviewed by Hamilton's pupil Clerk-Maxwell in the Preface

to his epoch-making *Treatise on Magnetism and Electricity* (1873)—
migrated to the Continent to find a congenial home as a provocative
subject of intellectual discussion, in an Austrian Empire, which, amid
a growing decadence and disruptiveness of a somewhat more spectacu-
lar sort than our Scottish species, was in the process of becoming the
new hot-bed of Western ideas.

Indeed, as far as central Europe was concerned, the widely influential
and forceful books produced in the England of those years with the aim
of finally extirpating the Scottish pretensions to philosophical eminence
—J.S. Mill's, *An Examination of Sir William Hamilton's Philosophy*
(1865) and T.H. Green's Preface to the *Treatise of Human Nature*
(1874)—had the unintended effect of awakening in Prague and
Vienna a certain interest in the very authors whom their polemics had
intended to discredit, since in the tortuous intellectual milieu of Mittel-
Europa, the metaphysical doubts and difficulties expounded by Hume
and by Hamilton, the last of the Reid school, in some respects seemed
to have about them a deeper ring of reality than the earnest exposi-
tions of the British liberal ideal. Accordingly in the discussions and
criticisms of the English-language philosophy on which Husserl was
brought up, the key-figures, one might say, were Hamilton and Hume,
the men who, in the words of the former, were intent on re-installing
on his throne the good god Difficulty, rather than the ethical-minded
men-of-affairs like Mill and Green who, it appears, were always right
on all the Trade Union issues of the day but by whom the metaphysical
problem as such had been relegated to a very secondary place. Faced
with the enthusiastic out-pouring of this pair of high-minded polemists,
the Austrians fastened with relief and curiosity on the problem of abstraction in Scottish philosophy as the one and only feature of it about
which Mill and Green had a good word to say—the former singling
out Hamilton's theory of abstraction by shifts of attention as the only
decent thing in his books, the latter treating Hume's distinctions of
reason theory as the only intelligible item in the whole *Treatise*.
Stimulated by the novelty of what they found in Hume and Hamilton
on the subject, the German-speaking philosophers of the Brentano
circle concentrated on it to the neglect of everything else in Mill and
in Green, treating the Scottish tension over the abstraction problem as
the most significant item in the whole tradition of British Empiricism.

Husserl, a relatively slow developer, seems to have begun, like others
of the Brentano school, especially Meinong in his 1877 *Hume-Studies* I,
by taking Hamilton's side against Hume in the controversy over the
nature of abstraction, and the intellectually creative period of Husserl's
life did not, one might say, get properly going until, just about the
beginning of the present century, he reacted against the Hamiltonian

ideas sponsored by Meinong, and switched to the Humean side, digging for stimulus in the unread pages of the *Treatise* and encouraging his pupils to do the same. With that, things suddenly began to happen, and from then on his thought began to move forward in a curiously double-sided progress, alternately historical and systematic, by turns backward-looking and forward-looking, in which each creative contribution to the twentieth-century problem of analysis was accompanied, consolidated and perhaps sometimes sparked off, by fresh discoveries in the hidden parts of Hume's text, discoveries which sought to get behind the stereotype interpretations handed down from Hamilton and the final scholastic period of the Scottish school. In the first place, the emergence of the characteristically Husserlian theory of perception in and through the variations of perspective views goes hand in hand with the break-through, in the *Logical Investigations*, to a proper assessment of the power and originality of Hume's theory of abstraction—an assessment which corrected Meinong's Hamiltonian misconceptions about the distinctions of reason doctrine. Then, in the second place, the unveiling of the material *a priori* by Husserl, as implicit in the theory of perception by perspective views, is closely bound up with the appearance, in the years before World War I, of a remarkable paper by Adolf Reinach, to which Husserl, in his obituary article on his pupil's death shortly afterwards at the Front, acknowledged the deepest debt for its achievement in having brought home to him the real meaning of Hume's doctrine of the relations of ideas, that is to say of necessary truths, as having a genuine affinity with the phenomenological type of material *a priori* developed by himself, and as having in it nothing of the analytical or tautological character attributed to Hume by Kant. Then, in the third place, some twenty years later with the final assimilation by Husserl of the import of these discoveries in the *Treatise*, and with the growing awareness on his part of the seminal role played by Hume in Western philosophy, the 1929 edition of the *Yearbook for Philosophy and Phenomenological Research* contains not only Husserl's *Formal and Transcendental Logic*, then given to the world for the first time, but also, immediately after it, the book-length article on Hume by Husserl's English postgraduate student, C. V. Salmon, a Germanified Oxonian—the two works being placed, side by side, in what I feel to be (given Husserl's editorship) a juxtaposition of a highly significant character. Here, the paradoxical dictum about 'the as yet, in its most important respect, unrecognised greatness' of *Treatise* I, contained in the *Formal and Transcendental Logic*, has its meaning highlighted and underlined by being followed up immediately by the pupil's lucid and exciting demonstration that the central problem of David Hume's philosophy is constituted by the impressively profound struggle of the *Treatise* to anticipate, a century and a half before its time, the central Husserlian distinction between consciousness of object and object of consciousness, that is, *Noesis* and *Noema*, which had grown out of the doctrine of perception by perspective views.

Moreover, this underlying affinity of the central problem of the Humean philosophy with that of the Husserlian phenomenology, first discovered by Salmon under the Master's supervision in 1929, and then independently rediscovered and re-stated by another pupil Aron Gurwitsch, ten years later, is not by any means the end of the story. In a final bursting out beyond Hume but through Hume to recapture the spirit of the great philosophical movement of which Hume had been the pathfinder and pioneer in the Scotland of his time, the book on *The Crisis of the European Sciences*, which is the crown of Husserl's career, not only in effect re-stated in terms of our twentieth century the problem so much insisted on by the Scottish philosophers of the classical school as central to the whole movement of modern civilisation, that is to say the problem of the morally disruptive effects of scientific reductionism as pre-figured in the Cartesian algebra, (the problem of guarding against the danger that natural science, in the pride of its world-conquering expertise, may turn its hand against the intellectual standards to which it owed its birth); but, in addition—what is just as remarkable—gave a new lease of life to the common sense critique of scientism carried through by the old Scottish school, and was indirectly to inspire, among some phenomenologists of the next generation, the project of uncovering the hidden excellence of the chef d'école of Scottish philosophy, Hume's opponent Thomas Reid, in much the same way as Husserl in his life-time had helped to uncover the hidden excellence of David Hume. Looked at in this light, Husserl's final years left behind them the legacy of a programme for a sort of phenomenological refurbishing of the philosophy of Scotland's classical age, which was, in the first place, to be excellently implemented in France by a classic article in 1954 by Professor Maxime Chastaing of the University of Dijon, a one-time pupil of J-P. Sartre, on *Thomas Reid, the Philosophy of Common Sense and the Problem of our Knowledge of Other Minds*, and also bore worthy fruit at the other side of the European Continent, in Poland, in the book on Reid—both sympathetic and stimulating as communicated to me in conversations with the author, Professor Hempelinsky then of Krackow—which, produced under the direction of Husserl's closest philosophical associate Roman Ingarden, sanctions a sort of posthumous identification of Husserl's phenomenology with Reid to match the affinity affirmed in Husserl's lifetime of his phenomenology with the philosophy of Hume.

Thus, carried forward from its first beginnings by the wave of intellectual excitement aroused by the discussion of Hume and Hamilton in the Brentano circle, chiefly through the work of Meinong, the phenomenological movement has, in an indirect way, time after time sought fresh inspiration in a return to the ideas of Hume and the Scottish school of common sense. Whatever value and influence Husserl's central work as a creative systematic philosopher has had on the English-speaking world, there can be no doubt of the influence and value of this secondary and historically oriented work (for all that it was a throw-away spasmodic effort) in the de-sedimentation of the *Treatise* texts—in the smashing of the second-hand Hamiltonian stereotypes of Hume—which, influencing that most remarkable historian of philosophy, Norman Kemp Smith, not only provided him with the means of transforming his early articles on Naturalism in Hume into the magisterial works of his later years on *The Philosophy of David Hume* and the *Dialogues*, but also in the long run, by the spillover of Kemp Smith's infectious enthusiasm for re-assessing the intellectual inheritance of the West, prepared the way for the subsequent realization, now at long last belatedly dawning on the Scottish Universities themselves, that there was gold in the dung-hill of the common sense philosophy as accumulated in the classrooms of Scotland in the course of a full century's discussion and re-discussion of Hume's *Treatise* Book I.

1.   *Letters*, ii. 452.
2.   *The Wealth of Nations*, bk. v, ch. 1, pt. 3, art. 3.
3.   'Of Essay Writing' in *The Philosophical Works of David Hume* ed. T. H. Green and T. H. Grose (London 1874–5) vol. IV, pp. 367–70.

Hume and the Ethics of Belief

THAT PHILOSOPHERS differ is scarcely news. But for all our familiarity with their habit of disagreeing, the range of their differences on a particular issue is sometimes so great as still to astonish us. The relationship between belief and decision is such a case. At one extreme, Bernard Williams tells us that it is logically impossible, incompatible with the very nature of belief, to suppose that we can, in any case whatsoever, decide to believe.[1] At the opposite extreme, Descartes argues that decision is necessarily inherent in the act of believing. 'The will', he writes, 'is absolutely essential for our giving our assent to what we have in some manner perceived'.[2] Somewhere between these extremes, Chisholm asserts that at least a particular class of beliefs— those beliefs which arise out of deliberation—are 'as much within [the believer's] control as is any other deed we attribute to him'.[3] And he claims Peirce as a predecessor, justifiably enough if we remember that Peirce once wrote that 'a deliberate, or self-controlled, habit is precisely a belief'.[4] Indeed, the pragmatic movement as a whole takes it for granted that there are circumstances in which we can decide to believe.

To sum up, then, we can point to leading philosophical representatives of the view (1) that it is logically impossible for us to decide to believe; (2) that there are circumstances in which we can, and circumstances in which we cannot, decide to believe; (3) that it is logically impossible for us to believe except as the result of an act of decision. Diversity can scarcely go further!

On the margins of philosophy, in theology, the position is very similar. The theologian, of course, concentrates his attention on a particular class of beliefs, those which bear upon the existence and nature of God. But for Locke and Hume, too, this class of beliefs is of the first importance, never far from their minds. Notice the way in which, in the *Enquiry concerning Human Understanding*, when Hume wants to illustrate how beliefs can arise out of resemblance and causation he takes as his leading example of the first 'the ceremonies of the Roman Catholic religion' and of the second, the use by devotees of relics 'to enliven their devotion' (*Enquiries*, pp. 51, 53). Save where they are stock, a philosopher's examples indicate his preoccupations. So the differences, at this point, between the interests of philosophers and the interests of theologians are not as marked as one might at first expect.

And it is not at all surprising that their opinions should subdivide in much the same manner.

There is a powerful Christian tradition to the effect that belief lies under our control, that we can sometimes properly be blamed for not believing as we should, for 'wilful misbelief', When Clement of Alexandria tells us that 'not only the Platonists; but the Stoics, say that assent is in our power',[5] this is in order to invoke their authority on his behalf. Cardinal Newman took the same view: 'assent is a free act, a personal act for which the doer is responsible'.[6] In somewhat different theological traditions, Kierkegaard, like Descartes, supposes it to be essential to belief that it is a free decision.[7] And for Tolstoy freedom has no meaning, unless we are free to decide whether to believe or disbelieve.[8]

Aquinas formulates the intermediate doctrine. Although, he argues, when the intellect is confronted by what is *known* to be true, first principles and the like, it has no choice but to assent, in those situations in which it is faced with conflicting opinions it can assent 'through an act of choice, whereby it turns voluntarily to one side rather than another'.[9] More rigorous, Augustinian theologians expound the thesis that we have no control over our beliefs; faith is a gift of God, of divine grace. So, making allowance for the typical Christian uncertainties about grace and freedom, the three major alternative views we discovered in philosophy are paralleled within theology.

At a different level, ordinary usage seems to be on the side of those who argue that although we are sometimes, as the phrase has it, 'forced to believe', in other circumstances we can make a choice: as in 'I refuse to believe . . .', 'I like to believe . . .', 'I cannot bring myself to believe . . .', 'I prefer to believe . . .', 'My present inclination is to believe . . .', 'I have made up my mind to believe . . .', 'I have decided to believe . . .'. And although English usage is not decisive evidence for anything except English speech-habits, this wealth of voluntarist idiom is somewhat surprising if in fact it is *logically impossible* to decide to believe.

Enough has by now been said to suggest at least that there is some sort of tension in our thinking on this point: on the one side a pull towards the view that, as a matter of everyday experience, we can and do decide to believe; on the other side—for Bernard Williams by no means stands alone—a pull towards the view that this is quite impossible, that although we can decide to make our beliefs public, or to keep them to ourselves, or to examine them, or to leave them unexamined, we cannot decide *what we shall believe*. And this is matched by a parallel moral uncertainty, whether we can properly condemn the holding of this or that belief, as Clifford so firmly maintains in *The Ethics of Belief*—'it is wrong always, everywhere, and for everyone, to

believe anything upon insufficient evidence'[10] — or whether beliefs lie
so far outside our control as to be no more subject to moral censure than
is our breathing.

Where there is so strong a pull in contrary directions, we can expect
to find inconsistencies within the writings of individual philosophers.
Locke is a case in point, which we cannot now explore in detail — his
argument is very complex — but should at least illustrate. In his *Letter
on Toleration* he is quite emphatic and uncompromising. We cannot
choose what to believe — 'to believe this or that to be true is not within
the scope of our will'.[11] One can readily see why the author of a defence
of toleration should want to take such a view. If men and women are
not free to believe *p* rather than *q*, then they cannot be blamed for their
beliefs; to persecute them merely for holding a particular belief would
be plainly unjust. But even outside the *Letter on Toleration* with its
special concerns, there are many occasions on which Locke no less
categorically denies that our beliefs lie under our control. Yet he also
tells us that we *ought* to regulate our beliefs in accordance with the
evidence (*Essay*, IV. xvi. 1, D2: 369).[12] Does not this 'ought' imply
'can'? Perhaps what Locke means by 'evidence' is the evidence we
could have before us, rather than the evidence we do *in fact* have before
us; perhaps he is urging us always to make sure we have all the evidence before us. But it is not so easy to set aside that passage in which he
explicitly lays it down that there is a class of cases in which 'assent,
suspense or dissent are often voluntary actions' (*Essay*, IV. xx. 15; D2:
454). This is the class of cases in which the evidence for *p*, as against
the evidence for *q*, is not decisive, but in which we are nonetheless
bound to come to a conclusion — the class of cases in which William
James also argued that we can properly choose what we shall believe,
It is interesting to observe, however, that these are precisely the circumstances in which we are least inclined to *blame* anyone who believes
p rather than *q*; there is room, we then say, for an honest difference of
opinion.

To come at last to Hume. Bernard Williams, we note, counts Hume
as an ally, except that Hume writes as if choosing to believe is *psychologically* impossible, whereas Williams, in the manner typical of recent
British philosophy, wants to argue that it is 'logically' or 'conceptually'
impossible, that we just would not count as 'our belief' any propostion
which we knew, or even suspected, we had acquired at will.

One must grant to Williams that he is correctly describing the
general tenor of Hume's reasoning. Consider, for example, the *reductio*
argument that Hume propounds in his Appendix to the *Treatise*. He is
there concerned to refute the view that a belief is distinguishable from
other ideas in virtue of its having 'some new idea such as that of

reality or *existence*' annexed to it. And his argument runs thus: 'The mind has command over all its ideas, and can separate, unite, mix and vary them as it pleases; so that if belief consisted merely in a new idea, annex'd to the conception, it wou'd be in a man's power to believe what he pleas'd' (*Treatise*, p. 625). There the argument ends, the *reductio* is complete. In other words, Hume here supposes it to be obviously absurd to hold that a man has the power to believe what he pleases—that any theory of belief which leaves open this possibility can at once be dismissed. One can easily enough find other passages in his writings to a similar effect. That belief is something that happens to us, rather than something we do, is implicit in his observation that *'belief is more properly an act of the sensitive, than of the cogitative part of our natures'* (*Treatise*, p. 183). The supposition that we can believe what we please is, he more directly tells us, 'contrary to what we find by daily experience' (*Enquiries*, p. 48).

Enough, it might well be thought, has been said. Hume's position in respect to belief and decision is, to an unusual degree, indisputable. Yet, dipping into Hume, scholars have sometimes supposed him to take quite the contrary view. 'A wise man', they read in Hume's *Enquiry concerning Human Understanding*, 'proportions his belief to the evidence' (*Enquiries*, p. 110). Surely 'proportioning' is a cogitative act, if anything is! And is not Hume, when he writes that sentence, exhorting us to decide not to believe until we have examined the evidence—as if, then, we had the power, at least, to *suspend* our belief? If this be so, if we can choose not to believe, does it not follow that belief is in some measure under our control?

After all, we might add, it is one thing to say that we cannot choose to believe at will, if what this means is that we cannot, in respect of each and every proposition, decide whether to believe it or not to believe it, and quite another thing to say that in *no* circumstances can we decide whether or not to believe a proposition. The first view, one can agree with Hume, is quite contrary to experience, so much so that I doubt whether any philosopher or theologian has ever seriously held it, although they may loosely have written as if they did. If the rain is pelting down, I cannot simply decide to believe that it is not raining, any more than, Dostoevsky to the contrary notwithstanding, I can simply decide to believe that $2 + 2 = 5$. But it does not follow that when the evidence is inconclusive as between p and q I cannot decide to believe p rather than q, that the judge's 'I have decided to believe you' or the friend's 'I refuse to believe he could act in that way' are unacceptable. This is the only point that is really in dispute—whether Hume ever admits that, as Locke admits, there are *some* circumstances in which belief is voluntary. Of the commentators on Hume, Price, for

one, argues as much,[13] or argues at least that there are places in which
Hume's philosophical procedure makes sense only on the assumption
that belief can sometimes be under our control. Hume's philosophical
practice, on Price's view, is to that extent inconsistent with his mechanical theory of belief. A more straightforward inconsistency, as we have
already pointed out, is at least suggested by Hume's observation that
'the wise man proportions his belief to the evidence'. So for all that our
initial tendency is to think of Hume, in Bernard Williams' manner, as
an exceptionally whole-hearted proponent of the view that we believe
as we must, it is worth exploring the matter a little further—the more
especially as, if there is a degree of tension in our ordinary thinking on
this question, we might expect to find it reflected, like most other such
tensions, in Hume's philosophy.

Let us begin by looking a little more closely at Hume's theory of
belief.[14] One thing that might surprise us at the outset is that Hume
should so obviously think of himself as a pioneer. No one else, he tells
us, has even suspected that there is any difficulty in determining in
what belief consists (*Treatise*, p. 628). We are surprised because Locke,
to say nothing of such of his predecessors as Plato, had talked about
belief at considerable length, even if sometimes, like Hume himself,
under the name of assent. But, Hume would reply, neither Locke nor
Plato had supposed there to be any difficulty attaching to the act of
believing as such—it was an act of the understanding and no more
need be said. He himself was the first to anatomize the act of believing, as distinct from 'placing' belief epistemologically in its relation
to knowledge.

Consider, in this light, Locke's definition of belief: 'The admitting or
receiving [of] any proposition for true, upon arguments or proofs that
are found to persuade us to receive it as true, without certain knowledge
that it is so' (*Essay*, IV. xv. 3, D2: 365). Hume would object to this
definition on three grounds: the first, that vague phrases like 'the admitting', 'the receiving' conceal the fact that we are not being told in
what *believing* consists; the second, that to define belief as admitting or
receiving a proposition as true upon *arguments or proofs* wrongly suggests that our beliefs are all of them the conclusions of arguments; the
third, that the phrase 'admitting or receiving'—'receiving' has here
the same force as in 'the Ambassador received the guests'—makes it
appear that our beliefs are accepted only after scrutiny, whereas in fact
they are automatic responses to particular forms of experience.

Hume can properly think of himself as an innovator, then, in at
least two respects: first, in defining 'belief' in purely psychological
terms, as a vivid perception rather than, along with Plato and Locke, as
a proposition we hold to be true on evidence less than sufficient to

constitute knowledge; and, secondly, in denying that beliefs necessarily
or normally have their source in argument or deliberation.

We can see at once how sharply Hume differs from his predecessors
by looking at his initial account of belief in his second, considerably revised, discussion of 'the senses and the memory'. 'The *belief* or *assent*
which always attends the memory and the senses', he there informs us,
'is nothing but the vivacity of those perceptions they present . . .'
(*Treatise*, p. 86). Locke had argued that the senses give us knowledge;
Hume will have none of this—they offer us beliefs, the belief that
something is the case. And this has the consequence that a belief has
all the immediacy, although not the infallibility, of an intuition; it does
not rest, anymore than for Locke knowledge need rest, on arguments or
proofs. The whole process is spontaneous, completely involuntary; a
vivid perception is at once a sensation or a memory and a belief. The
belief 'attends' our memory and senses not as an inference from them
but as an aspect of them. This is true, he later argues, even when the
belief depends for its existence on a constant conjunction of experiences,
as distinct from a single experience. 'The belief, which attends the present impression, and is produc'd by a number of past impressions and
conjunctions . . . arises immediately, without any new operation of the
reason or imagination' (*Treatise*, p. 102).

Further to point the contrast between Hume and Locke, we can draw
attention to the fact that in Locke's account of belief two distinct factors have always to be kept in mind. First, the objective probability of
the proposition to which we give our assent; secondly, the degree of
assurance we attach to that proposition. Ideally, and in large part in
fact, those two are proportionate one to another. When they are not,
this is because we get our calculations wrong: 'the foundation of error
will lie in wrong measures of probability' (*Essay*, IV. xx. 16, D2: 456).
How such errors can arise, how men can be so attached to false beliefs,
is a question that deeply troubles Locke; he tries to explain such per-
versity in a variety of ways. But in every case, certainly, the degree of
probability is one thing, the degree of assurance quite another.

In a familiar passage, Hume sweeps aside Locke's Janus-like analysis, and with it all Locke's problems about how degrees of assurance can
come to be dissociated from degrees of probability. 'Thus all probable
reasoning', he writes, 'is nothing but a species of sensation. 'Tis not
solely in poetry and music, we must follow our taste and sentiment,
but likewise in philosophy. When I am convinc'd of any principle, 'tis
only an idea, which strikes more strongly upon me. When I give the
preference to one set of arguments above another, I do nothing but
decide from my feeling concerning the superiority of their influence'
(*Treatise*, p. 103). This makes it look as if Locke's problem—how we

can have a degree of assurance which is not conformable to the probabilities—ought not, for Hume, to so much as arise. The question
makes no sense. *For the probability and the degree of assurance are by
the nature of the case exactly the same thing.*

There are, however, distinct oddities in Hume's account of what
happens when we find one set of arguments more convincing than
another. 'I decide from my feeling', he says. This makes it sound as if
something like the following happens: 'I ask myself: "Which is the
more vivid, my idea of *p* or my idea of *q?*" I decide that *p* is more vivid
than *q*. Therefore I decide to believe *p*.' But if I thus 'decide from my
feeling', as distinct from simply *feeling*, then a cogitative act is central
to the whole analysis. A thorough-going mechanical theory will have
to argue, rather, that what we call 'giving the preference to one argument over another' *simply consists* in a more vivid idea somehow
driving out a less vivid idea. If Hume does not say this, it is not merely,
I think, because he has momentarily fallen into the language of the
vulgar; he has a picture in the back of his mind, a picture which he
cannot entirely expunge, of a human being's hesitating between two
alternative views, uncertain which to accept, and finally deciding
between them. Hume moves such a decision from a decision about the
strength of evidence to a decision about vividness. To leave it entirely
out of account would be to do altogether too much violence to the facts.

One may add, too, that as Hume's argument proceeds we begin to
wonder whether he does *in fact* identify probability with degree of
assurance. As I interpret Hume, this is one of the points at which there
is a conflict between Hume the moral scientist—Hume the *mitigated*
sceptic—and the Pyrrhonian Hume.

Consider his distinction between 'philosophical' and 'unphilosophical' probability. The ground for such a distinction, one would naturally
be inclined to suppose, is that the first, though far from being demonstrative, generates beliefs that are rational, while the second generates
beliefs that we are not justified in holding, which we can be blamed, or
at least rebuked, for persisting in. Hume the Pyrrhonian sceptic will
not permit us to make any such distinction. In this spirit, he argues
that philosophical and unphilosophical probability involve the same
psychological mechanism. In each case all that happens is that our idea
is vivified; there is no rational ground for preferring the philosophically
vivified idea to the unphilosophically vivified idea. Yet under the head
of unphilosophical probability he includes what he calls 'prejudice' and
illustrates this by the example of a person who having met one dishonest Frenchman firmly believes, in consequence, that all Frenchmen
are dishonest. A Pyrrhonian would delight in the conclusion that it is a
mere prejudice on our part to condemn beliefs arising in such a fashion

as prejudices. But Hume the enlightened, Hume the moral philosopher, would by no means welcome it.

For the moment, I shall not carry this line of argument any further. Let us return, rather, to Hume's phrase, 'the belief attending the memory and the senses'. It is more than a little strange to speak of 'belief' in this connection. 'I believe I once went to Cambridge' would normally suggest something quite different from 'I remember going to Cambridge'—an element of hesitancy and doubt, a failure to remember, or at the very least to remember clearly. There is a similar element of hesitation, normally, in 'I believe there is a man on that hill' as compared with 'I can see a man on that hill'. One may well doubt whether the traditional dichotomy—either knowledge or belief—is refined enough to deal with such cases. But Hume is suggesting that even if we ordinarily suppose there is a difference of the sort that our choice of language in these instances suggests, that is, our choice of 'remembering' rather than 'believing', this supposition is erroneous; we are believing when we remember or perceive quite as much as when we go beyond what we can either remember or perceive; the word 'remembering' serves only to indicate the kind of belief that is in question.

To believe, for Hume, is to take something to have occurred (memory or retrodictive causal inference), to be occurring (sensation), or to be about to occur (predictive causal inference). That he thinks of belief in this way explains why, in the *Appendix* passage I have already quoted, when he asks whether believing could consist in annexing another idea to an unbelieved idea and so converting it into a believed idea, the candidates that come at once to his mind are 'reality' and 'existence', rather than let us say 'assurance'. To say that belief is nothing but a vivid idea is, for Hume, to say that taking x to exist, or to be about to exist, or to have existed, is identical with *having a vivid idea of x*.

At this stage in Hume-criticism, we need not describe in detail the difficulties Hume gets into when he tries to give an account of this 'vivacity' or the way in which he gradually works towards the somewhat different view that a belief is 'differently conceived' from other ideas. We can set aside the fact, too, that as his argument proceeds, he offers much narrower definitions of belief, whether as *'a lively idea related to or associated with a present impression'* (*Treatise*, p. 96), or as arising only from causation (*Treatise*, p. 107). These variations, these differentiations of the genus 'vivid idea', bear witness to the fact that he is not, in every mood, happy to identify 'a poetical enthusiasm' and 'a serious conviction'—as he *did* identify them when he wrote that ''tis not solely in poetry and music, we must follow our taste and sentiment, but likewise in philosophy'. *Serious* convictions, unlike poetic enthusiasms, arise, his second thoughts suggest, only when our belief is associated with a present impression or even, his third thoughts suggest, only when it arises out of causation. But he is not going back on his view that belief, whatever else it is, is a vivid idea; in the *Enquiry* he still suggests that this is at least one way of describing the distinctive character of a belief. For our purposes it does not greatly matter whether it can also be described as an idea 'conceived in a certain manner'—whatever this can mean on a Humean view—or even, as some of the things he says in the *Enquiry* might suggest, as an odd sort of sentiment, rather like love and hate. It is enough that belief, on any such interpretation, is still something which we find ourselves with, which happens to us. So for brevity's sake let us hold fast to the vivacity analysis, with the rider that the alternative expression—'manner of conceiving'—surely suggests that a belief is, after all, cogitative rather than sensitive.

Consider in the light of this analysis of belief Hume's observations at the very end of Book 1 of the *Treatise*. He is there asking what general conclusions he can draw from his argument as a whole. 'The *intense* view of these manifold contradictions and imperfections in human reason', he writes, 'has so wrought upon me, and heated my brain, that I am ready to reject all belief and reasoning, and can look upon no opinion even as more probable or likely than another' (*Treatise*, pp. 268–9). 'I am ready to reject all belief . . .'. What can this possibly mean? It might mean something like this: 'My brain is so heated as a result of my considering contradictions that I no longer have any vivid ideas.' But Hume makes it perfectly clear that this is not at all what he means. He is complaining, indeed, that his ideas are only too intense, only too vivid; otherwise he would have no problems. He has to dine, play back-gammon, converse, make merry with his friends before his sceptical views lose their vividness, turn 'cold and strain'd and ridiculous'. When he is 'ready to reject all belief' this cannot mean, either, that he is ready to stop himself from having any vivid ideas; that is impossible. What he is ready to do is something quite different: 'to look upon no opinion as more probable or likely than another'. And this brings out the fact that having a vivid idea and looking upon an opinion as probable are not after all the same thing.

It is notoriously difficult, of course, to determine what Hume wants to say about the degree to which, when we are philosophising, we can succeed in not believing, or can suspend our belief about, what at other times, so he tells us, we *cannot help* believing—nature not having left to us the decision whether to believe or not to believe.[15] We need only insist upon one fact: Hume certainly presumes that we can at least *question* our beliefs even when they are extremely vivid. So far, as Price argues, his philosophical practice is not consistent with his philosophical theory. For 'questioning a belief' cannot mean asking ourselves whether it is really vivid or really conceived in a certain manner; that is not the sort of thing that can be doubted. What else can it mean, then, except asking ourselves whether it is *really* probable? So being vivid and being probable cannot be identical. This same conclusion would seem to follow from another, particularly striking passage in the *Appendix*. 'A . . . reflection on *general rules*', he there tells us, 'keeps us from augmenting our belief upon every encrease of the force and vivacity of our ideas' (*Treatise*, p. 632). So to believe *p* rather than *q* is not, after all, equivalent to having a more vivid idea of *p* than of *q*; we can have a more vivid idea of *p* and yet *not* believe it; the scientist, relying on 'general rules', is constantly in this position.

In the less heated atmosphere of the *Enquiry*, Hume's metaphysical agitations are subdued. But at the same time it becomes more and more evident that he does not consistently think of belief as an automatic reaction, over which we have in no sense any control. A long note appended to his discussion 'Of the Reason of Animals' (*Enquiries*, p. 107) brings out this point very clearly. Its placing is interesting. Hume is ready to ascribe belief to animals. After all, they can remember, anticipate. That, not possessing language, they cannot give assent to propositions might lead a Locke to conclude otherwise, but not a Hume. But is Hume really prepared to say that the beliefs of animals, vivid as they can doubt can be, are in every way as good as the beliefs of human beings? And this can be absorbed into another question: Are the beliefs of one man quite as good as the beliefs of another? He is not now prepared to answer 'Yes'. Yet if all probable reasoning is nothing but sensation, there does not seem to be the slightest ground for denying to animals, or to the foolish, beliefs as rational as those of the wisest man. Can Hume, consistently with his theory, avoid this conclusion?

As a sceptic, he might not wish to do so. But in fact he makes the attempt, pointing to not one ground of distinction but many. After lengthy experience wise men, he says, becoming accustomed to the uniformity of nature, acquire a general habit of arguing from the known to the unknown. After 'even one experiment', they 'expect a similar event with some degree of certainty, where the experiment has been made accurately, and free from all foreign circumstances' (*Enquiries*, p. 107n). When there is a complication of causes, again, the wise man is better than the foolish man at considering the situation as a whole, seeing what goes with what. The forming of general maxims, too, is a delicate business; unlike the prejudiced, the wise do not allow themselves to be led astray by haste or narrowness of vision. And so on.

So we can certainly say this much at least of Hume: he does not invariably think of our beliefs as the automatic product of custom. He allows that a wise man, when he encounters p, can expect r rather than q because he has examined the situation carefully, not just because r is more vivid than q. So far, at least, belief can be cogitative rather than sensitive. But this still leaves it open to Hume to argue that, once the wise man has done his examining, his idea of r is automatically vivified —even if not, it would seem, by any of the processes Hume has explicitly described—without its lying in his power to prevent this from happening.

If, on this interpretation, a man can be condemned, and lie open to moral censure, for believing q rather than r, it will be for the reason Locke most often suggests: he has not looked carefully enough; he has failed to examine the situation as adequately as he should have done. Even in this case, Hume strongly suggests, the fact that some men are better endowed than others, have better powers of attention, observation and memory, has the consequence that to blame men for holding q rather than r would be like blaming an animal because it cannot predict an eclipse. But this is surely not the whole story. For it does not seem possible to explain, purely in terms of natural endowments, why some men, attentive and observant, confronted by a particular set of evidence, accept it as a proper foundation for believing q and others do not. Wisdom is not the same thing as having good 'faculties' of the sort Hume enumerates.

Now at long last we reach the crucial passage: 'a wise man proportions his belief to the evidence'. But before examining it, let us look first at the immediately preceding sentences: 'Some events are found, in all countries and all ages, to have been constantly conjoined together: Others are found to have been more variable, and sometimes to disappoint our expectations; so that, in our reasonings concerning matter of fact, there are all imaginable degrees of assurance, from the highest certainty to the lowest species of moral evidence' (*Enquiries*, p. 110). If this stood alone, we could read it in terms of the mechanical theory. Those conjunctions that are invariable, we might take Hume to be saying, produce extremely vivid ideas in us—we have a vivid idea of the effect whenever the cause occurs; other conjunctions are more variable and therefore produce less vivid ideas. 'Our reasonings concerning matters of fact' should then be read, in the spirit of Pyrrhonian scepticism, as '*what we are pleased to call* our reasonings'.

Then, however, it would be absurd to go on and say that 'the wise man proportions his belief to the evidence'. Let us attempt a Humean translation. 'A wise man is one the liveliness of whose ideas correlates with variations in his experience'. But on the interpretation we offered above, this correlation applies to *everyone*'s beliefs, the foolish as much as the wise, to animal beliefs as much as human beliefs. To translate in such a manner, then, would be entirely to rule out the obviously intended contrast between the wise man and the foolish man. On the face of it, it is only if we are being called upon to think of the wise man as one who has first looked at the evidence and then *decided* what to believe—or at least how strongly to believe—that Hume is telling us anything at all distinctive about wise men.

It is interesting to observe that this pronouncement about the 'wise man' prefaces Hume's discussion of miracles—interesting because in discussing miracles Hume is talking about the class of beliefs that most concerned Locke, those in which we accept, or reject, somebody's testimony. (Where Hume's cautionary remarks for inquirers have so far turned around the analysis of causes, Locke's, for the most part, turn around the criticism of witnesses.[16]) No doubt, half-realizing that he has shifted his ground, Hume attempts to assimilate arguments from testimony to causal arguments. To readers who not unnaturally boggle at this assimilation he replies in a notably off-hand manner: 'I shall not dispute about a word' (*Enquiries*, p. 111). It is enough that just as there is no necessary connection between cause and effect, so too there is no necessary connection between a testimony and its truth. But a good deal more is involved than a word. It is, indeed, a most implausible view that we come to accept certain testimonies only as a result of having experienced a constant conjunction between testimonies of that type and the truth. Implausible in terms of Hume's general theory; what exactly is 'the truth' in such a conjunction? Empirically implausible, too. At first, in fact, a child automatically believes what he is told; what he acquires as a result of experience is a tendency to be more critical of testimony, more hesitant in accepting it.

Hume recognizes, indeed, that our tendency is to accept testimony. We have, he says, 'a remarkable propensity to believe whatever is reported . . . however contrary to daily experience and observation' (*Treatise*, p. 113). But just how remarkable this propensity is, on his assimilation of arguments from testimony to causual inferences, he does not pause to consider. For his real concern, once more, is with the procedures of the wise.

When, again, we are suspicious about a testimony, we do not proceed to examine it with the help of the rules Hume lays down for 'judging of causes and effects'. We consider, as Hume himself tells us, the character of the witnesses, the initial plausibility of what they say, their remoteness in time from the events and so on. If it be replied, as Hume replies, that in doing so we rely on such experience-based maxims as are implicitly appealed to in 'The lady doth protest too much, methinks', these maxims, once more, are not causal; the falsity of what the lady says is in no sense a *consequence* of her multiple protesting to the contrary. No doubt, *we* may come to believe that what she says is false as a consequence of her protesting so much, but the maxim 'those who protest too much often make false statements' is not *itself* a causal maxim.

In the special case of miracles, so Hume tells us, what I do is ask myself whether it is more probable that the witness is either deliberately deceiving me, or is himself deceived, than that the events he describes really have occurred.[17] 'I weigh the one miracle against the other; and according to the superiority, which I discover, I pronounce my decision, and always reject the greater miracle' (*Enquiries*, p. 116). This is Lockeian in tone; there are two sets of probabilities, I weigh one against the other, discover that one is superior to the other and then. . . .

What follows the 'and then'? Hume is sufficiently definite: 'I pronounce my decision'. If this is the right way of putting it, then I *decide* to believe that the testimony is false rather than that the miracle occurred. True, he runs on thus: 'If the falsehood of his testimony would be more miraculous, than the event which he relates; then, and not till then, can he pretend to command my belief or opinion'. This might suggest that once we look at the facts, they determine the outcome, as Locke supposed, and leave us unable to make any decision, *commanded* as we are by the facts to believe in a particular way. But what, then, is the force of 'pretend' in 'pretend to command'? Does it not suggest '*properly* command'? If so, then Hume is saying that we *ought not* to prefer the testimony to the beliefs we have derived from experience, that the wise man will not do so.

Let us take still another look at Hume's description of what happens. 'I weigh the one against the other', the testimony against the likelihood. Who is this 'I'? Hume is certainly not describing, purely and simply, what he himself does as an individual. Just as when he wrote a little earlier that 'we frequently hesitate concerning the reports of others' (*Enquiries*, p. 112), he is a spokesman for the wise man—that wise man who lends 'a very academic faith to every report which favours the passion of the reporter' (*Enquiries*, p. 125). A Pyrrhonian is, in principle at least, an egalitarian; for him one view is as good as another. But in the jargon of our own days, Hume was an élitist. Although there are points at which he sceptically writes as if the wise and the foolish were in exactly the same position, passive victims of their experience, this, as we have already seen, is not at all his invariable opinion. And in this section of the *Enquiry*, it is not his opinion at all. Then is Hume simply describing the beliefs of those men we choose to call 'wise'? Wise men's ideas are enlivened by constant conjunctions, foolish men's beliefs have other sources. That is the end of it.

At certain points in the *Treatise* Hume tries to adopt this merely descriptive attitude: he is the elegant eighteenth-century spectator, contemplating from his coffee-house the strange antics of the passers-by. Or, if we like, he is the phenomenologist telling us what is included in our concept of wisdom. But if this were the whole story, his enterprise would be pointless. For he is *arguing against* those who accept miracles; he is exhorting the 'wise and learned', the 'judicious and knowing', if nobody else, to become more sceptical. True, he would not expect to convert 'the vulgar'; like Gibbon, he has a strong sense of 'man's knavery and folly'. But if his arguments are valid, then it will be wrong for the wise, at least, to accept testimony for miracles.

Confronted by Clifford's dictum that 'it is wrong always, everywhere, and for everyone, to believe anything upon insufficient evidence', Hume might, in his more sceptical moods, reply: 'Evidence is sufficient if in fact it induces men to believe; to say that it is wrong for men to believe on insufficient evidence is to say that it is wrong for them to believe in circumstances in which it is just not possible for them to believe'. But at other times, and especially in the *Enquiry*, his reply would be very different. The vulgar, he would then say, do not examine evidence; their beliefs are entirely the product of 'education'. It is not *wrong* for them to believe on insufficient evidence; that is how they are made. But the wise, if only as a result of experience, develop critical principles, 'general rules',[18] which enable them to proportion their belief to the evidence. At this point, however, 'evidence' does not mean simply 'that which engenders vivid ideas'; the wise resist the influence of their education, they resist vivid but implausible stories, they weigh evidence. And if they do not do this they act wrongly. For 'there is a degree of doubt, and caution, and modesty, which, in all kinds of scrutiny and decision, ought for ever to accompany a just reasoner' (*Enquiries*, p. 162).

In the end then, Price seems to be right. If men's beliefs were as automatic as Hume sometimes suggests, if they were always, purely and simply, the product of custom operating upon the imagination, many of Hume's philosophical procedures would be quite fruitless. There are times, certainly, when he suggests that this, by their very nature, is their fate; inevitably, we shall in the end ignore what he has taught us, submitting to our senses and imagination (*Treatise*, p. 269). It is certainly no part of his object to convert men in general into sceptical philosophers, especially those honest country gentlemen who represented Hume's social ideal—'employ'd in their domestic affairs, or amusing themselves in common recreations' (*Treatise*, p. 272). But he does want to destroy superstition; if philosophy is often ridiculous, so he tells us, superstition is both ridiculous and dangerous. That is precisely what leads him to write as if it is both possible and desirable to stand back from our vivid ideas, to decide, in certain circumstances, not to count them amongst our beliefs.

Hume, one might then say, is trying to persuade us to adopt a 'belief policy': the policy of examining critically all beliefs which arise from such suspect sources as 'education', that is, our upbringing. To that degree he is suggesting that however vivid an idea is, we ought to be prepared to set it aside, temporarily at least. Thus to set it aside is not, of course, the same thing as deciding to believe its contrary. But it does mean that belief lies in some measure under our control; we can deliberately prevent ourselves from believing, even when we are strongly tempted to believe. And this is how we *ought* to behave. Those who adopt a different policy, for example the policy of accepting whatever they are told, are properly subject to censure. So far, at least, there is an 'ethics of belief'.

The paper originally arose out of my supervision of a PH.D. thesis on *Belief* by D. R. Naulty; it owes a good deal to discussion with him and with my co-supervisor, Dr E. Curley.

1. Bernard Williams *Problems of the Self* (Cambridge 1973) ch. 9.
2. René Descartes *Principles of Philosophy*, trans. Ross and Haldane (Cambridge 1968) pt. 1, Principle XXXIV.
3. R. M. Chisholm 'Lewis' Ethics of Belief' in P. A. Schilpp (ed.) *The Philosophy of C. I. Lewis* (La Salle 1968) p. 224.
4. 'Pragmatism in Retrospect' (c. 1906) in Justus Buchler (ed.) *The Philosophy of Peirce* (London 1940) p. 280.
5. Clement of Alexandria *The Stromata or Miscellanies*, bk. II, ch. 12, in A. Roberts and J. Donaldson (eds.) *Ante-Nicene Fathers* (Michigan 1962) p. 360.
6. J. H. Newman *An Essay in Aid of a Grammar of Assent* (repr. New York 1955) p. 189.
7. S. Kierkegaard *Philosophical Fragments*, trans. D. F. Swenson (Princeton 1946) pp. 35–6.
8. L. Tolstoy *The Kingdom of God is Within You*, Conclusion, Section 5.
9. *Summa Theologica*, 11, 2, q1. 4. In the end, this is what Descartes also wants to say. See E. M. Curley 'Descartes, Spinoza and the Ethics of Belief' in E. Freeman and M. Mandelbaum (eds.) *Spinoza: Essays in Interpretation* (La Salle 1975) pp. 165–6.
10. W. K. Clifford 'The Ethics of Belief' in *Lectures and Essays*, vol. II (London 1879) p. 186.
11. John Locke *Letter on Toleration*, ed. R. Klibansky, trans. J. W. Gough (Oxford 1968) p. 21. The Latin reads: 'Ut hoc vel illud verum esse credamus, in nostra voluntate situm non est'.
12. References to Locke: *Essay Concerning Human Understanding* will be abbreviated in this form: 'IV. xvi. 1' means 'Book IV, chapter xvi, section 1; D2: 369' means the second volume, page 369 of the two volume Dover edition, New York 1959.
13. H. H. Price *Belief* (London 1969) pp. 239–40.

14. Only in outline, however, and merely touching upon its inconsistencies and fluctuations. For a fuller account see John Passmore *Hume's Intentions*, rev. edition (London 1968) *passim*, but esp. pp. 94–104.
15. Compare my discussion of Price in *Hume's Intentions*, p. 148.
16. Not entirely, of course. But in relative detail. Compare Locke's *Essay*, IV. xv. 4; D2: 365–6.
17. This is a misleading short-hand account of what Hume says, but detail would be out of place here. See, for that detail, Antony Flew *Hume's Philosophy of Belief* (New York 1961) ch. VIII.
18. For some of the problems here see *Hume's Intentions*, pp. 62–4.

Hume and the Sources
of German Anti-Rationalism

THE SUBJECT WITH which I intend to deal is, unlike the other issues discussed at this conference, central neither to Hume's thought, nor to his intellectual development, nor to his life, nor to the world in which he lived and wrote. My topic is concerned with certain ideas of Hume's in connection with his influence on, or rather, the use made of them by, a group of thinkers who, in most respects, utterly rejected all that Hume believed and stood for. The movement which they formed is, I think, best described as the German Counter-Enlightenment, which reached its height towards the end of the eighteenth century. Two, at least, of its leaders, Johann Georg Hamann and Friedrich Heinrich Jacobi, saw Hume as an out and out enemy, but, nevertheless, one with a difference: a man who, however little he may have intended it, supplied them with weapons, both offensive and defensive, against his close philosophical allies, the French Encyclopaedists, whom above all others they wished to confute. Their use of some of Hume's writings, if he had conceived of its possibility, would almost certainly have astonished and, indeed, horrified their author; the moral and intellectual distance between him and these German irrationalists could scarcely have been greater. The history of ideas is not without its ironies.

It is a commonplace, which I do not need to labour, that the culture of the West in Hume's lifetime was largely dominated by the ideas of the French Enlightenment. Whatever the differences that divided the French *philosophes* and their disciples in other countries (and these differences were deeper and more numerous than is often supposed), there existed nevertheless a wide consensus: it rested on an acceptance of what was, in effect, a secular version of the old natural law doctrine according to which the nature of things possessed a permanent, un-alterable structure, differences and changes in the world being subject to universal and immutable laws. These laws were discoverable in principle by the use of reason and controlled observation, of which the methods of the natural sciences constituted the most successful applica-tion. The most powerful instrument in the acquisition of knowledge was held to be mathematics. Whether this was due to the fact that the basic structure of reality was itself such that mathematics was an abstract representation, or symbolisation, of it, or, alternatively, whether mathematical methods were no more than the most reliable means of recording, predicting, and therefore controlling nature whose real character remained inscrutable, was a less crucial issue than what followed from either assumption: namely, that the true path to knowledge was that of the natural sciences, that is to say, all statements with claims to truth must be public, communicable, testable—capable of verification or falsification by methods open to and accepted by any rational investigator. From this it followed that all other types of authority were to be rejected, and in particular such foundations of faith as sacred texts, divine revelation and the dogmatic pronouncements of its authorised interpreters, tradition, prescription, immemorial wisdom, private intuition and all other forms of non-rational or transcendent sources of putative knowledge. This principle was held to apply to both the human and the non-human world: to abstract disciplines, such as logic or mathematics, to the applied sicences which established the laws of the behaviour of inanimate bodies, plants, animals and human beings, and to the normative disciplines which revealed the true nature of ultimate human goals, and the correct rules of conduct, public and private, social and political, moral and aesthetic. According to this doctrine, all genuine questions were in principle answerable: truth was one, error multiple; the true answers must of necessity be universal and immutable, that is, true everywhere, at all times, for all men, and discoverable by the appropriate use of reason, by relevant experience, observation and the methods of experiment, logic, calculation. A logically connected structure of rules, laws, generalisations, susceptible of demonstration or, at least in practice, of a high degree of confirmation (and, where required, of application appropriate to differing circumstances) could, at least in principle, be constructed, and could replace the chaotic amalgam of ignorance, laziness, guesswork, superstition, prejudice, dogma, fantasy, and, above all, what I think Helvétius called 'interested error', which enabled the cunning and the strong to dominate and exploit the stupid, ignorant and weak, and had throughout human history been largely responsible for the vices, follies and miseries of mankind. Only knowledge, that is, the growth of the sciences, could rescue mankind from these largely self-induced evils. Some believed that certainty in empirical matters was attainable, others that no more than high probability could be achieved; some were pessimistic about progress towards virtue or happiness, others were more sanguine. But the majority of the *philosophes* were agreed that if irrational passions could be controlled, and ignorance, prejudice, fear and greed diminished, an end could be made to the worst confusions in human thought and feeling, which led to blind fanaticism in thought and savage barbarism in practice.

This faith in the powers of reason and science was by no means

universally held, even in the mid-eighteenth century in Western
Europe—at least not with equal confidence or fervour: it was regularly
assailed by the insidious doubts of sceptics, by the hostility of the
orthodox defenders of the authority of Church and State, by the
defenders of variety, individual and cultural, and of local and traditional
values, as well as by the champions of the artistic imagination untrammelled by universal rules and regulations, who, by mid-century,
had begun to attack the citadels of neo-classicism. Nevertheless, it
would not, I believe, be inaccurate to say that the central tradition of
the Enlightenment rested on the assumptions of which I have supplied
so over-simplified and crude a summary. Despite pleas for historical
understanding and the celebration of the beauty and strength of early
epic poetry by such critics as von Muralt, Bodmer and Breitinger in
Switzerland, Lowth, Blackwell and the Wartons, father and son, in
England, and, most of all, by the founder of historicism, Giambattista
Vico in Naples; despite the growing interest in the Bible as the national
epic of the Jews, in Homer as the voice of the entire Greek people, in
the sagas of the Norsemen and the Celts, in oriental literatures, in
Shakespeare and Milton, in folk-song, myths, legends and, above all,
diverse cultural traditions which could not be made to fit into the
critical strait-jackets provided by the Parisian arbiters of taste, this reaction remained largely confined to the province of literature and the
arts; the central ideological edifice of the Enlightenment remained
relatively unaffected. The first formidable attack upon it, uncompromising, violent and fraught with lasting consequences, came from Germany. This is not the place in which to try to elaborate on the many
factors which led to this German backlash against the French cultural
domination of the Western world. It was certainly not unconnected
with the anti-rationalist currents in the Lutheran Reformation; nor
with the relative—cultural as well as economic—deprivation of
German-speaking populations in the hundred years that followed
Luther's revolt in contrast to the great cultural flowering of Italy,
France, England, Spain and the Low Countries, which bred in the
Germans a growing consciousness of their own provincialism, and with
it a sense of inferiority, deepened by the disasters of the Thirty Years
War. I am not a social historian. I am not qualified to speculate on either
the roots or the effects of the inevitable rise of resentment and wounded
self-esteem in German territories, particularly in relation to France,
then in the full pride of its power, wealth and artistic achievement.
Yet even to the eye of an amateur it seems obvious that this condition is
not unconnected with the rise of Pietism, one of the most introspective,
austere and self-absorbed of all the inner currents of Lutheranism. The
Pietists, profoundly unpolitical in temper, contemptuous of the world

and its varieties, sought direct communion of the individual soul with God. Liable to extremes of both emotion and self-discipline, they tended to be suspicious of hierarchy, ritual, learning and rational speculation—as against the living voice of the individual conscience with its absolute sense of moral and spiritual duty, infallible guide in the unending battle in and for the soul of sinful man between the word of God and the temptations of the world, the flesh and the devil. Pietism was particularly strong in East Prussia, where the attempt by Frederick the Great, in the middle years of the eighteenth century, to modernise that backward and semi-feudal province with the help of French-speaking officials, was resented and resisted among the devout, conservative population. Much of this sentiment was probably at the root of the revulsion against the materialism, utilitarianism, ethical naturalism and atheism of the French *lumières* which one finds in such thinkers as Hamann, Lavater, Herder and, indeed, Kant himself. They and their disciples Jacobi, Fichte, Schelling, Baader, were in fact the philosophical wing of German cultural resistance movements—of the *Sturm und Drang*, of 'pre-Romanticism' and, indeed, of Romanticism itself.

Let me say something about the mysterious figure of Hamann, the Magus of the North, as Kant and others have called him, who was, perhaps, the most influential leader of this emotionally charged, basically religious opposition, a man described as the first *émigré* of the Aufklärung, the leader of the Vendée of the Enlightenment. Born in 1730 in Königsberg, he received, like his older friend and one-time patron, Kant, a strictly Pietist upbringing. In the 1750s and 60s he was looked upon as a promising young publicist in the service of the German *Aufklärung*. He first made his name with a translation of a French treatise on commerce, accompanied by a disquisition of his own on the effects of trade, and the social value of merchants. He admired Lessing, was taken up by Moses Mendelssohn, Nicolai and the other leaders of liberal German culture in Berlin; Kant and his friends had high hopes of their young *protégé*. However, during a brief sojourn in London in 1757–8, Hamann went through a spiritual crisis, returned to the Pietist faith of his early years, and came back to Königsberg a convinced opponent of the Enlightenment. During the rest of his life—he died in 1788—he published a series of violent attacks upon scientific materialism, universalism and secularism. These were written in an idiosyncratic, obscure, rhapsodical, sybilline prose, full of at times untraceable allusions, private jokes, elaborate puns, meandering digressions into dark paths, which appear to lead nowhere in particular; all this in language which he doubtless intended to contrast as sharply as possible with the, to him, now detestable elegance and brilliance, shallow clarity and spiritual emptiness of the *habitués* of the Paris *salons*—blind leaders of the blind, men cut off from the true, the inner life of man. He was by temperament not merely indifferent, but deeply opposed, to those who seek to find some intelligible order in the universe, capable of being reduced to, and communicated by means of, a theoretical system. He belonged to those thinkers (perhaps more often found east than west of the Rhine) whose hatred of tidy, rational schemas leads them to look for the exceptional and the irregular, if only because these serve to undermine reliance on general laws, and to confute those who suppose that they can catch and order the teeming variety of reality within their artificial constructions. Monist, dualist, pluralist systems were, for him, equally delusive chimeras, efforts to confine the unconfinable, contain the wildly conflicting, unpredictable, often chaotic, data of direct experience, and reduce them to regularities and symmetries by means of logical or metaphysical links—he describes them as walls of sand built to hold back the waves of an ocean.

A more profoundly anti-scientific or anti-rational outlook can scarcely be conceived: all knowledge for Hamann can be obtained solely through direct confrontation with reality provided by the senses, by instinct, by the imagination, by the immediate, uncontradictable insight of the poet, the lover, the man of simple faith. His favourite quotation is Corinthians 1.27—'God has chosen the foolish things of the world to confound the wise'—that is, Descartes, Voltaire and their disciples in free-thinking Berlin. Like William Blake, Hamann believed that truth is always particular, never general; genuine knowledge is direct, gained through some species of immediate acquaintance; the senses, outer and inner, do not refer: they present data directly, and any attempt to organise such data into systems distorts their concrete actuality. 'To cut the cord between faith and the senses is the first symptom of our upside-down type of thought.'[1] Belief (in Hamann's sense) is 'a basic instinct (*Grundtrieb*) without which we could not act at all'.[2] Words are symbols which convey a voice speaking; they are either a method of communication between real persons, immortal souls, or they are mere mechanical devices, the classifying instruments of an impersonal science. Hamann was a passionate Christian pietist, and believed that men had or could have direct experience of God, everywhere and at all times: the words of the Bible were God's voice speaking directly to them, and so was the whole of nature to those who had eyes to see and ears to hear; so, too, was the history of mankind, which was a divine language to convey spiritual truths to an untrammelled understanding, not corrupted by the formulae of the sophists of Paris. It was not words that were the main obstacle to the vision of reality, as Bacon, Locke, Berkeley had maintained. Direct perception was far more violently distorted by concepts, theories, systems; such book-keeper's devices might have their uses in organising or controlling economic or political activities—regions that no longer interested Hamann—but they failed to reveal the real world. They were mere fictions, *entia rationis*, man-made dummies, mistakenly identified with the real world. Only insight which sprang from feeling —at its height, from love for a person or a thing—could reveal and illuminate. It was not possible to love the ghostly network of formulae, general propositions, laws, concepts and categories that the French philosophers had erected between themselves and reality. The task of the philosopher was to explain life in all its contradictions, all its peculiarities, not to smooth it out, or substitute for it hypostatised abstractions, idealised entities, useful, perhaps, for limited ends, but figments. God is a poet, not a mathematician; 'only spiders like Spinoza' make systems that shut out the real world, 'catch flies and build castles in the air'.[3] Men have mistaken words for concepts, and concepts for realities. No system, no elaborate construction of scientific generalities, will, in Hamann's view, enable a man to understand what is conveyed by a gesture, a look, a tone, a style, or to understand a line of poetry, a painting, a vision, a spiritual condition, an *état d'âme*, a form of life—how can men, caught in such webs of abstractions, achieve communion with their fellows, still less with God, who speaks to them in the simple human language of the Bible, in the burning words of inspired visionaries, of nature, and of history, if only men knew how to look and to listen? What is real is always particular; what matters is the unique, the individual, the concrete, that therein a thing differs from other things; for that is its essence and its point, and not that which it has in common with other things—all that the generalizing sciences seek to record. 'Feeling alone gives to abstractions and hypotheses hands, feet, wings'.[4] God speaks to us in poetical words, addressed to the senses, not in abstractions for the learned. Men like Kant (an intimate friend) suffer, he tells us, from a 'gnostic hatred of matter',[5] re-arrange reality into artificial patterns and live in a world of figments. Systems, Hamann insists over and over again, are mere prisons of the spirit, they lead not only to false ideas but sooner or later to the creation of huge bureaucratic machines, built in accordance with rules which ignore variety, the unique, asymmetrical lives of men, and force living creations into the mechanism of some repressive political system, in the name of some intellectual chimera, unrelated to the flow of history or the real lives lived by men. To understand a man, a group, a sect, one must grasp what shapes them—'the union of language, tradition and history'. Every court, every school, every profession, every sect, has its own vocabulary. How does one enter them? With the

passion of a friend, like a lover, an intimate, with faith, not by means
of rules. Reality is an unanalysable, dynamic, changing organism, incapable of being represented by the static metaphors of mathematics
and the natural sciences. All absolute rules, all dogmatic precepts are
fatal: they may be needed in the conduct of ordinary life, but nothing
great was ever achieved by following them. The English critics, Young
above all, had rightly maintained that originality entailed breaking
rules, that every creative act, every transforming insight, could be
obtained only by setting aside the commandments of the arrogant
masters of theory. Hamann declared that rules are like vestal virgins;
unless they are violated, there will be no issue. Nature is no ordered
whole: so-called sensible men are blinkered beings who walk with a
firm tread because they are blind to the true and profoundly disturbing
character of reality, sheltered from it by their man-made contraptions;
if they glimpsed it as it is—a wild dance—they would go out of their
minds. How dare these pathetic pedants impose on the vast world of
continuous, fertile, unpredictable, divine creation their own narrow,
dessicated categories? There is no knowledge save by direct perception
—a direct sense of reality which Hamann calls *Glaube*, faith, the direct
capacity which all men have for unquestioning acceptance of *data* and
not *ficta*.[6] Faith is analogous to sight or taste—the physical senses offer
me my immediate experience of the physical world, while faith—
Glaube—is needed to reveal to me my inner life, as well as the meaning of what others say to me by means of symbols, gestures, ritual acts,
works of art, books or any other expression of the imagination or the
passions. *Glaube* is for Hamann a kind of sense; faith, like the senses,
cannot be refuted by reason, 'it is not its creature'; its findings need no
evidence, it does not rest on grounds, it is not subject to doubt; it may
be delusive, but it cannot be corrected by calculation or rational argument, certainly not by the constructions of the scientists, which are, at
best, mere practical devices for utilitarian purposes, which say nothing
to the soul or the senses through which alone God and nature speak to
us.[7] The wiseacres of Paris, like their allies in Berlin, who dissect
nature, deal with dead matter: they know a great deal and understand
little. Man is not born to reason, but to eat and drink and procreate, to
love and hate, agonise and sacrifice and worship. But they know nothing of this in Paris, where the monstrous *cogito* has obscured the
'sublime *sum*'.

Hamann attempted no less than a total reversal of the values of the
Enlightenment; in place of the abstract and general he wished to place
the particular and the concrete: in place of the theoretical constructions,
stylised patterns and idealised entities of the philosophers and scientists
—the directly given, the unmediated, the sensuous. He was in the

strict sense of the term a reactionary, that is, he wished to return to an older tradition of the ages of faith: quality in place of quantity, primacy of the given, not of the analytic intellect, the immediately perceived secondary qualities, not the inferred primary ones; the free imagination, not logic. His deepest conviction was of the indissolubility of spirit and matter, the sensuous and the spiritual attributes of man, and of the omnipresence of God, transcendent and personal, not the de-personalised world soul of the pantheists, or the remote Clockmaker—the rationally demonstrated, somewhat shadowy Supreme Being of the deists.

I have tried to convey the general drift of this most unsystematic father of German Romanticism, with his revulsion against the French *raisonneurs* and his celebration of the irregulars of life, the outsiders and vagabonds, outcasts and visionaries, whom he favours because they are closer to God than liberal theologians who seek to prove his existence by logical methods. 'Those who seek to prove the existence of God by means of reason' wrote a German pietist thirty years earlier, 'are atheists', and this is what Hamann himself believed. Religion was the direct experience of the presence of God, or it was nothing. From *Glaube*—belief or faith—to revelation was but a short step. Hamann's religion was that of the burning bush, not that of Thomist logic or 'natural' semi-Lutheran religion; it sprang from a Dionysiac experience, not Apollonian contemplation. Driven to the extreme to which he drives it, this attack on all generalisation leads inevitably to the denial of the possibility of all language and thought. Hamann ignores this. He is obsessed by the conviction that the fulness of life, the transforming moments of sudden illumination, are lost in analysis and dissection. No wonder that he was greatly admired by Goethe and by the romantics and criticised sternly by Hegel, that he inspired Herder and Jacobi and, most of all, Kierkegaard, who called him 'The Emperor'.

What, you may ask, has all this to do with David Hume, whose temperament, beliefs and entire outlook were exceedingly remote from this ecstatic view of life, who was repelled by nothing so much as zeal, fanaticism, religious enthusiasm, against which (so his best biographer tells us) he had reacted so strongly, as a result of his own strict Presbyterian upbringing? And indeed, it *has* nothing to do with Hume. But Hume, so it turned out, had, all unknowing, a good deal to do with it.

HUME'S WORKS, like those of other British writers, were much read in the mid-eighteenth century by German intellectuals. The *Treatise* was translated into German only in 1790, but translations of some of *The Moral, Political and Literary Essays*, in the form of *Vermischte Schriften*, were published in German in 1753–6, and of the *Enquiry concerning Human Understanding* in 1755. A German version of *The*

Natural History of Religion was published in 1757 and 1759, and an anthology of Hume's writings (compiled by J.G.Bremer), perhaps translated from the French, appeared in 1774. A complete version by K.G.Schreiter of the posthumous *Dialogues on Natural Religion* came out in 1781. Hamann was a lifelong student of Hume. He read him partly in translation, but mainly in English—he certainly read the *Treatise* in the original, probably during his early London sojourn. His first mention of Hume occurs in 1756, after he had read the German translation of the *Essays*. In a letter to Jacobi of 1787 he wrote 'I studied Hume even before I wrote my *Socratic Memoirs* [i.e., in 1759] and this is the source to which I owe my doctrine of faith [*Glaube*]. . . . I was full of Hume when I was writing the *Socratic Memoirs*. . . .[8] Our own existence, and that of all things outside us must be *believed*, and cannot be demonstrated in any other fashion.'[9] It may be an exaggeration to claim that Hamann actually derived his notion of *Glaube* as fundamental to all knowledge and understanding solely from Hume. But equally there is no doubt that Hume's doctrine of belief, particularly such assertions as, for example, the statement in the *Treatise* that 'Belief is more properly an act of the sensitive than of the cogitative part of our natures',[10] made a profound impression upon Hamann, played a part in his return to fervent Christian faith, and certainly reinforced his anti-intellectualism by providing him with an anti-Cartesian weapon of great power. The doctrine that reason is unable to progress by means of purely logical steps from one statement of fact about the world to another—and that consequently the entire ontological structure of the Cartesian, or indeed, any other rationalist metaphysics was built on a central fallacy—that, to Hamann and his followers, was a boon of inestimable value; they used it as a battering-ram against the hated Wolffian philosophy that dominated German universities and that seemed to them to de-spiritualise the world, to reduce its irregular, living texture to an artificial pattern of bloodless categories, or, alternatively, in its empirical version, to the deathly materialism of Holbach or Helvétius, in which there was, for Hamann, no colour, novelty, genius, thunder, lightning, agony, transfiguration. In the course of this he transformed Hume's psychological and logical concepts into religious ones; for Hamann, belief, faith, revelation, were ultimately one.

Nevertheless, Hume's scepticism, above all his denial of the existence of necessary connections in nature, and his severance of logical relations from those of the real world, which had shocked Kant out of his dogmatic slumber, delighted Hamann, since for him this cleared the path to the existence and power of the basic human faculty of belief, without which there was neither thought nor action, neither an external world nor history, neither God nor other persons, nothing but an unrefuted solipsism. Hamann had no illusions about Hume's general position; no man who demanded that philosophy, when dealing with the human mind, adopt the methods of the natural sciences, could be anything but an enemy; but Hume was an enemy who, however unintentionally, had uncovered the truth on a crucial issue. 'Hume', Hamann wrote to Herder in 1781 (evidently meaning to contrast him with Kant), 'is always my man, because he at least paid homage to the principle of faith, and incorporated it in his system.'[11] No doubt Hamann unwarrantably identified Hume's doctrine of belief with the full doctrine of Pauline faith in things unseen. Still, belief and acceptance of reality without *a priori* demonstration was the basis of Hume's epistemology. To have so powerful an ally in the camp of the enemy, indeed, in the shape of an unbeliever through whose mouth God had chosen to reveal a central truth, was itself a marvellous gift. Towards the end of the Preface to the second edition of the *Critique of Pure Reason*, in a famous sentence, Kant says 'It remains a scandal for philosophy and human reason in general that the existence of things outside us . . . must be taken only on faith, and that if it occurred to someone to doubt it, we could produce no counter-argument sufficient to prove it'. What is a scandal for Kant, is at the very heart of Hamann's doctrine; in support of it he quotes Hume's words in the *Enquiry*: 'It seems evident that men are carried by a natural instinct or prepossession to repose faith in their senses';[12] and he tells Kant: 'to eat an egg, to drink a glass of water, the Attic philosopher Hume needs faith. If he needs faith to eat and drink, why does he belie his own principle when judging of things higher than eating or drinking?'.[13] In other words, if the reality of the external world is guaranteed by belief as a form of direct acquaintance, why should this also not hold of our belief in God, the belief or faith of those who daily and hourly see God in His creation, or hear His voice in His sacred books, in the words of His saints and prophets, to be found among the humblest and most unregarded of mankind? Whatever his errors, Hume is surely right about belief; without it, Hamann tells Kant in 1759, there can be no action: 'if you want a proof for everything, you cannot act at all—Hume realises this'.[14]

Even though Hume's concept of belief is none too clear, as he himself admits in the *Treatise*, it is nevertheless far removed from Hamann's quasi-intuitive, infallible, Pauline-Lutheran *Glaube*. Hume at times speaks of belief as a peculiar and not further describable 'feeling' or 'superior *force* or *vivacity* or *solidity* or *firmness* or *steadiness*' and the like; but the reasonableness or justification of beliefs about reality rests not so much on the evidence of introspection of this kind, as on repeated conjunctions of impressions, and the association of the resultant ideas, that is, on regularities in experience and the construction therefrom of a systematic network of reliable expectations without which neither human thought nor action is possible. Although inductive methods, which rest on the undemonstrable belief that the future will imitate the past, cannot yield certainty, their job is to generate various degrees of probability. It is by these that, for Hume, at least in some moods, rational beliefs (which, in his somewhat loose fashion, he tended to identify with custom, habit, experience, nature and the like) are to be distinguished from mere fantasy or guesswork or prejudice or superstition. Since the existence of one thing can never logically entail the existence of any other, these methods are all that is available to us for building a body of knowledge. It is by applying this criterion to the assertions of theologians, whether orthodox Christians or deists, that Hume justifies his most sceptical and destructive conclusions.

Nothing could be further from Hamann's fervent defence of *Glaube* as the only path to the external world, to other persons, to God. At times he almost acknowledged this. 'I do not know', he wrote in 1787 to Jacobi, 'what Hume or either of us understands by *Glaube*—the more we speak and write about it, the less we shall manage to seize hold of this lump of quicksilver; *Glaube* cannot be communicated like a parcel of goods, it is the kingdom of heaven and hell within us.'[15] This is very remote from Hume's world, something of which, in some sense, Hamann is not unaware, for he systematically ignores everything in Hume which is antipathetic to him, that is, almost all that is most characteristic of the Scottish philosopher. Thus he says nothing about Hume's insistence on 'the received maxims of science, morals, prudence and behaviour',[16] which Hamann himself looks on as so many philistine obstacles to the authentic vision of truth. Hamann has nothing to say on the crucial distinction made in the *Treatise* between superstition and prejudice on the one hand, and on the other belief supported by direct experience and the evidence of constant conjunction. He ignores Hume's psychology of belief as the effect of nature, custom, tradition, and the like; he detests the associationist physchology with its mechanical approach and hair-splitting (as he calls it). As might be expected, he will have nothing to do with Hume's notion of the self as a bundle of sensations, the plaything of desires and passions; Hamann's self is an immortal soul known by direct *Glaube*, with an inner life concerned with matters not dreamt of in Hume's philosophy. Hume for Hamann is an unbeliever whose theological views are therefore of no concern to him; consequently he ignores the inconsistency between Hume's apparently deistic argument in the *Natural History of Religion*, and its virtual dissolution in the *Dialogues* (pointed out by Kemp-Smith and others) and replacement by Philo's total agnosticism; nor does he pay attention to Hume's violent diatribes against precisely the type of Christianity that he and his friends most fervently espoused.

Hume's positivism and his anti-clericalism are equally remote from Hamann's own spiritual concerns. He mentions neither the celebrated passage in Section XII of the *Enquiry* about committing everything that is neither quantitative nor empirical to the flames, nor the equally famous designation of historical religions as 'sick men's dreams' and 'playsome whimsies of monkies in human shape',[17] about which Hume declared that 'in a future age, it will probably become difficult to persuade some nations, that any human, two-legged creature could ever embrace such principles. And it is a thousand to one, but these nations themselves shall have something full as absurd in their own creed, to which they will give a most implicit and most religious assent'.[18] In theory Hume is speaking only of absurdly irrational systems and religions, but irrationality was not a defect in Hamann's eyes: indeed, he accepted and glorified it. His interest in Hume is intense and life-long, but narrow, confined to Hume's argument against the conception of reason held by the rationalist thinkers, the followers of Descartes and Leibniz and Spinoza. Hume is acclaimed for showing that reason is not an organ of discovery, and for reducing it to its proper role as a mere capacity for recombination, elucidation, consistency, taxonomy, lacking all power of creation or revelation. Hume, Hamann wrote in 1759, is 'a spirit for tearing down, not building up, that is indeed his glory'.[19] Hume is a destroyer of metaphysical illusions; it was precisely because Kant, in his effort to build a system of his own, which to some degree restored the very *a priori* links discredited by Hume, that Hamann clearly preferred Hume to his old Königsberg friend, whom he sometimes calls—whether or not this is intended as a compliment—a Prussian Hume.[20] Hume is, of course, one of the pillars of the Enlightenment, a fighter on the wrong side of the barricades; nevertheless, Hamann sees him as being, despite himself, a kind of ally. 'Just as nature,' Hamann writes to Lindner in 1759, 'furnishes an area of poisonous weeds with antidotes in close proximity, and the Nile knows how to couple the crocodile with his treacherous enemy, so Hume falls on the sword of his own truths';[21] like Socrates, Hume shows how wide is the realm of human ignorance—a very useful weapon, Hamann remarks, against 'our clever heads and scribes'. Hume's immortal service is his destruction of *a-priorism*, the notion of logically or metaphysically guaranteed truths about the world: this, for Hamann, removes the rationalist barriers to direct communication with nature and with God, liberates the creative imagination in which such communication can be embodied, and brings down the house of cards of the builders of metaphysical fictions. Hume's relativism, his phenomenalism, his doctrine of the role of belief in the growth of scientific knowledge—all this is nothing to Hamann. It is the cauterising scepticism which Hume is held to share with Socrates, that confession of ignorance of first causes, or of the ultimate purpose of things, which prepared the soil for the daimon of Socrates, for the revelation of the divine, the Pauline vision, that excited Hamann. His hatred of laws, rules, system, is almost obsessive: it is this love of an open texture, whether of the individual imagination or of social relationships that are spontaneous, founded on natural human feeling, that is echoed in the two centuries that followed by Herder and his disciples—populists, romantics, influenced by Rousseau, nostalgic seekers after a vanished organic society, denouncers of all forms of alienation.

In all this, it is direct contact of the individual with things and persons and God, the movement of both history and nature, which he calls 'faith', that dominates Hamann's thought. He says that faith—*Glaube*—in its most intense form is something which must lead and illuminate us in a fashion far more immediate, more inward, darker and more certain than 'rules' of any kind. This notion of belief is, of course, something very different from that strain in Hume in which he speaks of belief as a more or less mechanical, inescapable acceptance of external reality, which men share with animals; or indeed, from the epistemology of Reid and the Scottish school. Yet they had the root of the matter in them: 'truth to tell' (Hamann wrote later in his life), 'I look with pity on the philosopher who demands from me evidence that he possesses a body and that there exists a material world. To waste one's time and wit on these kinds of truths and evidences is at once sad and ridiculous.'[22] It is because Hume shows the absurdity of demanding demonstrative proof of the existence of any thing or person, human or divine, and, unlike Kant, does not draw ontological lines between types of reality with no basis in experience, that Hamann claims him as an ally. This accounts for the fact that in his references to Hume, he shows no trace of the kind of attitude displayed towards him by his British detractors, nothing resembling Beattie's outburst against the 'vile effusion of a hard and stupid heart', or Warburton's and Hurd's denunciations—evidently he is not, to Hamann, one of the three demons driven by the angel into the bottomless pit of Reynolds' celebrated allegorical painting.

Hamann's particular use of Hume is perhaps best illustrated in his treatment of the words which form the concluding paragraph of the tenth section of the *Enquiry*, entitled 'Of Miracles'. In this, according to Kemp-Smith 'probably the most notorious passage in all Hume's writings', Hume asserts that 'Upon the whole, we may conclude that the *Christian religion* not only was at first attended with miracles, but even at this date cannot be believed by any reasonable person without one. Mere reason is insufficient to convince us of its veracity: And whoever is moved by *Faith* to assent to it, is conscious of a continued miracle in his own person, which subverts all the principles of his understanding, and gives him a determination to believe what is most contrary to custom and experience.'[23] No unprejudiced reader could fail to notice, as, indeed, Kemp-Smith points out, that both the content and tone of this passage are ironical and clearly designed to discredit faith in miracles. Hume's general argument is that the probability of human mendacity or delusion or fantasy or credulity is, on the evidence available, far greater than the probability of the events in question, the prodigies and miracles reported in the Old Testament, which are incompatible with the laws of nature as established by experience; and since the testimony of those who have claimed to have observed miracles cannot be regarded as being more reliable than the mass of the testimony of observation on which acceptance of the laws of nature is founded, the weight of the former cannot stand up against the weight of the testimony for the latter.

Hamann, and after him Jacobi, did not, as they well might have done, question the *validity* of this argument; they simply turned it round. They seized eagerly upon this very text as an argument for the miraculous nature of faith, a doctrine of which Hamann's most ardent admirer, Kierkegaard, became the most celebrated proponent. For Hamann, miracles are not a breach of the natural order, for he does not believe in causality, either as a relation of real objects or as a category of the mind—a truth for which, again (less plausibly in the latter case), he claims the authority of Hume. For Hamann everything is a work of God, working not through secondary causes, but by the direct action of His will. What is there in nature, he asked, in the commonest and most natural events, which is not a miracle for us, a miracle in the strictest sense? Everything that happens need not have happened unless God had willed it so: we accept it as real because we have been given *Glaube*—in itself a miracle—which indelibly impresses it upon our minds, our senses, imaginations, memories and intellect. Hume's 'continued miracle in his own person' is precisely what the thinkers of the Counter-Enlightenment, most passionately believed, or wished to believe. Writing to his friend Lindner in 1759 about this passage, Hamann says 'Hume may have said this scornfully or earnestly, nevertheless it is orthodoxy, and a testimony to the truth from the mouth of an enemy and persecutor of it—all his doubts are but a proof of his proposition.'[24] And three weeks later, in a letter to Kant, he cites the same sentence from Hume's essay—'a passage which should prove that even in jest, without knowing or wishing to do so, one can tell the truth'.[25] Hume is 'a Saul among the prophets',[26] a witness to a truth which he does not himself understand; for does he not rightly declare that faith—true Christian faith—is neither custom nor commonsense, but a miracle of the spirit? Yet Hume did not see that this applied to himself too, did not realise that it undermined his own scepticism; he may have intended these words against Christianity, but—such is God's grace—he thereby added to the believers' armoury.

It is probably in this spirit that Hamann began to translate the *Dialogues Concerning Natural Religion*, which Hume's nephew David published in 1779, three years after the author's death. The first edition of the *Dialogues* appeared on 21 July; a year later, on 7 August 1780, Hamann completed his own work on the text. It is not a complete translation, only a résumé and a rendering of about a quarter of Hume's text. He circulated it in manuscript privately to his friends, and it remained unpublished until 1951, when Nadler included it in his edition of Hamann's works. So far as we can tell, this was the only version of Hume's *Dialogues* known to Kant—there is no evidence that he was acquainted with Schreiter's full version of 1781. 'The *Dialogues* is a work full of poetic beauties', Hamann wrote to the publisher Hartknoch in 1780, 'and like Green[27] I consider it not so very dangerous. I am translating it like a fifty-year-old Swabian clergyman, for the benefit of my open-hearted (*freimüthige*) colleagues and countrymen. . . .'[28] Kant is said to have been delighted and influenced by it, although the *Prolegomena* of 1783 shows that he did not fully accept the refutation of the argument from design, which Hume develops in it. As for Hamann, any attack upon rational theology and deism was grist to his mill and that of the other defenders of revelation against both atheists and proponents of natural religion, between whom he and his allies professed to see little difference. The very notion of natural religion angered Hamann, who compared it to the idea of natural language—a typical fiction of the philosophers, logic-choppers who had not enough sense of reality to know that languages were intimately connected with particular places and times, particular environments, particular forms of historical growth, were organic expressions of particular groups of human beings in unique relationships to one another, something which no general formula could convey. The real enemies were the deists, who invented an abstraction, a First Cause, or The Divine Clockmaker who set the universe in motion; but what had this *ens rationis*, this figment of the philosophers, to do with the God who spoke to men's hearts, the God whose only begotten son died to redeem us from our sins? 'It seems evident', said Hume in the twelfth section of the *Enquiry concerning Human Understanding*, 'that men are carried by a natural instinct or prepossession, to repose faith in their senses; and that, without any reason, or even almost before the use of reason, we always suppose an external universe. . . .' Even animals do this. 'But this . . . opinion of all men is soon destroyed by the slightest philosophy, which teaches us that nothing can ever be present to the mind but an image of perception.' For Hume this is an argument against common sense realism. But to Hamann this and similar passages may well have seemed the very opposite: warnings, the more striking if they were not consciously so intended, against the corrosive touch of philosophy and its delusive constructions, particularly when they touch on matters of ultimate concern, such as the relationship of man to God.

So also with the *Dialogues*. In the concluding passage of the *Dialogues*, in a paragraph added by Hume in one of his final revisions, Philo says 'A person, seasoned with the just sense of the imperfections of natural reason, will fly to revealed truth with the greatest avidity: While the haughty dogmatist, persuaded that he can erect a complete system of theology by the mere help of philosophy, disdains any further aid, and rejects this adventitious instructor. To be a philosophical sceptic is, in a man of letters, the first and most essential step towards being a sound, believing Christian.'[29] Hamann does not, as far as I know, refer to this passage: yet it is difficult not to think that he could have regarded it as anything but yet another piece of Christian evidence provided by an enemy, unintended testimony to a truth sufficient to destroy the scepticism or agnosticism which is Philo's official position in the *Dialogues*. Hume's scepticism seemed to him to sweep away far more effectively than Kant's cautious arguments the rickety constructions of reason which obstruct the inpouring of faith; into the vacuum so created *Glaube* can enter. In one of his last letters to Jacobi, which I have quoted already, Hamann says 'When I wrote the *Socratic Memoirs* I was full of Hume, and the following passage in my little book refers to this: *"Our own existence and the existence of all things outside us* must be *believed* and cannot be determined in any other way."*'[30] This is the heart of the *Dialogues* for Hamann. 'One must start *a posteriori*, not *a priori*—that is the mistake of other philosophers.'[31] Causality, determinism, are barriers to the comprehension of the miraculous nature of reality. 'Do you not realise, philosopher, that there is no physical bond between cause and effect, means and ends, but a mental, ideal one, one of blind faith, as the world's greatest writer of his country's history and of the 'natural church' has maintained?'[32] The 'blind faith' is 'the faith that is not the work of reason and not open to attacks by reason, since faith no more happens according to reasons than taste or sight.' That is why 'Hume was always my man', not Kant—'our fellow-countryman who is constantly blasting away with his causality'[33] (*seine Kausalitätsstürmerei*).

IT IS A STRANGE paradox that has thus made Hume one of the patron saints of German fideism and irrationalism. Yet so it was. Hamann's disciple, Friedrich Heinrich Jacobi, continues this line of thought; and since, according to one of the posthumous essays of the late Arthur Lovejoy, Jacobi was one of the most widely read thinkers of his time both in Germany and outside it, it is not a matter for surprise that his views entered the current of German and French philosophical intuitivism, which fed various streams of modern vitalism, irrationalism and existentialism. Jacobi (1743–1818) was not a thinker of the first or even second order. He is more interesting as a philosophical novelist, man of letters, middleman of ideas and indefatigable letter-writer. His correspondence with Kant, Herder, Hamann, Goethe, Mendelssohn, his famous controversy with Mendelssohn about Lessing's real beliefs (the so-called *Pantheismsstreit*), his attacks on Kant, Fichte, Herder and Schelling (and the ferocious counter-attack by the last named), and his rediscovery of such forgotten thinkers as Spinoza and Bruno, stimulated thinkers more gifted than himself and threw a great deal of light on the German philosophical scene at the turn of the eighteenth century. In 1786 he published a book, which he entitled *David Hume über den Glauben, oder Realismus und Idealismus Ein Gespräch*.[34] In this work, particularly in the Introduction to the philosophical dialogue which forms its main content, there is a paean to Hume as the apostle of non-rational faith. The mere fact that Hume's name occurs in the title of this treatise is evidence of the place occupied by him in the pantheon of early German romanticism. Jacobi was a realist in epistemology, but he was also a fervent anti-rationalist theist, brought up, like Kant, Herder and Hamann, in the pietist tradition, and he faithfully followed Hamann's practice of self-observation as well as his use of texts from Hune in the campaign against the shallow materialists and deists in France and their followers in Germany, particularly among liberal Lutheran pastors. His book carries an epigraph from Pascal: 'Reason refutes the dogmatist; nature refutes the sceptic'. It was the latter position that Jacobi developed at some length. The late Professor Philip Merlan, who in a short and interesting article examined the relations of Hamann, Hume and Jacobi,[35] took the trouble to point out that nature, unlike reason, could not refute, it could only cause us to avoid the truth and accept illusions, for truth remained truth, and illusions remained false, however comforting or indispensable they might turn out to be.

This, however, is, I believe, a misunderstanding of Jacobi's meaning. His thesis is that there is but one kind of genuine knowledge, and that is our natural *Glaube*: 'We are born in faith as we are born in society';

there are forms of intuitive certainty that reason is incapable of either confirming or refuting, such as my awareness of my own identity, of my causal efficacy revealed in deliberate effort and action,[36] and of the freedom of my will. And I am similarly certain of the existence of God, of the rational world and of other sentient beings. These beliefs, according to Jacobi, are not merely presupposed in all that we do or feel or think, but are with us from birth, are all that bind us to reality, and are wholly independent of hypotheses or postulates or theoretical constructions of any kind, such as, for example, the hypothesis of the uniformity of nature, which is a necessary postulate of the propositions of the natural sciences—for hypotheses are subject to verification or falsification, from which true *Glaube*, faith or belief, loss of which is inconceivable, is wholly free. Our certainty of our own existence and of our own unique personality is a 'feeling'—*ein Gefühl*—a sense of reality; and it guarantees the reality of whatever it reveals. Our infallible conviction of our own self is the touchstone of all other knowledge: we measure the reliability of other beliefs by it, not the other way about, for all inference and evidence cannot be as strong as what we know by acquaintance with our own personality. The task of philosophy is to 'reveal existence', *Das Dasein zu enthüllen*; and it is such feelings—*Gefühle* or *Gesinnungen*—that do this; there is no way of establishing the truth 'beyond and above' this. To support this he quotes Hume's *Treatise*,[37] where belief is described as 'something *felt* by the mind which, distinguishes the ideas of the judgement from the fictions of the imagination. It gives them more force and influence; makes them appear of greater importance; infixes them in the mind; and renders them the governing principle of all our actions.' He quotes, too, from Section XII of the *Enquiry* the relevant passages on men's 'natural instinct' and on their 'prepossession to repose faith in their senses'. 'This very table, which we see white, and which we feel hard, is *believed* to exist, independent of our perception, and to be something external to our mind, which perceives it. . . .' Jacobi goes on to say that 'we believe in our senses, and therefore in the existence of a sensible world. And similarly we believe in our inner sense, and therefore in the existence of a world beyond the senses.'[38] This seems to him to follow from Hume's premises; and such belief (he says nothing about Hume's difficulties with solipsism) seems to him, as it does to Hamann, to pass insensibly into *Offenbarung*, that is, revealed truth given directly without benefit of reason. This is then contrasted with the generalisations and abstractions of Plato or Spinoza, builders of logically coherent systems of idealised figments that are death to the sense of reality.

Jacobi's method of drawing sustenance from the enemy's resources is well illustrated by his treatment of Hume's celebrated refutation of the argument from design. Jacobi characteristically turns it on its head in the manner of Hamann, to reinforce his own conception of faith, *Glaube*. Hume in the *Enquiry*[39] argues that since it is an argument from analogy, it cannot be applied to something that, *ex hypothesi*, is unique, namely the deity. Analogies can be sought only between entities which belong to a species containing other actual or possible members. Let me quote Professor Wollheim's succinct formulation of this argument in his edition of Hume on religion:[40] 'The only cases where we can validly argue from a particular event to its cause, is where the event is one of a series of events which have been observed to be constantly conjoined with events similar in kind to the cause. In other words, we cannot attribute a cause to an event, if that event is unique in human experience. But it is obvious that "the frame of nature" is, in this sense, unique . . . therefore the religious hypothesis . . . turns out to be an unwarranted inference.' And this, indeed, is the burden of Hume's three-pronged criticism of what in *The Dialogues* he calls 'the religious hypothesis'.

Jacobi positively welcomes this mode of reasoning. He agrees that ordinary knowledge is founded on what he calls 'comparisons', and since God is unique, no comparison with Him is possible. It is not an instance of a general concept. But neither, Jacobi avers, is my own mind: it, too, is unique, wholly individual, and cannot be reached from any external starting point. This is precisely why I know God, as I know myself, by an immediate *sense* of their existence; not by analogy or any other kind of inference, nor, in the case of my self-identity, by memory or in any other indirect fashion. I am not to myself an idea capable of being described, still less analysed; my certainty of my own existence cannot be separated from my certainty of what I am, of the mind, indeed the unique substance, that I directly know myself to be. This knowledge is the basis of all other awareness: it is direct and transcendent; no wonder that Hume and Kant, who look for the self in ordinary sense experience or the shadow world of logical categories, cannot find it. This inversion of Hume's empiricism and scepticism in order to prop up faith is typical of the entire strategy of this group of dogmatic religious transcendentalists: they call in Hume as a kind of outside specialist, expert at demolishing what they most deeply abhor— the theories of knowledge and reality of the rationalist metaphysicians. For Jacobi, reality is revealed by what he sometimes calls *Wesenheitsgefühl*—the immediate feeling of essential being—which he regards as a gift of God. He speaks of *Glaube*—the direct apprehension of God, oneself, the external world—as a kind of *salto mortale*, a leap of faith, without which we remain imprisoned in the imaginary worlds of logical, mathematical or metaphysical constructions—Hamann's castles in the air—remote from reality, in which many worthy and respected thinkers live all their lives. From this, Hume's scepticism can save us. That, indeed, Jacobi tells us, is his claim to immortal fame.

To Sum Up this peculiar relationship: it is doubtful whether the German opponents of the Enlightenment needed Hume to establish their position, but it is a historical fact that their founding fathers, Hamann and Jacobi, were fascinated by his arguments against their principal enemies, the deists, whom they abhorred more than out-and-out atheists, perhaps because the latter at least did not seem to them to vulgarise and dilute that which the existence and presence and direct knowledge of God meant to the true believer. They simply took from Hume's writings what they needed. Mrs Shirley Letwin, in a recent essay on Hume,[41] has justly observed that 'every great philosopher has been rendered into diverse characters'. Lessing, Herder, Goethe had done this for Spinoza, who after being the secret inspirer of French materialism was turned into something approaching a pantheistic transcendentalist, the father of German Absolute Idealism. In Hume's case the metamorphosis is no less complete. Represented by some as 'the most devastating sceptic who not only destroyed the pretences of traditional philosophy, but also showed that knowledge of any sort is an illusion', he is turned by others into 'a dogmatic empiricist who believed that man could achieve incontrovertible truth'.[42] Support can be found in Hume's writings for both these interpretations, and for others also. Burke's distrust of philosophical abstractions, his faith in nature, good sense, history, civilisation, and his hostility to absolute rules and *a priori* generalisations, and, still more, to radical reform in the name of eternal principles or unstable, capricious popular passions —all this has its roots in Hume as well as Montesquieu and Hooker. Mill, and following him, Russell, owe him much of their faith in scientific method and their rejection of dogmatism, *a priorism* and the false analogies drawn by theologians, as well as their suspicion of the tendency to mistake convention and habit for eternal principles, their acceptance of probability as the nearest approximation to unattainable empirical certainty, their crusading hatred of irrationalism, their approval of the calmer passions and their inclination towards naturalism and a modified utilitarianism. But for Hamaan and his disciples Hume was simply a more destructive critic than Kant of the older rationalism. He seemed to them to have finally undermined the notion of unalterable categories of experience, as well as any form of dualism, the doctrine of two worlds, whether of a Cartesian, Leibnitzian or Kantian kind; there was only one world, that of direct confrontation with reality; and although Hume's notion of this world was radically different from their own, the recognition of its unity, and of the Platonic fallacy which underlay all attempts to determine frontiers that divided reality from everyday experience, was of supreme importance to them. For these mystical nominalists there were no walls between the natural and the spiritual worlds. God spoke to them in symbols which they understood, those of nature, history, sacred books, for their eyes and ears were open to His words. Armed with faith, they needed no proof nor evidence of the reality of what they saw before them. They perceived tongues in trees, books in the running brooks, sermons in stones and (by a slight emendation) God in everything. These were not metaphors to them: the God they worshipped was personal; they looked on pantheism as a species of atheism. Hamann and his allies wanted no barriers to the all-penetrating power of faith, a faith which brooked no rules, obeyed no laws, was inconceivably remote from the tidy world of human contrivances—institutional order, utilitarian calculation, the artificial constructions of the logic- and evidence-bounded natural sciences, the clear and sensible organisation sought after, in their various fashions, by the King of Prussia and his officials, by Bentham, by the radical thinkers of Paris, perhaps by Hume too. The ideals of the Enlightenment seemed to at least one of its German opponents, Lenz, no better than a form of postponed death; Holbach's system struck the young Goethe as Cimmerian, grey, corpse-like, the end of all vitality, freedom and imagination. Hume's scepticism was the most devastating weapon against these enemies of the spirit that some among these forerunners of romanticism thought that they had found; Hume had removed the *a priori* bonds needed to guarantee the indestructible validity of the rationalist edifice (and indeed, after him, despite the efforts of later philosophers, the old confidence never fully returned). But to the thinkers of whom I am speaking the eliminating of the *a priori* cement seemed to render one supreme service: to clear the ground for the victory of religious faith.

Nothing could have been further from Hume and his outlook. The history of his influence on a handful of German antinomian thinkers is no more than a footnote in any account of his philosophy, although an exceedingly odd one. It is of somewhat greater importance to the history of irrationalist ideas in Europe, both religious and secular, during the nineteenth and twentieth centuries, of which this revolt against reason marks the modern beginnings. It is strange to reflect that the calm, reasonable, placid, moderate, ironical Hume, with his firm sense of reality, and his lucid and disciplined prose, should have attained semi-canonical status as one of the founding fathers—if not a strictly legitimate one (but then Hamann had an ambivalent attitude to all conventions, and especially to legitimate paternity)—of this turbulent, extravagant, heaven-storming movement, the very existence of whose leaders remained, so far as one can tell, wholly unknown to him. Which was, perhaps, just as well, for he would hardly have approved of them or their views; indeed, he could scarcely have felt anything but his habitual revulsion before such storms of uncontrolled spiritual enthusiasm. If, in addition, he had known of their insistent and admiring acknowledgement to him of a major intellectual debt, he might have looked upon this as one of the unintended, and unwelcome, yet, perhaps, not altogether unpredictable consequences of their own ideas, which even the most reasonable, careful, self-protective and accommodating thinkers cannot always wholly escape.

1. *Hamann's Schriften*, ed. F. Roth and G. A. Wiener (Berlin and Leipzig 1821–43) vol. V, p. 370, hereafter referred to as *Schriften*.
2. *Schriften*, vol. IV, p. 326.
3. *Schriften*, vol. III, p. 192. The pun on the name 'Spinoza' and 'spider'—*Spinne*—is very characteristic.
4. *Schriften*, vol. II, p. 187.
5. *Schriften*, vol. III, p. 285.
6. *Schriften*, vol. V, p. 668; vol. I, p. 365; vol. IV, p. 326.
7. See *Johann Georg Hamann. Sämmtliche Werke*, ed. Josef Nadler (Vienna: Herder 1944–57) vol. II, pp. 73–4.
8. *Johann Georg Hamann's, des Magus im Norden, Leben und Schriften*, ed. C. H. Gildemeister (Gotha 1857–73) vol. V, pp. 496 and 506.
9. *Schriften*, vol. II, p. 35.
10. *Treatise*, p. 141.
11. Letter of 10 May 1781, *Schriften*, vol. VI, p. 187.
12. *Enquiries*, p. 151ff.
13. *Schriften*, vol. I, p. 441.
14. *Johann Georg Hamann. Briefwechsel*, ed. W. Ziesemer and A. Henkel (Wiesbaden 1955) vol. I, p. 379.
15. Letter to Jacobi of 27–30 May 1787, *Schriften*, vol. V, p. 517. On this see W. M. Alexander *Johann Georg Hamann: Philosophy and Faith* (The Hague: Martinus Nijhoff 1966), p. 130ff.
16. Which Mrs S. R. Letwin rightly stresses; see her article 'Hume: Inventor of a New Task for Philosophy' *Political Theory* 3, no. 2 (May 1975).
17. *Dialogues*, Introduction, p. 11.
18. ibid.
19. Letter to Linder of 21 March 1859, *Schriften*, vol. I, p. 356.
20. See *Schriften*, vol. VI, pp. 156–8.
21. Letter to Linder of 3 July 1759, *Schriften*, vol. I, p. 356.
22. *Schriften*, vol. VII, p. 419.
23. *Enquiries*, p. 131; see *Dialogues*, p. 47.
24. Letter of 3 July 1759, Ziesemer and Henkel *Briefwechsel*, vol. I, p. 356.
25. *Briefwechsel*, p. 380; see Alexander, op. cit., p. 152 n. 2.
26. *Briefwechsel*, p. 380; see *Schriften*, vols. I, p. 443, and III, p. 391.
27. Kant's friend, the English merchant, who lived in Königsberg.
28. Letter to Hartknoch of 29 July 1780, quoted by J. Nadler in *Johann Georg Hamann, der Zeuge des Corpus Mysticum* (Salzburg: Otto Müller 1949) p. 341.
29. *Dialogues*, pp. 227–8.
30. *Schriften*, vol. I, pp. 405–6.
31. Gildemeister *Leben und Schriften*, vol. V, p. 232.
32. Nadler *Sämmtliche Werke*, vol. III, p. 29.
33. *Schriften*, vol. VI, p. 187.
34. I have used the text published as Volume II of Friedrich Heinrich Jacobi's *Werke* (Leipzig 1815) pp. 1–310.
35. P. Merlan 'Kant, Hamann-Jacobi and Schelling on Hume' *Rivista Critica di Storia della Filosofia* (1967) Fasc. IV, La Nuova Italia Editrice (Florence 1968) p. 484.
36. Something of this kind used to be argued by Whitehead and Stout, and it has had its later exponents.

37. *Treatise*, p. 629.
38. *Werke*, vol. II, p. 152.
39. *Enquiries*, p. 140.
40. R. Wollheim (ed.) *Hume on Religion* (London: Collins, Fontana 1963) Introduction, pp. 32–4.
41. Shirley R. Letwin, op. cit.
42. ibid.

Additional Bibliographical Material

Blum, Jean. *La vie et l'œuvre de J.-G. Hamann, le 'Mage du Nord', 1738–1788*. Paris: Librairie Felix 1912.
Hamann's Socratic Memorabilia. A Translation and Commentary. Baltimore: Johns Hopkins Press 1967.
Hegel, G. W. F. *Hamann's Schriften in Sämtliche Werke*, ed. H. Glockner, vol. 12, pp. 203–75. Stuttgart 1930.
Knoll, Renate. *Johann Georg Hamann und Friedrich Heinrich Jacobi*. Heidelberg: Carl Winter, Universitätsverlag 1963.
Leibrecht, Walter. *God and Man in the Thought of Hamann*, trans. James H. Stam and Martin H. Bertram. Philadelphia: Fortress Press 1966.
Merlan, Philip. 'From Hume to Hamann' *The Personalist* XXXII, no. 1 (January 1951).
—'Hamann et les Dialogues de Hume' *Revue de Métaphysique et de Morale* (1954).
—'Johann Georg Hamann (1730–1788)' *Claremont Quarterly* 3 (1955).
Metzke, E. *J. G. Hamann's Stellung in der Philosophie des 18 Jahrhundert*. 1934.
O'Flaherty, James C. *Unity and Language: A Study in the Philosophy of Johann Georg Hamann*. University of North Carolina Studies in the Germanic Languages and Literatures, no. 6. Chapel Hill 1952 (reprinted in hard back, New York: AMS Press Inc. 1966).
Smith, Ronald Gregor. *J. G. Hamann: A Study in Christian Existentialism*. New York: Harper & Brothers 1960.
Unger, Rudolf. *Hamann und die Aufklärung*, 2 vols. Jena: Max Diederichs 1911 (reprinted Tübingen: Max Neimayer 1963).

The Beginnings of Hume's Philosophy

IT HAS BEEN GENERALLY accepted in recent research on David
Hume that the famous words, 'When I was about 18 Years of Age,
there seem'd to be open'd up to me a new Scene of Thought, which
transported me beyond Measure', appearing in a letter to a physician
(probably Dr Arbuthnot) dated March or April 1734,[1] mark the
beginning of Hume's philosophy. Only the content of the 'new scene of
thought' has remained a matter of scholarly dispute. Norman Kemp
Smith, who was the first author to insist on the importance of this letter,
writes: 'To come now to the question of the primary sources of Hume's
teaching, the thesis for which I shall argue is that it was under the
direct influence of Francis Hutcheson that he was led to recognise that
judgments of moral approval and disapproval, and indeed judgments of
value of whatever type, are based not on rational insight or on evidence,
but solely on feeling; and that what then "open'd up to [him] a new
Scene of Thought, which transported [him] beyond Measure" (giving
birth in due course to the Treatise), was the discovery that this point
of view could be carried over into the theoretical domain, and could
there be employed in the solution of several of the chief problems to
which Locke and Berkeley had drawn attention, but to which they had
not been able to give a satisfactory answer.'[2]

The letter itself does not at all support this interpretation. Ernest
Campbell Mossner follows Kemp Smith and is more precise: he thinks
that Hume discovered in 1729 'the extension of sentiment or feeling
beyond ethics and aesthetics (to which it was limited by Hutcheson) to
include the entire realm of belief covering all relations of matter-of-
fact', especially the relation of cause and effect. 'The intense excitement with which Hume greeted his discovery concerning the nature
of causation in the spring of 1729 is explainable in terms of its implications. . .'.[3] Here, Smith and Mossner are describing what *must* have
happened in 1729, not what can be documented by the sources we have
at our disposal. Without refuting the preceding interpretations, Duncan Forbes gives the following opinion in his recent book *Hume's
Philosophical Politics*: '. . . natural law teaching and Newtonian or
Baconian experimental science came together, and allied to Hume's
religious scepticism, produced his famous "new scene of thought", and
one aspect of this was a modern theory of natural law'.[4] Again, it is a
presupposition of the interpreter that fills up the gap and decides the
content of Hume's inspiration.

In what follows I intend to show that in the phrase 'a new scene of thought' Hume was not referring to the beginning of his philosophy. In fact he considers the turning point to have occurred, not in 1729 when he was 'about 18 years of age', but rather in 1731. Indeed, he severely criticizes the period referred to in the phrase and regards it as belonging to a previous phase of his development. I shall, furthermore, try to define more precisely what were Hume's ideas in the years 1729–31 and 1731–34. Finally, I hope to show the origins of the dialectic of empiricism and scepticism in Hume's philosophy.

WRITING IN 1734 from the vantage point of a twenty-three-year old Hume says: 'When I was about 18 Years of age, there seem'd to be open'd up to me a new Scene of Thought . . .'. The period during which he was in a state of high intellectual excitement lasted only a few months, after which there was a sudden change: he experienced a strange 'coldness', a 'lowness of Spirits'. Then again he found his 'Spirits at their highest Pitch', the 'Ardor', the 'higher Flights of Genius' returned, but he sank again into a depression. These mental states, the succession of flights of genius and apathy, led to a physical illness, which Hume describes in some detail in the same letter.[5] Towards the end of 1730 he slowly began to recover. On his return from Edinburgh to Ninewells in the spring of 1731 he expected a further recovery and, together with this, a greater stability in his intellectual life: 'But in this I was much mistaken'. Why were these expectations not fulfilled? His convalescence progressed, but now there was a virtually qualitative change, which manifested itself in his development from a puny youth into, in his words, a 'most sturdy, robust healthful-like Fellow'. At the same time he becomes sociable, a 'good companion'. He has left the phase of flights of genius and subsequent depression behind him and now Hume, the cool philosopher we know, is born. 'Having now Time and Leizure to cool my inflam'd Imaginations' — the 'now' refers to his return to Ninewells in the spring of 1731 — Hume decides to tread a completely new path in moral philosophy similar to the trail blazed in modern natural philosophy. The object of his investigation must first of all be human nature. Only in this way can one escape the arbitrariness of subjective 'Fancy' and the illusion of making progress in knowledge by trusting to the greatness of one's own genius. With this step Hume makes a decisive break not only with all previous moral philosophy but also with his own efforts in this field. At last in the spring of 1731 he finds himself. It is only now that what he writes counts for him: 'Within these three years I find that I have scribbled many a Quire of Paper', he declares in the spring of 1734.

It is clear, then, that Hume himself places the beginnings of his philosophy in 1731, and interprets these beginnings as the critical turning from his earlier flights of genius to his own philosophy. Let us return once again to the crucial phrase 'a new scene of thought'. It is strange that no one has hitherto remarked on the qualifying word 'seemed' in 'There seem'd to be open'd up to me . . .'. The expression 'a new scene of thought' itself indicates a critical attitude on the part of the author. Superstition, not philosophy, '*opens* a world of its own, and presents us with new *scenes*, and beings, and objects, which are altogether new', writes Hume in the *Treatise* (p. 271, italics added).[6] The expression implies a negative evaluation and therefore should not be taken as an indication of the beginning of Hume's philosophy.

In order to determine the character of Hume's philosophy more precisely it will be necessary not only to analyse the phase beginning in 1731 but also to identify those factors from his earlier period that Hume believed he had overcome. What indeed was this new scene of thought? I think we must conclude that it was based not on some new idea or discovery but rather on a subjective experience comparable to Rousseau's Vincennes experience or to the visions of the mystics.[7] Now, the only sure documents of the early life of Hume are his letters, and I think they can give us the decisive hint. The letter written to Michael Ramsay in July of 1727 shows Hume as living in a world which we may call one of poetical-philosophical criticism: 'sometimes a Philosopher, sometimes a Poet' is his motto in reading.[8] 'Greatness and Elevation of Soul' he gives as the goal towards which he is striving. He finds congenial the spirit of Longinus of whom Hume says that he himself wrote in the grand and lofty style of those poets whom he as a critic portrays. 'I read some of Longinus already and I am mightily delighted with him; I think he . . . is himself an Author that may be cited for an Example to his own Rules by any who shall be so adventurous as to write upon his Subject.'[9] It seems probable that in 1729 Hume let himself get involved in the adventure of trying his hand at literary criticism, writing in the exalted and enthusiastic style of a young genius who was trying to express his experience of the Great and Sublime. He may have written in such a fashion in order to go beyond sober critics like Pope and Addison. I think this is the only explanation of the content of the 'new scene of thought' that is based on the texts of Hume and not in the imagination and thoughts of the interpreter.

According to the new maxim one must examine human nature in order to frame on this basis a theory of criticism and morality that will avoid the caprice of subjectivity. Herewith Hume provides us with the basic plan of his *Treatise*. Books I and II lay the foundations by investigating ideas and impressions. Book III, published separately, provides an application of the results of these investigations to the field of morality. Hume intended to write a fourth book on criticism.[10] Human nature, he writes in 1734, 'I resolved to make my principal Study, and the Source from which I wou'd derive every Truth in Criticism as well as Morality'.[11]

He wants to inaugurate a new era in the field of moral philosophy similar to that which had already taken place in natural philosophy. 'I found that the moral Philosophy transmitted to us by Antiquity, labor'd under the same Inconvenience that has been found in their natural Philosophy, of being entirely Hypothetical, & depending more upon Invention than Experience'. 'Has been found', says Hume—but by whom? I think it is of the greatest importance to know of whom Hume was thinking here as a model for his non-hypothetical philosophy. Recent investigations would have us believe that his model was Newton. But that it was Bacon, rather than Newton, whom he had in mind can be shown by comparing the passages from the letters of 1734 with a reference to Bacon found in the introduction to the *Treatise*. We read in the latter that moral philosophy in antiquity did not begin to develop until over a century after natural philosophy. Thales inaugurated the latter, Socrates the former. In modern times the span of time between the re-establishment of these disciplines is the same. Modern natural philosophy was founded by Bacon and now moral philosophy, with the exception of a few precursors, makes its appearance again.[12]

In Hume's own philosophy, history has arrived at a second Socrates who inaugurates 'a total alteration in philosophy', a complete 'revolution'.[13]

Was it then a 'Newton-faced' generation he belonged to? If we consult the General Catalogue of the British Museum,[14] we discover the surprising fact that there had been many editions of the *Opera omnia* and of single works of Bacon up to the end of the seventeenth century, and then there was a gap, new editions beginning again in 1730. There were four editions of the *Complete Works* (in Latin) from 1665 to 1694, then in 1730 we have the *Opera omnia* in Amsterdam, and in the same year the first edition of the *Complete Works* with English text as well as Latin in London, followed by the *Philosophical Works*, an English edition, in 1733.[15]

So Bacon was an author rediscovered at exactly the time Hume had his crisis and decisive turning point. Perhaps we may say that Bacon saved him from the idols of his own imagination teaching him that all we can know must be based on experience. 'I believe 'tis a certain Fact that most of the Philosophers who have gone before us, have been overthrown by the Greatness of their Genius . . .', Hume writes in the letter of 1734; he could find in Bacon 'Quin et ab ingeniorum acumine et agilitate, dum suo motu feruntur, periculum metuimus. Itaque

hominum ingeniis non plumas aut alas, sed plumbum et pondera addi-
mus'.[16] The 'high flights of genius' are a source of errors, a philosopher must found his science on experience that can be controlled, not
on his own imagination. 'Etenim verum exemplar mundi in intellectu
humano fundamus; quale invenitur, non quale cuipiam sua propria
ratio dictaverit. Hoc autem perfici non potest, nisi facta mundi dissec-
tione atque anatomia diligentissima. Modulos vero ineptos mundorum
et tamquam simiolas, quas in philosophii phantasiae hominum extru-
xerunt, omnino dissipandas edicimus.'[17]

But what about Newton? I think I have been able to show clearly
that Hume saw himself as the Bacon of moral philosophy; this does not
exclude a Newtonian influence in particular parts of Hume's philosophy. The proof that Hume took Bacon as his model in the 'Attempt
to introduce the experimental Method of Reasoning into Moral
Subjects' is independent of the claim that Newton had an influence on
certain ideas of Hume.

In his essay, 'A Bacon-Facing Generation: Scottish Philosophy in the
Early Nineteenth Century', J. Charles Robertson writes: 'Reflecting
a widespread development in the eighteenth century, the Scottish
experimentalists insisted that a proper understanding of Nature must
include a thorough investigation into *human* nature or, as it was sometimes put, a knowledge of the very "principles of understanding". In
this, Bacon was still their guide and mentor. He inspired confidence in
the experimental method as a means of reforming the "plan of philosophical inquiry" throughout all branches of science and not merely in
natural philosophy'.[18] Before Reid and Diderot, d'Alembert and Kant,
Hume rediscovered Bacon as the leading figure of modern science. Of
course, experimental reasoning was not the same in moral and natural
subjects.

'Moral philosophy', Hume writes in the Introduction to the *Treatise*,
'has, indeed, this particular disadvantage, which is not found in natural,
that in collecting its experiments, it cannot make them purposely, with
premeditation[19]. . . . We must therefore glean up our experiments in
this science from a cautious observation of human life. . . . Where experiments of this kind are judiciously collected and compared, we may
hope to establish on them a science, which will not be inferior in certainty, and will be much superior in utility to any other of human
comprehension' (pp. xxii–xxiii).

We shall now see how Hume conceived his observational and comparative study of human nature in the early thirties.

A PERFECT EXAMPLE of the experimental philosophy Hume has in
mind in the letter to a physician is the letter itself, with its penetrating

analysis of his own psycho-somatic development. A further example is
another letter of 1734, written from France to Michael Ramsay. There
Hume propounds the paradoxical thesis, contrary to the generally
accepted opinion of the time, that 'the French have more real Politeness and the English the better Method of expressing it'.[20] The reasoning behind this inversion is an ingenious analysis of social role-playing,
of the relation between feeling and its customary expression, and the
spectator's reaction to this. One has to analyse the letter as a piece of
'criticism' in the tradition of Longinus (without the striving for greatness and elevation), Addison and Pope;[21] and then one may observe
that Hume tries to base his observations on general rules of human
nature. 'The Mind pleases itself by the Progress it makes in such Trifles,
& while it is so supported makes an *easy Transition* to something more
material.'[22] Here we have an example of the use of the principle of the
association of ideas in connection with belief. The 'easy transition' from
one idea to another, or from impressions to ideas, as anyone acquainted
with Hume's writings knows, is the very heart of his whole psychology.
'For in the same manner, as Soldiers are found to become more coura-
gious in learning to hold their Musquets within half an Inch of a place
appointed; & your Devotees feel their Devotion encrease by the Observance of trivial Superstitions, as Sprinkling, Kneeling, Crossing, etc.,
so men insensibly soften towards each other in the Practice of these
Ceremonies.'[23]

Hume would have read Mandeville, one of the authors he names in
the *Treatise* as his predecessors (Introduction, p. xxi, n. 1). Compare
the remarks on the process of socialisation in the letter to Ramsey and,
for example, the Fourth Dialogue Mandeville added to his *Fable of the
Bees*. Twice Hume speaks of the expression 'your humble servant',
which Mandeville takes as a point of comparison in his Dialogue.[24]
Mandeville also wrote a book on *The Origin of Honour*, published in
1732,[25] and Hume analyses the phenomenon of honour in modern
France.

I would like to suggest redating two shorter pieces of Hume's to the
period of about 1734. The first of these is generally dated much earlier
than this, the second many years later. The former is 'An Historical
Essay on Chivalry and Modern Honour', which E. C. Mossner classifies
as a college composition.[26] The reasons Mossner gives allow us to consider the date as still open to question. I am of the opinion that both 'the
maturity of thought, keenness of analysis and essential sureness of
style', to use Mossner's very own words, and the cool observation found
in this essay force us to re-date the essay to the period after 1731. Like
the letter written from France to Michael Ramsay in 1734, the Essay
on Chivalry is a synkrisis, or to put it in modern terms, a comparative

study of human behaviour, including some indications of the underlying principles of human nature, as for example the easy transition of
ideas and impressions. Furthermore, we find in the essay echoes of the
letter to the doctor written in the same year. 'Thus we find when,
without Discretion, it indulges its devout Fervours, that, working in
such fairy-ground, it quietly burys itself in its own Whimsies and
Chimera's, & raises up to itself a new set of Passions, Affections,
Desires, Objects & in short a perfectly new World of its own. . . .' This
is the very same way in which Hume criticized his own condition in the
period of 1729 to 1731.

During the 'twilight of reason' the mind, left uncorrected by either
understanding or experience, forms strange new ideas and 'schemes' of
behaviour among which are a grotesque heroism and a 'chimerical and
affected politeness'. Hume attempts to give a psychologically naturalistic explanation of these forms of behaviour. The key to understanding
them and the mediaeval spirit out of which they grew lies in recognizing that barbaric thought-patterns assimilated those of the late
classical period. This train of thought is in complete accord with that
found in the two letters of 1734.

My second suggestion concerns a section from the *Essays* (later
Enquiry) *Concerning Human Understanding* published in 1748, in
that part of Section 3 in which Hume applies the previously stated laws
of association to the field of literary criticism (paragraph 4 ff., omitted
by Selby-Bigge, but printed in the edition of Hendel). Instead of examining the principle of association in greater detail Hume wants to 'consider
some of the effects of this connexion upon the passions and imagination',
as he puts it in the transitional paragraph (cf. the last paragraph). The
whole dissertation on the unity of literary works, which is based on the
law of association, does not contain any explicit cross-references to other
parts of the work. It stands quite on its own. In the previous part of the
section Hume speaks only of the association of *ideas*. He does not
demonstrate that the passions, or rather impressions of reflection, par-
ticipate in the same mechanism. But in the analysis of poetry passions
as well as ideas are links connected with one another. Also, Hume even
considered that the *Enquiry* could appear without this part. I am
therefore led to believe that it, like Section 10, 'Of Miracles', is a product of the thirties and that it was planned, perhaps, as a part of a book
'Of Criticism' for inclusion in the *Treatise*.

The origin of Hume's philosophy lies in the field of morality and
criticism, understood as the observation of 'mores', actual human
behaviour, which Hume tries to derive from general principles of the
human mind, as, for example, the tendency of ideas to connect with one
another in 'easy transitions'.

Now, in all this, we have been concerned with the empiricist side of Hume's philosophy. What about Hume the sceptic?

The practice of ethology, the policy of cool objective observation and expression with which Hume attempts to re-establish moral philosophy by investigating human nature led him, as we saw, from the field of criticism to the analysis of the processes involved in cognition. It is precisely this policy which also led to a result that must have surprised even him. This is the final point we shall discuss here.

According to his original plan of 1731 Hume wanted to analyse the processes of the human mind as they actually occur, and not to allow himself to be carried away, as previous moral philosophy had been, into constructing moral philosophy out of his own fanciful inventions. In his observational analysis of the human mind in its cognitive behaviour he encountered an unexpected phenomenon: the analysing spectator increasingly fell into insoluble difficulties. Basic contents of consciousness such as the law of causality, the perception of space, the identity of objects and even of one's self proved to be questionable (one might even say, given the method chosen, necessarily questionable). To the eye of the pure spectator all phenomena present themselves as single facts in time and space, without any connection. The links we suppose to be there in reality prove to be the contradictory products of the imagination—the very faculty Hume no longer wished to trust.[27] Was he thereby thrown back into the crisis of 1730–31? In point of fact Hume does refer back to that experience in order to describe the scepticism to which the empirical analysis of the human mind in its cognitive behaviour had led him. He speaks of 'philosophical melancholy and delirium' and of the chimeras into which he had fallen. The cool observation of the mind reflecting on itself leads to a situation similar to that produced by sublime and fanciful speculation: one isolates oneself from other men, loses one's way in life and ultimately loses oneself in visions of vanishing Cheshire cats and Boojums. For Hume, the solution of this seemingly insoluble difficulty and perhaps of a renewed existential crisis, lies in a new Element as he himself describes it in the *Treatise*: 'Most fortunately it happens, that since reason is incapable of dispelling these clouds, nature herself suffices to that purpose, and cures me of this philosophical melancholy and delirium, either by relaxing this bent of mind, or by some avocation, and lively impression of my senses, which obliterate all these chimeras. I dine, I play a game of back-gammon, I converse, and am merry with my friends; and when after three or four hours' amusement, I wou'd return to these speculations, they appear so cold, and strain'd, and ridiculous, that I cannot find in my heart to enter into them any farther' (p. 269). It is confidence in the activity of life as an independent reality. Life itself and the actions necessary to its sustenance remain untouched by these insoluble problems into which observing reason falls. Hume learnt that human action not only has a curative function for body and soul, but is also a domain which cannot be disturbed by sceptical doubts. He characterizes his confidence in action and 'the occupations of common life' as 'belief', and by so doing he puts himself in the mainstream of the sceptical tradition that flows from Sextus Empiricus to Montaigne and Bayle: human understanding gets into a quagmire in its search for knowledge, but, of course, life is not thereby destroyed. Practical life according to Sextus Empiricus, and revelation according to Montaigne and Bayle are areas whose foundations cannot be doubted. And also, according to Hume, the facts of ordinary life are the firm foundation that saves the philosopher when the whirlpool of doubt threatens to engulf him.

1. *Letters*, i. 13.
2. N. Kemp Smith *The Philosophy of David Hume* (London 1941) pp. 12–13.
3. Ernest C. Mossner *The Life of David Hume*, 2nd edition (Oxford 1970) pp. 76–7.
4. Duncan Forbes *Hume's Philosophical Politics* (Cambridge 1975) p. 17, cf. pp. 59, 63.
5. Perhaps the letter to the physician could provide the basis for a psychoanalytical investigation similar to that undertaken by Erikson in the case of Luther. We still lack an analysis of the psychosomatic symptoms and insights revealed in this letter; nor has there yet been any attempt to relate Hume's struggle for identity to the polar structure of this letter.
6. cf. Addison, 'Imagination . . . makes new Worlds of its own' (*Spectator*, no. 419).
7. cf. *Letters*, i. 17.
8. *Letters*, i. 10.
9. *Letters*, i. 11. Hume could have found this opinion either in Pope (*Essay on Criticism*, verse 680) or in the *Spectator* no. 103 (' . . . as it is the Praise of Longinus, that he speaks of the Sublime in a Stile suitable to it'). The same quotation from Virgil that Hume used in his letter may be found in the *Spectator* no. 414. Information about the influence of Longinus is given in the edition of D. A. Russel (Oxford 1964), especially Introduction xiii–xlviii, and in the book of Samuel H. Monk *The Sublime. A Study of Critical Theories in XVIII-Century England* (Ann Arbor 1960).
10. *Treatise*, p. 118, announces ' . . . when we come to treat of the passions [Book II] and the sense of beauty'. On p. 276 the reflective impressions are divided into the calm and the violent, 'Of the first kind is the sense of Beauty and deformity in action [Book III, Of Morals], composition, and external objects'. On p. 504 we read, 'This we shall have occasion to explain more fully afterwards, when we come to treat of *beauty*'. The *Treatise* does not contain the promised fuller treatment of beauty.
11. Hume does not say how he conceives the logical relation between the

source and the truths derived from it. His criticism of *all* previous moral philosophy eliminates the possibility of Hutcheson having played the decisive part in Hume's intellectual development at this juncture. Hutcheson stresses even in the title of his *Inquiry* of 1725 its affinity to ancient moral philosophy ('according to the sentiments of the Ancient Moralists'). When Hume writes in the *Early Memoranda*, 'The Moderns have not treated Morals so well as the Antients merely from their Reasoning turn, which carry'd them away from Sentiment' (ed. E. C. Mossner in *Journal of the History of Ideas* IX (1948) 492–518 (517)), we must be in a later phase of his development during which he came to esteem Hutcheson.

12.   "'Tis no astonishing reflection to consider, that the application of experimental philosophy to moral subjects should come after that to natural at the distance of above a whole century; since we find in fact, that there was about the same interval betwixt the origins of these sciences; and that reckoning from THALES to SOCRATES, the space of time is nearly equal to that betwixt my Lord Bacon and some late philosophers in *England*, who have begun to put the science of man on a new footing, and have engaged the attention, and excited the curiosity of the public.' (*Treatise*, Introduction, pp. xx–xxi). The reference to 'some late philosophers . . . ' is not in total harmony with the chronological scheme Hume used before. Only that scheme is in accordance with the fact that Hume saw himself as the inaugurator of a new philosophy. The opinion expressed in the sentence preceding the above quotation. that the 'science of man is the only solid foundation of the other sciences', is an idea that Hume developed only after 1734.

13.   *Letters*, i. 26.

14.   British Museum General Catalogue of Printed Books (Photolithographic edition to 1955) vol. 9 (London 1965) pp. 779–809.

15.   An edition of the *Scripta in naturali et universali philosophia* in Amsterdam 1685 is followed by *Letters and Remains of the Lord Chancellor Bacon* in 1734 (London); the re-edition of the *Law Tracts* begins in 1737 (last edition 1681). When Hume went to France in 1734, he could find two new editions of the *Essais . . . sur divers sujets de politique et de morale*, Paris 1734 (the last previous edition being from 1621!). The Humean title 'The Essays Moral, Political and Literary of David Hume' (1741) sounds like an imitation of the Baconian work.

16.   Francis Bacon *Works*, ed. Spedding, Ellis and Heath (London 1857–74) vol. III, p. 638; cf. p. 572.

17.   Francis Bacon *Works*, vol. I, p. 218 (*Novum Organum* I, cxxiv); cf. further vols. III, p. 570 and II, p. 13. The reference to Thales and Socrates may perhaps be traced back to Bacon himself, cf. *Novum Organum* I, lxxix. At the end of Section I of the *Enquiry Concerning the Principles of Morals* Hume repeats his argument of 1734. 'The other scientifical method, where a general abstract principle is first established . . . is a common source of illusion and mistake. . . . Men are now cured of their passion for hypotheses and systems in natural philosophy, and will hearken to no arguments but those which are derived from experience. It is full time they should attempt a like reformation in all moral disquisitions; and reject every system of ethics, however subtle and ingenious, which is not founded on fact and observation.' The polemic against the deductive

method of 'abstract science' clearly contains features of Bacon's own critique.

18. J. Charles Robertson 'A Bacon-Facing Generation: Scottish Philosophy in the Early Nineteenth Century' *Journal of the History of Philosophy* (1976) 41.

19. Bacon had hinted at this difference in a passage about human imagination: ' . . . and in this it is hard (as we began to say) to make any new experiment; for I cannot command myself to believe what I will, and so no trial can be made' (*Works*, vol. II, p. 654).

20. *Letters*, i. 20.

21. The phrase, 'The English Politeness is alwise greatest, where it appears least' is taken from traditional literary criticism; cf. Longinus *On the Sublime*, ch. 17. The background of literary criticism becomes clearer in the comparison with the rules of dramatic poetry.

22. *Letters*, i. 21.

23. ibid. Here Hume is dealing with the stimulation of the believer's imagination by means of ceremonies; compare Bacon *Works*, vol. IV, pp. 400–1; 'With this is joined the inquiry how to raise and fortify the imagination . . . it may be speciously pretended that ceremonies, characters, charms, gesticulations, amulets, and the like, do not derive their power from any tacit or sacramental contract with evil spirits, but serve only to strengthen and exalt the imagination of him who uses them. As likewise in religion the use of images to fix the cogitations and raise the devotions of those who pray before them has grown common.' Hume takes up the same theme in *Treatise* I. iii. 8 ('Of the causes of belief').

24. Bernard Mandeville *The Fable of the Bees . . .* , ed. F. B. Kaye (Oxford 1924, reprint 1966) vol. II, p. 183.

25. Bernard Mandeville *An Enquiry into the Origin of Honour and the Usefulness of Christianity in War* (London 1732).

26. E. C. Mossner 'David Hume's "An Historical Essay on Chivalry and Modern Honour"' *Modern Philology* XLV (1947) 54–60 (57); cf. Mossner *Life*, pp. 46–8. The only reason Mossner gives for dating this work to the college period is the youthful handwriting. But considering that we do not possess an exact handwriting analysis of Hume's manuscripts Mossner's argument is not cogent. Hume would not have kept this fragment (he never finished the piece!) for sentimental reasons, as Mossner suggests, but for the same reason he kept the *Essay on Miracles*: he thought that he could use it later and indeed worked the material into his *History of England* (1762, Appendix); cf. Mossner *Life*, p. 47.

27. Of course, I simplify the complicated process of Hume's development after 1731, and the influence of Malebrache and Berkeley, and, above all, of John Locke.

Hume and the Deists : a Reconsideration

IN A RECENT STUDY, James O'Higgins has given an interesting
account of the relations between Hume and the deists.[1] He submits that
'between Hume and the deists there lay a considerable gulf, although
there were similarities between his opinions and theirs'.[2] Hume's
approach to religion, he argues, was not that of the deists, mainly
because Hume was sceptical about the possible achievements of human
reason.[3] While I do not wish to question the truth of his conclusion, I
doubt if it is the whole truth of the matter. If the gulf was as deep and
the similarities were as slight as O'Higgins tries to make out they were,
how can we explain the fact that Hume was labelled a deist by contemporaries as well as by subsequent historians? There must have been
positive features in him that agreed with some current notion of deism
and thus invited the label. No account of the relations between Hume
and the deists can therefore be satisfactory that does not survey those
features. As O'Higgins seems to me to give a somewhat selective account
of Hume as well as of the deists,[4] it is my intention in this paper to give
some preliminary hints of a more comprehensive view of the matter.

SEVERAL ANECDOTES related by biographers show that Hume was
commonly known as a deist.[5] At several junctures in his life he was
openly charged with deism. As early as 1744, when he was a candidate
for the chair of Moral Philosophy in Edinburgh, the 'accusation of
heresy, deism, scepticism, atheism &c &c &c.' was started against him;
in 1752, when he was nominated for the office of Keeper of the Advocates' Library, the 'violent cry of deism, atheism, and scepticism' was
raised; in 1765, he was appointed secretary to the Embassy in Paris 'in
spite of atheism & deism' (as well as various other faults which are not
relevant here).[6] In 1749 Philip Skelton dealt briefly with him in a
work with the suggestive title *Ophiomaches: Or Deism Revealed.*[7] A
few years later, he was even raised to the rank of a 'principal deistical
writer' and treated at appropriate length by John Leland.[8] Both these
works had a wide circulation and influence.[9] Skelton and Leland can
be said to have started a tradition which was alive throughout the
nineteenth century and is even now faintly discernible.[10]

How did Hume react to these charges? The accusations of 1744, he
(somewhat optimistically) says in a letter, 'never took, being bore
down by the contrary authority of all the good company in town'.[11] A

few months later, however, he showed some concern. In *A Letter from a Gentleman to his Friend in Edinburgh* (1745), he deals, at some length, with the allegation of scepticism and atheism but answers the charge of deism only obliquely, if at all, by hinting that it is scarcely compatible with that of scepticism. He points out that in Socrates, Cicero and Huet scepticism goes together with a strong sense of religion, and adds: 'In reality, whence come all the various tribes of hereticks, the Arians, Socinians and Deists, but from too great a confidence in mere human reason, which they regard as the standard of every thing, and which they will not submit to the superior light of revelation?'[12] This is one among a number of fideistic remarks in Hume, but perhaps the only one intended to ward off the charge of deism.

Occasionally, however, he seems to have accepted the charge. Giving an account to John Clephane of how he was elected Keeper of the Advocates' Library, he says: ''Twas vulgarly given out, that the contest was betwixt Deists and Christians; and when the news of my success came to the play-house, the whisper ran that the Christians were defeated. Are you not surprised that we could keep our popularity notwithstanding this imputation which my friends could not deny to be well founded?'[13] And in 1764, when he had won the friendship of Lord Hertford, he stated with some satisfaction: 'Nobody, henceforth, need be afraid to patronise me, either as a Scotsman or a deist.'[14] At other times he was uneasy about the imputation. In 1757 he asked a friend to give his compliments to Dr Leland and tell him that he had certainly mistaken his character,[15] and when Mrs Mallet, the wife of Bolingbroke's editor, introduced herself to him in 1758 or 1759 with the words 'We deists ought to know each other', he sternly replied: 'Madam, I am no deist. I do na style myself so, neither do I desire to be known by that appellation'.[16]

IN VIEW OF THE manifest disagreement about Hume's relation to the deists it will not be inappropriate to call to mind what he said in another context: 'From this circumstance alone, that a controversy has been long kept on foot and remains still undecided, we may presume that there is some ambiguity in the expression, and that the disputants affix different ideas to the terms employed in the controversy.'[17] What idea was affixed to the term by those who charged Hume with being a deist, or by Hume when denying that he was a deist?

Let me begin with Hume. Strangely enough, his use of the term seems never to have been investigated, although he obviously used it with various meanings. Relating the charges raised against him in 1744, 1752 and 1765 Hume mentions several 'hard names', which, he says, 'confound the ignorant'.[18] The mere multiplicity suggests that

these names served as terms of reproach with little or no precise meaning. O'Higgins rightly hints that in his letters Hume adopted the
language of his opponents and used deism 'in a popular sense, as the
equivalent of unbelief'.[19] That was common usage in the eighteenth
century, not only in polemical literature,[20] but also in Hume's writings,
for example, when he said of Cicero that 'he avoided, in the common
conduct of life, the imputation of deism and profaneness'.[21] It would,
however, be rash to equate deism and unbelief as far as Hume is concerned, for with what right did he then deny that he was a deist when
meeting Mrs Mallet? It is true he never 'styled' himself a deist, and he
surely had his reasons 'not to be known by that appellation', but could
he sincerely deny that he disbelieved the Christian faith? On that occasion, at least, Hume must have affixed a more positive idea to the
term.

As a matter of fact, there are several instances of a positive use of the
term in his writings. The passage quoted above from *A Letter from a
Gentleman* links the deists with the Arians and Socinians, in accordance
with a seventeenth-century usage that equated deist and Antitrini-
tarian.[22] The point of mentioning these people apparently lies in their
being 'tribes of hereticks', for a heretic is a Christian with a difference,
but still a Christian. To use the word 'deist' in this sense perfectly fitted
the apologetic purpose of the pamphlet, for it put Hume on common
ground with his opponents. It would, however, again be rash to conclude that Hume in 1745 still considered himself a Christian.

The term is used in still another sense in Hume's *Essays*, for example,
in the essay 'Of Superstitition and Enthusiasm'. Comparing the two
with regard to their political consequences, Hume remarks that superstition, by subjecting men to the priests, paves the way to tyranny,
whereas enthusiasm, being opposed to authority, favours liberty (once
its first fire is spent). This is illustrated by an example from English
history: 'Our sectaries, who were formerly such dangerous bigots, are
now become very free reasoners; and the Quakers seem to approach
nearly the only regular body of deists in the universe, the literati or the
followers of Confucius in China.' In a note Hume explains the allusion:
'The Chinese literati have no priests or ecclesiastical establishment.'[23]
This would be immediately understood by the reader, for in the early
eighteenth century both the Quakers and the followers of Confucius
were repeatedly applauded by the deists for upholding natural religion,[24]
and condemned by the orthodox for neglecting exterior worship and
traditional institutions.[25] If Hume understood by *deist* an adherent of
natural religion, and by *natural religion*, knowledge of the existence of
God, the divine attributes and the divine will in relation to man, he
could very well maintain that he was no deist. He did not think such

knowledge was attainable, nor did he believe that natural religion by itself could influence life.[26]

In the same essay, Hume links the deists with the independents as 'most opposite in their religious principles, yet united in their political ones' during the civil wars.[27] This remark is expanded in the *History of Great Britain*, where he lists the groups making up the republican party: the independents, the millenarians, and the 'deists, who had no other object than political liberty, who denied entirely the truth of revelation, and insinuated that all the various sects, so heated against each other, were alike founded in folly and error'. He names H. Marten, T. Chaloner, J. Harrington, A. Sidney, J. Wildman, and H. Nevil as 'the heads of this small division'.[28] Hume, I think, would have agreed with their religious principles but not with their political aspirations. Is it possible that this was at the back of his mind when he made his disclaimer in the face of Mrs Mallet? After all, several of the deists earlier in the eighteenth century were known as 'commonwealthmen'.[29]

NOW WHAT IDEA did Hume's opponents affix to the term when they called him a deist? Those who seem to be responsible for his literary reputation as a deist speak the language of eighteenth-century polemical literature. Skelton does not offer a formal definition but gives, from the mouth of the deist in the dialogue, a 'Deistical Creed' comprising five articles gathered from Shaftesbury and Tindal; they differ in structure as well as in content from the famous five articles laid down by Lord Herbert, but keep within what was commonly considered as deism: the acceptance of natural religion and the rejection of revelation.[30] Leland's account is more explicit but on substantially the same lines. He mentions the origins of deism in sixteenth-century France and calls it a characteristic of the modern deists 'that they reject all revealed religion, and discard all pretences to it, as owing to imposture or enthusiasm. In this they all agree, and in professing a regard for natural religion, though they are far from being agreed in their notions of it'.[31]

Thus deism has two sides, which we may call 'constructive deism' and 'critical deism',[32] and any judgment of the relations between Hume and the deists seems to depend on which of the two sides is emphasized. If the emphasis is on constructive deism, Hume can be called a deist, if at all, only with strong qualifications; if the emphasis is on critical deism, he can be called a full-fledged deist. How far Hume subscribed to constructive deism (or, to use his own term, Theism) is still an open question. The negative interpretation of the *Dialogues concerning Natural Religion* given by N. Kemp Smith has been accepted for a long time, although it has recently been challenged by Nelson Pike.[33] But even on a positive interpretation of the *Dialogues*, it is improbable that Hume went further than assenting to the rudiments of natural religion delineated in Part XII.[34]

In the eighteenth century the emphasis was very much on critical deism, because natural religion was common ground for the deists and the orthodox. A strong current of Anglican theology (best represented by the Boyle Lectures) cultivated natural religion as a suitable basis for revealed religion. What distinguished the orthodox from the deists was not so much the content and method of natural religion but the view that it was not sufficient for salvation. The deists, on the other hand, refused to go beyond natural religion because they found the evidences of revealed religion not convincing and some of its doctrines repellent. Hume's writings and letters no doubt show him as a critical deist. The section 'Of Miracles' not only was understood but was intended as an attack on the main proof of Christianity.[35] Leland attests that it had been 'mightily admired and extolled, as a masterly and unanswerable piece',[36] and even Dr Johnson admitted that its central thesis was right.[37] Nor can it be denied that Hume found some of the doctrines and institutions of Christianity unacceptable; he spoke of superstition, fanaticism, and intolerance in the tones of an inveterate deist. If his opponents had known his private letters they would surely have been confirmed in their opinion that he was one of the hated tribe. They read the note on priests in the essay 'Of National Characters' with indignation,[38] but what would they have thought of his intention 'to write a Supplement to *Gulliver*, containing the Ridicule of the Priests'? Swift himself might have written it, Hume says, if he had not been a parson. 'But Priests are so jealous, that they cannot bear to be touched on that Head; and for a plain Reason: Because they are conscious they are really ridiculous.'[39]

Instead of quoting further evidence for what seems obvious, I wish to raise a final question: does the common definition of deism fit the deists' views and intentions? Although very few writers have considered this, I do not think it can be taken for granted.[40] After all, the commonly accepted definition has been given by theologians and reflects theological bias.[41] In truth, scarcely anybody ever said, in so many words, that Christianity originated from imposture or that there was no such thing as revelation. Of course, those who did not say so, yet may have thought so; but how do we know they did? If we take the trouble to study their works we find that the evidence often points the other way. Lord Herbert expressly allowed for revelation,[42] and from 1730 onwards several writers spoke of 'Christian deism', which they did not feel to be a contradiction in terms.[43] If the rejection of revelation was not a necessary condition for deism, neither was rationalism. Lord Herbert founded religion on natural instinct, John Trenchard on ignorance and fear, Thomas Chubb on practical reason rather than on demonstrative proof.[44] Nor did all the deists think that natural religion flourished in the beginnings of history.[45] What characterized all of them was the aim of making a clean sweep of superstition and priestcraft, intolerance and religious persecution, by placing morality on a footing independent of revelation.[46] Rationalism was a means to this end no more. Hume was in sympathy with the end but not with the means; therefore, he developed means of his own. I submit that if we take our concept of deism from the works of the deists, not of their opponents, we may find Hume in greater agreement with the deists than is presently acknowledged. What separated him from them was not his rejection of rationalism but his final despair of any means to eradicate evils as deeply rooted in human nature as those mentioned above.[47]

1. J. O'Higgins 'Hume and the Deists: A Contrast in Religious Approaches' *Journal of Theological Studies* 22 (1971) pp. 479–501.
2. O'Higgins, p. 479.
3. O'Higgins, p. 492.
4. O'Higgins, for example, entirely fails to mention the section 'Of Miracles' and starts from a definition of deism that excludes the doctrines of some of the more prominent deistical writers, such as Lord Herbert, Thomas Chubb, and Thomas Morgan.
5. E. C. Mossner *The Life of David Hume* (Edinburgh and Austin 1954) p. 570. The well-known story of how Hume slipped into the bog and was rescued by an old fish-wife has two variant readings; see Mossner *Life*, p. 563 and J. Hill Burton *Life and Correspondence of David Hume* (Edinburgh 1846) vol. II, p. 458. That Hume was considered an atheist is likewise shown by anecdotes: see Mossner *Life*, pp. 411, 603.
6. *Letters*, i. 57, 165, 510.
7. London 1749, vol. II, pp. 20–2. Skelton originally did not mention Hume; he included him, just before going into print, at the instigation of John Conybeare, a divine known for having answered Matthew Tindal. Curiously enough, 'Hume the infidel' is said to have advised Andrew Millar to publish Skelton's work; see Mossner *Life*, p. 232.
8. *A View of the Principal Deistical Writers of the Last and Present Century* (London 1755) vol. II, pp. 1–135. See also Leland's *Supplement to the First and Second Volumes of the View of the Deistical Writers* (London 1756) pp. 68–127. After the publication of vol. I in 1754, Leland was 'put in mind of a considerable omission [he] had been guilty of in not taking notice of Mr. Hume, who was looked upon as being one of the most subtil writers that had of late appeared against Christianity' (Preface to vol. II, p. iii).
9. *Ophiomaches* saw a second edition in 1751 and was translated into German by M. Th. Chr. Mittelstedt *Die offenbarte Deisterey* (Braunschweig and

Hildesheim 1756). Leland's work reached the fifth edition in 1766 and was reprinted as late as 1837; see T. E. Jessop *A Bibliography of David Hume and of Scottish Philosophy* (London 1938) p. 108. There is a German translation by H. G. Schmidt *Abriß der vornehmsten deistischen Schriften, die in dem vorigen und gegenwärtigen Jahrhundert in England bekannt geworden sind* (Hannover 1755), which was reviewed by Lessing in the *Berlinische Privilegirte Zeitung*; see Lessing's *Sämtliche Schriften*, ed. K. Lachmann and F. Muncker (Stuttgart 1890) vol. v, pp. 443–5. In the 1750s, German authors commonly mentioned and criticised Hume along with the deists; see the preface to Part III of G. W. Alberti's *Briefe betreffend den allerneuesten Zustand der Religion und der Wissenschaften in Gross-Britannien* (Hannover 1752), in which part of the section 'Of Miracles' is translated into German. Hume's treatment of miracles was also criticised by Th. Chr. Lilienthal in *Die gute Sache der . . . göttlichen Offenbarung, wider die Feinde derselben erwiesen und gerettet*, Achter Theil (Königsberg 1758) pp. 970–1110. In the same year, Daniel Cornides defended *Theses philosophicae inaugurales Humio atque Bolingbrokio deistarum recentissimorum coryphaeis oppositae* at the university of Erlangen, which dealt mainly with Hume's first *Enquiry*: the author acknowledged Hume to be greatly superior 'ingenio et acumine' to the other deists on account of his argument against the proof from miracles (p. 9), but called him 'sophistam et deistarum pessimum' for his views on liberty and necessity (p. 11). Hume is briefly mentioned, along with Bolingbroke, in Chr. M. Pfaff's *Academische Reden über den Entwurff der Theologiae Antideisticae* (Franckfurt 1759) p. 50.

10. G. V. Lechler accorded a chapter to Hume in his *Geschichte des englischen Deismus* (Stuttgart and Tübingen 1841) pp. 425–36. He stressed his importance as 'die Vollendung des Deismus, sofern sich dieser in ihm aufhob und verneinte' (p. 425), a view which has a tincture of Hegelian dialectic. Lechler's *Geschichte des englischen Deismus* has long been the standard work on the deists (there is a reprint by Georg Olms Verlag, Hildesheim 1965); it had a considerable influence even on English speaking authors. Among those who made use of it and placed Hume in the tradition of deism are A. S. Farrar in *A Critical History of Free Thought in Reference to the Christian Religion* (London 1862) pp. 208–16; J. Hunt, who called Hume the 'most sagacious of all the deists' in his *History of Religious Thought in England from the Reformation to the End of the Last Century* (London 1873) vol. III, p. 184; and J. Orr in *English Deism. Its Roots and its Fruits* (Grand Rapids 1934) pp. 165–71. J. M. Robertson in his *History of Freethought Ancient and Modern*, 3rd edition (London 1915) vol. II, p. 174 seems to exaggerate both ways when he states: 'Hume wrote explicitly as a deist; and only in his posthumous *Dialogues* did he pass on to the atheistic position.' See also his *Dynamics of Religion*, 2nd edition (London 1926) p. 155. R. N. Stromberg gives a well-balanced account of Hume's position in *Religious Liberalism in Eighteenth Century England* (London 1954), in two sections of a chapter entitled 'The Definition of Deism' (pp. 64–9). The implicitly suggested classification is supported by the interpretation that Stromberg gives to Hume's religious ideal: 'The enlightened few will be deists if anything' (p. 68).

11. *Letters*, i. 57.

12. Ed. E. C. Mossner and J. V. Price (Edinburgh 1967) p. 21.

13. *Letters*, i. 166.

14. *Letters*, i. 428; see also the anecdote in J. Hill Burton *Life*, vol. II, p. 444.

15. *New Letters of David Hume*, ed. R. Klibansky and E. C. Mossner (Oxford 1954) p. 43. Hume occasionally complained of being treated as an 'infidel writer' on account of a few pages in an oeuvre of many volumes (e.g., *Letters*, i. 351), but took it in good humour when his complaint met with a witty reply; see Mossner *Life*, p. 545.

16. Mossner *Life*, p. 395.

17. *Enquiries*, p. 80.

18. *Letters*, i. 59.

19. O'Higgins *Hume and the Deists*, p. 479.

20. e.g., in *The Deist Stretched upon a Death-bed: Or a Lively Portraiture of a Dying Infidel*, a pamphlet directed against Hume in 1755; see Mossner *Life*, p. 343.

21. *The Natural History of Religion*, ed. H. E. Root (London 1956) p. 59.

22. See the quotations from Thomas Blount (1656), Elisha Coles (1676) and John Kersey (1702) in C. Welsh 'A Note on the Meaning of Deism' *Anglican Theological Review* 38 (1956) 161–2. This usage is also mentioned in Diderot's *Encyclopédie*, art. Déistes. The passage quoted in the text from *A Letter from a Gentleman* is echoed in Part I of the *Dialogues concerning Natural Religion*, where Philo remarks that 'during ignorant ages, such as those which followed the dissolution of the ancient schools, the priests perceived, that Atheism, Deism, or heresy of any kind, could only proceed from the presumptuous questioning of received opinions, and from a belief, that human reason was equal to everything' (*The Philosophical Works of David Hume*, ed. T. H. Green and T. H. Grose (London 1907) vol. II, p. 389).

23. *Phil. Works*, vol. III, p. 149. Hume's account of the Quakers in the *History of England* mentions the absence of priests among them but does not refer to deism or Confucianism (London 1848, vol. V, pp. 447–51).

24. For the deists' esteem of the Quakers see, e.g., M. Tindal *Christianity as Old as the Creation* (London 1730) p. 172; for Confucius, ibid., pp. 341–2, and also Bolingbroke *Works*, ed. D. Mallett (London 1754) vols. IV, p. 206 ff., v, p. 228 ff. J. M. Robertson remarks: 'The praise of Confucius is the note of deism; and (Gilbert) Burnet rightly held that no orthodox Christian in those days would sound it' (*History of Freethought*, vol. II, p. 111).

25. For the orthodox assessment of the Quakers as deists see G. Keith *The Deism of William Penn and his Brethren* (London 1699) and Ch. Leslie *A Short and Easie Method with the Deists*, 4th edition (London 1709), p. 54. In *A Representation of the Present State of Religion, with regard to the excessive Growth of Infidelity, Heresy and Profaneness* it is said that the Quakers 'in several of their Treatises, in their Catechisms and Primers, have taught the Rudiments of the Christian Faith in such a manner, as to make it seem to be little more than a complicated System of Deism and Enthusiasm' (London 1711, p. 5). See further C. J. Abbey and J. H. Overton *The English Church in the Eighteenth Century* (London 1878) vol. I, p. 560 ff.

26. In his early memoranda Hume notes that 'no religion can maintain itself in vigour without many observances to be practis'd on all occasions' (E. C. Mossner 'Hume's Early Memoranda, 1729–1740: The Complete

Text' *Journal of the History of Ideas* IX (1948) 503). The text quoted belongs to a series of notes written down probably between 1730 and 1734.

27. *Phil. Works*, vol. III, p. 150. In the very next sentence, Hume remarks that 'the leaders of the Whigs have either been deists or profest latitudinarians, that is friends to toleration and indifferent to any particular sect of Christians'. The description neatly fits both the deists and the latitudinarians, although the deists, in both respects, went further than the latitudinarians; see G. Gawlick 'The English Deists' Contribution to the Theory of Toleration' *Studies on Voltaire and the Eighteenth Century* 152 (1976) 823–35. That Hume connected Whig principles with indifference to the Christian sects is shown by his letter to John Clephane in which he admits that in the *History of Great Britain* his 'views of things are more conformable to Whig principles' and anticipates the conclusion readers will draw from his treatment of religion: 'As I run over all the sects successively, and speak of each of them with some mark of disregard, the reader, putting the whole together, concludes that I am of no sect; which to him will appear the same thing as the being of no religion' (*Letters*, i. 237, O'Higgins, *Hume and the Deists* p. 479, gives 18 February 1757 as the date of this letter). This seems to lead back to the identification of deism and unbelief.

28. *History of England*, vol. v, p. 356. Of Chaloner the regicide J. Aubrey reports that 'he was of the Naturall Religion' (*Brief Lives*, ed. O. Lawson Dick (London 1958) p. 61).

29. viz., John Toland, John Trenchard, and Thomas Gordon; see C. Robbins *The Eighteenth-Century Commonwealthman* (Cambridge, Mass. 1961) pp. 88–133, and I. Kramnick *Bolingbroke and his Circle* (Cambridge, Mass. 1968) pp. 236–60.

30. *Ophiomaches: Or Deism Revealed*, 2nd edition (London 1751) vol. I, pp. 34–5. For Lord Herbert's five articles, see, e.g., *The Antient Religion of the Gentiles* (London 1705) pp. 3–4.

31. *A View of the Principal Deistical Writers*, 5th edition (London 1766) vol. I, p. 2.

32. These terms were first used by Leslie Stephen in his *History of English Thought in the Eighteenth Century* (London 1876). There they are the headings of Chapters III and IV respectively, which treat of two different groups of deistical writers. My use of the terms differs from Stephen's, it will be noted.

33. See N. Kemp Smith's introduction to the *Dialogues* (Oxford 1935, 2nd edition Edinburgh 1947, reprinted Indianapolis n.d.), and Nelson Pike's commentary in the Bobbs-Merrill Text and Commentary Series (Indianapolis 1970) esp. pp. 204–38. It should be noted that even prior to the posthumous publication of the *Dialogues*, Hume's adherence to natural religion was questioned. In spite of his complaint, the *Treatise of Human Nature* already seems to have 'excited a murmur among the zealots', for in *A Letter from a Gentleman* Hume found it necessary to assure the public that his theory of causality did not endanger the argument from design (p. 23). Leland, who reckoned Hume among the 'principal deistical writers', nevertheless charged him with striking at the foundations of natural religion (*A View of the Principal Deistical Writers*, vol. I, pp. 259, 272, 283).

34. *Phil. Works*, vol. II, p. 467. Whether these rudiments add up to a system

of natural religion in the traditional sense of the word is a matter of interpretation. Hume himself obviously wished to retain only the minimum content of religion, as a letter, written to William Mure of Caldwell in 1743, shows, which equates religion with 'the Practice of Morality and the Assent of the Understanding to the Proposition *that God exists*' (*Letters*, i. 50). If we accept this as natural religion and define deism as the acceptance of natural religion and the rejection of revelation, it makes sense to call Hume a deist. But if we define deism as the doctrine that natural religion is sufficient for salvation (see Stromberg *Religious Liberalism*, p. 55), it hardly makes sense to call Hume a deist, for the God he accepted could scarcely be said to be concerned with the destiny of man.

35. J. C. A. Gaskin has shown, convincingly, I think, that in the section 'Of Miracles' Hume was 'in part concerned to answer (Thomas) Sherlock's *Tryal of the Witnesses*', one of the foremost contributions to the deistic controversy on the orthodox side ('David Hume and the Eighteenth-Century Interest in Miracles' *Hermathena* 99 (1964) 80–92). In addition, several passages in that section seem to be designed in reply to Charles Leslie's *Short and Easie Method with the Deists*, a pamphlet first published in 1698 and printed as late as 1884 (the British Museum Catalogue and the National Union Catalogue together list about fifty different editions of the work). It has been noted that Hume's specific criticism of the proof from miracles was parallelled in deistic literature; see J. M. Robertson *History of Freethought*, vol. II, p. 180, whose conclusion that Hume developed a proposition laid down before him in 1741 is, however, unwarranted because Hume himself dates his own argument as early as 1734 (*Letters*, ii. 361).

36. *View of the Principal Deistical Writers* vol. I, p. 284.

37. James Boswell *The Life of Dr Johnson*, ed. S. Roberts (London/New York 1949) vol. II, p. 137. Johnson thought that the proof from miracles retained some force as it went together with the proof from prophecy (and the internal evidence). Had he studied the first *Enquiry* more attentively he might have seen that Hume classified prophecies as 'real miracles' (*Enquiry*, pp. 130–1), so that if he dealt a decisive blow against one proof, the other fell as well.

38. *Phil. Works*, vol. III, pp. 245–7. See also the letter to John Clephane in which Hume draws a comparison between priests and apothecaries on the one hand, philosophers and physicians on the other (*Letters*, i. 150).

39. *Letters*, i. 153. Several of the deists expressed a similar view of the priesthood by quoting the saying attributed to Cato Censorius: 'Mirari se aiebat, quod non rideret haruspex haruspicem cum vidisset.' See G. Gawlick 'Cicero in the Enlightenment' *Studies on Voltaire and the Eighteenth Century* 25 (1963) 664. For Hume's interest in the history of the church see Mossner *Life*, pp. 484–5 and M. Morrisroe 'Hume's Ecclesiastical History: A New Letter' *English Studies* 53 (1972) 431–3.

40. A notable exception is A. R. Winnett 'Were the Deists "Deists"?' *Church Quarterly Review* 161 (1960) 70–7. O'Higgins simply adopts what he calls 'the most complete analysis and definition of deism' from Samuel Clarke's Boyle Lectures for 1705 (*Hume and the Deists*, p. 479). As a matter of fact, Clarke gives no more than a classification of the deists in four groups distinguished by varying degrees of conformity with the traditional Christian concept of God; see his *Discourse concerning the*

Unchangeable Obligations of Natural Religion (London 1706) pp. 19–42.

41. There are very few explications of the meaning of deism from the pen of the deists themselves. This is partly due to circumstances. Originally the name of deist was assumed by those who did not commit themselves to any form of revealed religion but wished to stress that they were not atheists. Very soon, however, it became a term of reproach and was avoided by those who were entitled to it. As far as I know, Lord Herbert, 'the father of English deism', never used the name. The few authentic statements of deism, e.g., Ch. Blount's 'Summary Account of the Deist's Religion' in *Oracles of Reason* (London 1693) pp. 87–96, the anonymous *Deism Fairly Stated and Fully Vindicated* (London 1746), and a few scattered remarks by Thomas Chubb, were largely neglected by contemporary as well as modern authors.

42. *De Veritate* (London 1645) p. 225. Note his proviso that revelation must not counteract the moral tendency of natural religion. In his auto-biography (ed. S. Lee, 2nd edition (London 1906) pp. 133–4), Herbert tells us that he was encouraged, by a sign from heaven, to publish *De Veritate*. No matter what degree of authenticity the story may have, Herbert would not have told it if he himself had thought it inconsistent with his deism. Incidentally, it was John Leland who brought this part of Herbert's unpublished autobiography to public notice. Leland had 'no doubt of his Lordship's sincerity in this account' (*View of the Principal Deistic Writers*, vol. I, p. 24).

43. The term 'Christian deism' was first used, as far as I know, by M. Tindal in *Christianity as Old as the Creation* (London 1730) pp. 368 ff. Eariler in the eighteenth century, one of the speakers in Shaftesbury's *Moralists* declared himself 'averse to the cause of theism, or the name of a deist, when taken in a sense exclusive of revelation' and had no 'patience to hear the name of deist (the highest of all names) decried and set in opposition to Christianity'; see *Characteristics*, ed. J. M. Robertson (London 1900) vol. II, p. 19. Vol. I of Thomas Morgan's main work has the form of a dialogue between 'Philalethes a Christian Deist, and Theophanes a Christian Jew'. For an explanation of what Morgan means by 'Christian Deism' and in what sense he even acknowledges the necessity (!) of revelation, see *The Moral Philosopher*, 2nd edition (London 1738) pp. 144, 411. In *The Life of John Buncle, Esq.*, a fictitious biography giving an account of the author's religious views, Thomas Amory distinguishes between 'Christian deism' and 'anti-Christian deism' (London 1756, vol. I, pp. 222, 380 ff.).

44. Of the three, Trenchard seems to come closest to Hume. His *Natural History of Superstition* (London 1709) invites comparison with Hume's *Natural History of Religion* but is neglected by historians of philosophy.

45. The exception is Trenchard; see n. 44.

46. In my article 'Der Deismus als Grundzug der Religionsphilosophie der Aufklärung' I have tried to give a short account of deism that is free of traditional distortions (printed in *Hermann Samuel Reimarus (1694–1768), ein 'bekennter Unbekannter' der Aufklärung in Hamburg* (Göttingen 1973) pp. 15–43). Very much remains to be done, though.

47. Hume's pessimism with regard to the 'Enlightenment' becomes apparent in his letters over the years; see, e.g., *Letters*, ii. 310; *New Letters*, pp. 131, 199.

La Méthode Newtonienne
et les Lois Empiriques de l'Anthropologie
dans Traité II

APPLIQUER UNE méthode newtonienne pour élever à la science une théorie générale des passions, telle est la tâche que Hume se propose dans le Livre II du *Traité*. Selon Norman Kemp Smith, l'entreprise aurait tourné mal. Hume aurait-il manqué son but? Du point de vue théorique, les lois de l'association qu'il établit seraient fantaisistes et inutilement compliquées. Du point de vue téléologique, ce Livre II serait un échec puisqu'il serait pour le moins inutile par rapport aux 'ethical problems'. Au reste, Kemp Smith attribue à Hume dans ce Livre II une fin oblique: il aurait simplement pour rôle d'illustrer une méthode, celle qui a été employée dès le Livre I; comme tel, il serait subordonné à l'épistémologie. En conséquence à tous égards le Livre II serait un échec. En fait de connaissance théorique, il serait stérile. Et la fin morale qu'on pourrait légitimement en attendre serait manquée.

Comment excuser Hume? Le plus expédient est de faire de ce Livre II du *Traité* un péché de jeunesse—mais il faut alors rendre compte de la maturité relative du reste de l'œuvre, dont on peut démontrer qu'il est une partie intégrante. Ou bien l'on essaie de limiter, malgré Hume lui-même, l'importance qu'il attache aux lois de l'association, dans leur fondement et dans leur application—mais l'interprète peut-il s'y hasarder sans porter atteinte à la valeur scientifique de la théorie générale des passions? Il se trouve, enfin, selon Kemp Smith, que l'application de la méthode de Newton à la philosophie morale n'est pas newtonienne en esprit, et qu'au reste Newton ne l'aurait pas reconnue. Et Kemp Smith de conclure à une heureuse 'récession' du caractère newtonien de la philosophie de Hume prise dans son ensemble. Le Livre II étant ainsi excisé, l'œuvre alors épurée, l'auteur est maintenant disculpé. Une telle interprétation du Livre II du *Traité* ruine la portée de la théorie générale des passions. Du point de vue historique pourtant, il faut relever que la *Dissertation sur les passions*, de 1757, affirme encore le caractère scientifique de la théorie, de même méthode qu' 'any part of natural philosophy'.[1] Mais, à suivre Kemp Smith, l'interprétation du *Traité*, de sa structure (rapport entre Livres I et II d'une part, d'autre part I–II et Livre III) et de sa genèse condamnerait l'anthropologie de Hume comme une anthropologie sans homme. Quel est donc

le motif du grand commentateur pour infliger un si mauvais traite-
ment au Livre II? Le but de Kemp Smith est-il de sauver l'âme
humaine du 'mécanisme' pour pouvoir, avec Newton et contre Hume,
sauver l'âme de Hume lui-même?

L'Introduction de Hume au *Traité* nous enjoint de la prendre
comme un tout; le principe de méthode que l'auteur y prescrit (fonder
sur l'expérience la science de la nature humaine) nous autorise à lire
l'ouvrage comme un traité d'anthropologie empirique (même s'il est
encore bien autre chose), divisé comme suit: (1) l'homme comme
animal intelligent, (2) comme animal soumis aux passions, (3) comme
animal politique.

Le Livre I, partie de l'anthropologie, est une logique. C'est une
théorie générale de l'entendement, ou une théorie de la connaissance.
Le Livre I tout entier montre que l'entendement a un fonctionnement
pragmatique. Mais c'est un fait, irréductible, que l'homme a une idée
de la vérité invincible à tout le pragmatisme. Le signe de cette grâce
dont la nature l'a marqué est la passion unique que l'homme ne partage
pas avec les autres animaux: la curiosité ou l'amour de la vérité. La
curiosité, voire le scepticisme (nom simplement plus osé de cette
passion) est peut-être le charisme de la créature.[2]

Symétriquement, c'est encore un fait irréductible que l'homme a une
idée de la vérité invincible à tout le moralisme. L'anthropologie du
Livre II exclut par principe, comme intempestive, toute référence aux
problèmes éthiques.

Or, l'animal intelligent tente de dépasser les bornes de l'expérience:
son esprit n'est pas lesté une fois pour toutes. Il fluctue avec les passions
et oscille entre l'empirisme (Berkeley, comme école du scepticisme, est
un bon remède contre cette faiblesse[3] et le délire de la raison. Le Livre
II est donc indispensable pour comprendre le Livre I. C'est ainsi que,
conjointement:

(*a*) comme théorie de la connaissance, le Livre I (puis l'*Inquiry*)
peut fonder une critique de la religion dans les limites de l'entendement,
i.e. une religion naturelle. Elle sera mise à jour dans les *Dialogues*, sur
lesquels anticipe l'Introduction du *Traité*: c'est dire que, de l'écrit de
jeunesse à l'oeuvre posthume, la pensée vivante de Hume est une;

(*b*) Le Livre II, comme anthropologie, peut fonder l'*Histoire Naturelle de la Religion*, qui expose la connaissance empirique que nous
prenons de l'animal religieux: (1) parce qu'il est doué de curiosité,
d'amour désintéressé de la vérité, il peut se libérer de certaines passions.
(2) parce qu'il est susceptible d'être ainsi émancipé, le 'problème' de la
liberté, écarté comme dispute métaphysique simplement verbale,
trouve son sens dans la morale et la politique.

L'animal moral et politique est doué d'un sens singulier: le gout. Il y a en lui une sorte d'*a priori* affectif. L'homme a un sens du beau invincible à tout l'utilitarisme. Ce sens irréductible est le point d'Archimède sur lequel s'appuiera tout le traité d'Adam Smith: 'how selfish so ever man may be supposed . . .'. Le sens du beau fait pendant, en philosophie pratique, à la curiosité en philosophie spéculative.

Ces remarques préliminaires doivent suffire à nous préserver de toute méfiance. Nous n'avons pas à 'concéder' à Hume quelque texte que ce soit de son œuvre. Reconnaissons-lui le Livre II du *Traité* tout entier, et, par principe, présumons plutôt que, s'il ne l'a pas remanié, c'est qu'il en était satisfait: il ne se contentait pas de peu.

Montrons brièvement, sur quelques exemples, l'application de la méthode newtonienne. Réduite à l'essentiel, 'the true system', la vraie théorie des passions indirectes est d'une 'irresistible evidence': Les passions cardinales sont produites par une double relation d'idées et d'impressions. Une fois établi[4] suivant les *Regulae Philosophandi* une et quatre de Newton, le principe de la théorie, il reste à l'appliquer, à 'composer' le système de ces passions à monter, comme un mécanisme, la structure formelle des quatre passions cardinales. La double relation d'idées et d'impressions ne suffit pas à dégager cette structure. A leur production est nécessaire une autre condition, un élément qui a une 'equal influence' à celle des causes originaires des passions: *la sympathie*.[5] Pour que se produisent ces phénomènes que sont l'orgueil et l'humiliation il faut un champ de forces: le champ concret, le lieu naturel des passions, est la société. Mais le système fermé, auquel se réduit le carré des passions cardinales dans cette première étape de la composition, est un système mécanique, de mouvement réversible: '*in whatever order we proceed* . . . , the experiment is not in the least diversify'd.'[6] On peut y faire abstraction du temps. Le montage de ce système est effectué de la même manière dont Newton, dans l'*Opticks*, fait réapparaître la lumière solaire '*but yet in a contrary order*', après l'avoir analysée, pour administrer la preuve expérimentale qu'elle est, par nature, un composé.[7] L'expérimentation en idée de Hume est, aussi, analogue à celle que doit employer l'astronome faute de pouvoir manipuler les planètes: Enlevons la lune, nous supprimons les marées. Réintégrons la lune dans le champ de la gravitation, nous retrouvons ces marées. Avec l'observation, c'est le calcul qui remplace le montage de l'expérimentation. Chez Hume, c'est l'évidence qui donne à l'analyse la même certitude qu'aux calculs en philosophie naturelle.

Or la réversibilité des passions, constatée dans l'expérimentation quatre,[8] est aussitôt mise en question (exp. cinq et six). Nous étions passés de l'amour (pour mon frère, par exemple) à l'orgueil: Si maintenant nous tentons d'effectuer un retour, 'the whole chain is broken': le passage n'est pas si 'naturel' dans cet ordre qu'à l'inverse. Comme

l'avait écrit La Rochefoucauld, 'on passe souvent de l'amour à l'ambition, mais on ne revient guère de l'ambition à l'amour.[9] Cela veut dire
que je rapporte aisément la conscience que j'ai de mon frère (idée plus
obscure) à la conscience de moi-même (idée plus vive): le passage est
'smooth and open', la transition est donc facile de l'amour que je lui
porte à la fierté que j'ai de moi. En revanche, si étroite que soit la
relation entre mon frère et moi, je sors plus difficilement de ma conscience de moi vers la conscience que j'ai de lui. Je 'rapporte' plus
aisément mon frère à moi-même que je ne me 'porte' vers lui. La relation d'idées est bien ici, pourtant, réciproque: s'il est mon frère, je suis
également le sien. Mais cette relation est polarisée de façon irréversible.
Il me faut, en termes newtoniens, quitter mon centre de gravité et
rejoindre sur son orbite un objet qui tourne à une certaine distance de
moi. La relation réciproque signifie une gravitation réciproque, mais
inégale. Ce n'est pas une 'relation parfaite',[10] celle en vertu de laquelle
on passe de la même manière de A en B et de B en A, avec une totale
réversibilité, ce qui serait le cas dans une gravitation réciproque égale.

Il nous faut pousser plus loin, dans une nouvelle expérimentation,
la septième, l'épreuve de l'argument élaboré dans les expérimentations cinq et six. Nous pouvons énoncer cette double proposition:
L'imagination passe plus aisément d'un objet éloigné à un proche, que
l'inverse; elle passe plus aisément d'un moindre à un plus grand, que
l'inverse. Ces deux propositions, dit Hume, ont 'the very same reason'[11]
—entendons: la gravitation. Elles constituent ensemble une *loi*
empirique, Hume dit même un *principe*.[12] Comment l'expérimentation sept met-elle en question l'ensemble des expériences cinq et six?
Dans deux cas possibles: la solution de ces deux problèmes peut être
construite selon la règle du parallélogramme des forces.[13]

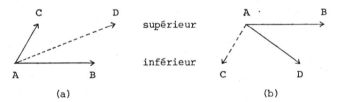

(*a*) Hypothèse: une passion pour un objet inférieur, côté AB, et une
relation d'idées (relation inférieur-supérieur), côté AC. Selon la *composition* du parallélogramme des forces, il devrait en résulter la diagonale AD (passion pour un objet supérieur). Or elle ne se 'construit'
pas: la passion pour l'inférieur ne se transfère pas au supérieur. La
relation d'impression est empêchée dans son action.

(*b*) Hypothèse: côté AB (une passion pour un objet supérieur) et
diagonale AD (le transfert de la passion à un objet inférieur). Selon la

résolution du parallélogramme, il devrait résulter l'autre côté AC (relation supérieur-inférieur). Or on ne peut pas le 'construire'. La relation d'idées, contraire à la propension naturelle de l'imagination, est empêchée dans son action.

Dans cette seconde étape, le mécanisme de la gravitation mentale est donc confirmé: ce qui ne réduit pas l'homme à une machine: L'intrusion du temps rend le cours des passions irrévocable: le mécanisme ne peut rendre compte de la totalité du fonctionnement des passions. Telle est la limite d'application de la méthode newtonienne, non son échec.

Dans la Section IV de la *Dissertation sur les passions* de 1757, viendront, à titre d'illustrations, des exemples de production et transformation des passions. Or, privilégiant les expérimentations cinq et six, Hume montrera la rupture de continuité qui s'impose ici, et le caractère irréversible dans le temps, donc non mécanique, du système des passions humaines.

Le principe de comparaison[14] est le second élément, opposé et complémentaire par rapport à la sympathie, nécessaire à la constitution du champ de forces des passions. Il sera requis pour rendre compte des passions dans leur structure réelle, et dans 'the variations of these variations' à l'infini,[15] la pitié, la malice, par exemple.

L'explication de ces passions nouvelles, produites par mélange et variation des passions cardinales, fait apparaître une nouvelle structure, qui dessine la valeur vitale des passions. Le carré abstrait des passions cardinales tracé en II.11.2 se tord en une croix des passions construite sur ses diagonales. Amour et humiliation affaiblissent l'âme, tandis que celle-ci trouve force et vigueur dans la haine et l'orgueil.[16]

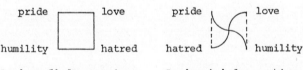

Le 'carré' des passions   La 'croix' des passions

Il faut, pour saisir le sens de cette torsion, (1) remonter au champ des forces que constituent la sympathie et la comparaison. Nous avons vu dans l'expérimentation six que si l'autre (mon frère) n'est pas un objet quelconque, la sympathie cependant ne suffit pas à produire l'identification des deux soi. La sympathie est la communication universelle, plus ou moins intense ou étendue suivant les circonstances. C'est l'éther qui porte l'homme. C'est ce qui le fait vivre et ce qui le tue (cf. Le sens de l'humiliation). Fondamentalement, deux principes s'opposent: la sympathie et la comparaison. C'est dans leur équilibre qu'il faut situer l'orgueil pour comprendre sa signification comme marque de vitalité, et sa fonction qui est d'entretenir l'attachement à la vie et à soi. Le soi vit de l'opposition,[17] où il se manifeste par le désir de se comparer, ou, comme dit Rousseau, de se distinguer. (2) La croix des passions est à interpréter en termes de temps. Les passions qui revigorent l'âme lui ouvrent l'avenir; celles qui l'affaiblissent la dévouent au passé. Le 'choc du futur', 'future shock', normalement, nous entraîne plus que le poids du passé ne nous freine.[18] D'où l'effet des passions sur notre jugement: elles le faussent. C'est que leur fonction est d'abord de nous attacher à la vie—même au prix d'une duperie sur la réalité. D'où, aussi, la pauvreté de la section sur la passion amoureuse, dont Hume, heureusement, a traité ailleurs. De Shakespeare à Rousseau, romanciers et dramaturges montrent que l'homme est un animal qui peut mourir d'amour. Mais la philosophie morale, l'anthropologie, expliquent pourquoi, en règle générale, la mort vient rarement délivrer les hommes de cette souffrance.

La troisième étape dans la composition de la nature humaine nous conduit jusqu'à la structure concrète des passions; le champ des forces est le 'monde des réalités', par opposition à celui des idées—province de l'entendement—celui où se meut la volonté.[19]

Dans cette troisième partie du Livre II, ce ne sont plus seulement des lois de la gravitation mentale, ce sont encore des lois empiriques que Hume réussit à établir. Et une autre méthode y est introduite, la phénoménologie, ce que nous ne pourrons exposer ici.

1. *The Philosophical Works of David Hume*, ed. T. H. Green and T. H. Grose (London 1874–5) vol. IV, p. 166.

2. *Enquiries*, p. 32.

3. *Enquiries*, p. 122 n.

4. *Treatise*, p. 285.

5. *Treatise*, p. 316.

6. *Treatise*, p. 337 (italics added).

7. *Opticks*, bk. I, pt. II, prop. V, theorem IV, exp. 10.

8. *Treatise*, pp. 336–7.

9. *Maximes*, 490 (5th edition).

10. *Treatise*, p. 355.

11. *Treatise*, p. 342.

12. *Treatise*, p. 343.

13. ibid.; cf. Newton *Philosophiae Naturalis Principia Mathematica*, vol. I, axiom III, cor. I & II; Henry Pemberton *A View of Sir Isaac Newton's Philosophy*, ed. I. B. Cohen (New York 1972) p. 30 and drawing on p. 74 — the rule of the parallelogram here follows the Second Law of Motion; Colin MacLaurin *An Account of Sir Isaac Newton's Discoveries* (London 1748) bk. II, ch. XI, §§8–11, cor. I & II.

14. *Treatise*, p. 372.

15. *Treatise*, p. 347.

16. *Treatise*, p. 391.

17. *Treatise*, p. 435.

18. *Treatise*, p. 432.

19. *Treatise*, p. 413.

Hume and his Predecessors
on the Causal Maxim

IN A WELL-KNOWN SECTION of the *Treatise*[1] (1.iii.3) Hume under-takes to prove that the causal principle, which he equates with the dictum that 'whatever begins to exist must have a cause of existence', is not what would nowadays be called a logically necessary truth. He argues that it is not one of those 'intuitively certain' propositions whose truth can be established by mere inspection of the ideas they contain; nor is it one of those 'demonstrably certain' propositions whose truth can be shown to follow from some other propositions themselves 'intuitively certain'.

Hume realises that, if he is right, any attempt to show the causal principle to be 'demonstrably certain' must be fallacious, and to clinch his point he goes on to examine in the same section four arguments that purport to do just this. The first of these, which he ascribes to Hobbes, relies on the principle that 'all the points of time and place' are 'equal'. Hume's second argument, ascribed to Clarke ('and others'), says that if anything came into existence without a cause it would be produced by *itself*, but to be so it would have to 'exist before it existed, which is impossible'. The third argument is attributed to Locke, and says that if a thing came into existence without a cause it would be produced by *nothing*, but 'nothing can never be a cause'. All these arguments are rejected by Hume in the belief that they involve a *petitio*: they take for granted the principle of causality they set out to prove. To these arguments Hume adds a fourth whose proponents are dismissed as 'still more frivolous' but not named: every effect, they say, must have a cause, since 'cause' and 'effect' are correlative terms. He points out that this does not show that every being must be preceded by a cause, just as from the conceptual truth that every husband must have a wife it does not follow that every man must be married.

The demolition of these arguments in the *Treatise* must have filled many readers with admiration; we have the spectacle of a young David Hume confronting the philosophical giants of his age and dealing them mortal blows in rapid succession. But what is remarkable is Hume's coyness in revealing the identity of his illustrious opponents: their names are dropped one by one in separate footnotes added to the relevant arguments, without the slightest indication where in their vast writings his reported arguments are to be found. The matter was

noticed by Green and Grose, who seem to have been the first to supply
the missing references.[2] That was in 1874; other references have since
been offered by Hendel,[3] by Laird,[4] and more recently by Watkins[5]
and Ferguson.[6]

The aim of this paper is to show that none of the accused philosophers
is guilty. Hume's three opponents certainly upheld the principle of
causality, but (with the possible exception of Clarke) not as a logically
necessary truth. Rather they regarded it as an ultimate metaphysical
truth about the whole universe: they did not attempt to derive it from
anything more basic, and could not consistently have done so.

Accordingly we shall find upon examination, that every reference
suggested on behalf of Hume is either mistaken or irrelevant. The
havoc will be more conveniently made through an imaginary dialogue,
in which the real Hobbes, Clarke and Locke are jointly interviewed by
a present-day critic. Our Critic is a professional philosopher who has
just completed a research paper on the Mystery of the Footnotes, and is
very glad of the opportunity to discuss his findings with Hume's real
opponents.

Critic: The first charge is laid against Mr Hobbes, who is reported
by Hume to have argued as follows:

> All the points of time and place, . . . in which we can suppose any
> object to begin to exist, are in themselves equal; and unless there
> be some cause, which is peculiar to one time and to one place, and
> which by that means determines and fixes the existence, it must
> remain in eternal suspence; and the object can never begin to be,
> for want of something to fix its beginning. (*Treatise*, p. 80)

I have been able, with the help of Green and Grose, to track down the
argument in Hobbes's writings. It occurs in an essay entitled 'My
Opinion about Liberty and Necessity', where Hobbes asserts eight
propositions, of which the sixth reads:

> Sixthly, I conceive that nothing taketh beginning from itself, but
> from the action of some other immediate agent without itself.
> (*EW*[7] iv, p. 274)

His 'reason' for upholding this position is given a couple of pages later.

> Also the sixth point, that a man cannot imagine anything to begin
> *without a cause*, can no other way be made known, but by trying
> how he can imagine it; but if he try, he shall find as much reason,
> if there be no cause of the thing, to conceive it should begin at one
> time as another, that he hath equal reason to think it should begin
> at all times, which is impossible, and therefore he must think
> there was some special cause why it began then, rather than
> sooner or later; or else that it began never, but was *eternal*. (ibid.,
> p. 276)

As far as I can see, Hume's account is a moderately good rendering of this argument.

Hobbes: I can see no resemblance whatsoever between the two arguments you have reproduced. For one thing, Hume states his premises in terms of space ('place') and time, whereas my reasoning has to do with time alone. As well, Hume derives an absurdity, which nowhere figures in my own argument, namely that the object would never begin to exist at all but must 'remain in eternal suspense'.

Critic: But these are trifling alterations. Frankly, I think they yield an improved version of your argument without seriously distorting it. Indeed, your actual argument could have served Hume's purpose equally well, for it is open to the same telling objection that Hume levelled against his own reformulation of it.

To show this, let p stand for the proposition that a cause is necessary for fixing the time or place at which an object begins to exist, and q for the proposition that every object that begins to exist has a cause. Then both your actual argument and Hume's version of it have the same crucial part, which may be restated thus: It is obvious that p entails q; hence if q were false p would be false; but, it is assumed, p cannot be false (its falsity is 'intuitively absurd'); hence q cannot be false either, and must be a logical truth.

Hume found this argument question-begging, and to my mind he was quite right. For, since p entails q, their logical status must be the same ('they are both upon the same footing'): either both propositions are necessary or neither is. Hence it is illegitimate to assume that one of them is a necessary truth in order to show that the other is (*Treatise*, pp. 80–2).

Hobbes: So according to Hume, I attempted to prove that q, the causal maxim, is a logical truth by deducing it from p, and taking it for granted that p is a logical truth. But in point of fact I never held this maxim to be a logically necessary truth: it is for me an ultimate law of nature, and, as I pointed out in *De Corpore*, ultimate principles 'cannot be demonstrated' and 'need no demonstration, though they need explication' (*E W* i, pp. 80–1).[8]

However, it strikes me that your reconstruction does not do justice even to the Hume-reported argument. For you omit what looks like an important premise, namely that 'all the points of time and place' are 'equal'.

Critic: I am not sure how to take the alleged premise. The 'points' are, of course, 'equal' in magnitude since they are either extensionless or durationless, but how is this relevant to the conclusion? A more plausible rendering would be that space and time are causally neutral ('indifferent'): which is the stipulation that spaces and times do not count as causes. But this is compatible with both determinism and in-determinism.

Hobbes: Actually, within my system, your first interpretation is in-admissible. For what I call a 'point of time' (or an 'instant') is not an indivisible durationless moment, but any finite interval of time taken as an undivided whole; and similarly with 'points of place' (see *E W* i, p. 206). Hence it would have been an arrant contradiction for me to assert that all the points of time and place are equal in magnitude. It is significant that the assertion does not occur in that quoted passage of mine where I speak, not of 'points' being equal, but of a man having 'equal reason' (or 'as much reason') to imagine one situation as another.

Indeed what I say in that passage was not intended to be a deductive proof of the causal maxim at all; that would have been to abandon my belief that it is an ultimate principle. Rather, it offers as a 'reason' what some recent writers would call an 'epistemic justification', a notion which may be illustrated by means of a simple example. Suppose I were to say 'I know that there is a ladder outside this window', and were asked how I knew this. I might then answer: 'Because I have seen it', or 'Because I have been told that there is one by some reliable person who has seen it'. In either case my answer would be an epistemic justification for my claim to know that there is a ladder outside the window.[9] It constitutes the 'evidence' for my claim, and, notoriously, such evidence (almost) always falls logically short of what one claims to know.

Now we have a similar situation here. The two passages you have quoted occur in an essay in which I try to reconcile liberty with causal necessity. At *E W* iv, p. 274, I express my *conviction* that the principle of causality is true (and please note that where I say 'I conceive that . . .' I mean 'I maintain, or am convinced, that . . .', a sense of 'conceive' which is now considered obsolete[10]). Anyone who questions my claim to know this is offered an epist emicjustification, which in the present case brings out an important fact about the imagination. I would para-phrase that passage from *E W* iv, p. 276, as follows. If you try to imagine an object O beginning to exist at a certain time t without a cause, you will find your imagination incapable of executing the task. Now in my view the idea of time is parasitic upon the idea of change and succes-sion;[11] so that the idea of pure time, absolutely empty yet with fixed temporal positions for objects to occupy, is nonsensical. Thus your mental picture would contain no item corresponding to the time t un-less it contained, beside the object O, at least some other discernibly different object O' immediately prior and contiguous to O in a succes-sive series of changing objects; but then your picture would be larger than it is supposed to be. If the mental picture is confined to O alone, it will be compatible with O having started at any other time *t'* before or after *t*, or even with O being eternal and thus having started at *no* time at all. The point is that your mental picture, if it were adequate, *ought* to exclude these alternatives, but it cannot.

It is surprising that Hume, whose views on time and space were similar to mine,[12] did not appreciate my point. But I must remind you that my views on causation are rather different from his: this is a matter of fact which is easily cleared and ascertained.[13]

Critic: I realise that. But before we leave Hume's first argument I wish to sound Dr Clarke about the suggestion that *he* used it in his Second Reply to Leibniz.[14]

Clarke: It should be plain to any reader of that *Correspondence* that I never quarrelled with Leibniz over the truth of the principle of causality (or 'sufficient reason' as he would say), which we both regarded as ultimate. What I objected to was his view that even the actions of God are subject to it, that God never acts without a rational motive. I thought it very presumptuous of him to provide answers on behalf of God.

Critic: Do you mean to say that you never *ever* offered a proof of the principle of causality? I confess I have not been able to find anything like Hume's second argument in your famous *Demonstration*.[15] Its peculiar premise, however, does occur under your Proposition III, where you say that 'to be produced by itself' is 'an express contradiction'.[16] You do not say why; but earlier you had asserted that the cause must have existed before;[17] so the contradiction presumably consists in the thing's having existed before it began to exist.

Clarke: No, I had a different reason in mind. I regard causality as a relation between non-identical ('external') objects; hence to speak of an object as producing itself implies that it is both itself and not itself, which is 'an express contradiction'.

Unlike Locke and Hume, I do not want to say that a cause must always precede its effect. But I do insist that whatever exists contingently must have an 'external' cause, even if it were eternal, in which case its external cause could not precede it but would be co-eternal with it.[18] This enabled me to confute those atheists who opposed the Christian doctrine of the creation by maintaining that the material world is an eternal series of finite beings in succession, and therefore had no beginning. To which I replied *ad hominem* that, even so, the entire chain, taken together, would exist contingently; for 'where no part is necessary . . . the whole cannot be necessary'.[19] The entire chain would thus require another independent, non-contingent being as its external cause, and so there is at least one eternal 'immutable and independent being'.[20]

I call such a being 'self-existent', or 'necessary', by which I mean 'a being the supposition of whose non-existence is an express contradiction'.[21] And to avoid possible misunderstanding I went on to explain that 'to be self-existent' is not the same as 'to be produced by itself': the latter is a self-contradictory notion, but the former is not.[22]

Critic: You seem to equate causal independence with logical necessity, and so infer that only what is logically necessary is uncaused. But I will not pursue this point.

Some commentators believe that what you did produce was the third argument, which Hume actually ascribed to Locke.[23] They have in mind the following passage in your Proposition I:

... It is ... certain that *something has existed from all eternity*. ... For since something now is, it is manifest that something always was. Otherwise [i.e. if there had ever been nothing] the things that now are [or what they arose from] must have risen out of nothing, absolutely and without cause. Which is a flat contradiction in terms; for to say a thing is produced, and yet that there is no cause at all of that production, is to say that something is *effected* when it is *effected by nothing*, that is, at the same time when it is *not effected at all*. Whatever exists has a cause of its existence: either in the necessity of its own nature, and then it must have been eternal; or in the will of some other being, and then that other being must ... have existed before it.[24]

Clearly this does not contain anything like Hume's third argument. 'Nothing' is in no way reified, or considered and rejected as a possible kind of cause; and 'effected by nothing' is immediately equated with 'not effected at all'. What the passage *does* contain is Hume's fourth, unascribed argument. Here you fallaciously infer from 'whatever is *effected* must have a cause' that 'whatever *exists* has a cause'. For some cause or reason Hume did not ascribe this argument to you.

Clarke: But surely the conclusion of my reasoning is not the causal maxim but Proposition I, which appears in italics *over* it.

Critic: But equally you end up with the causal maxim, which appears without italics *under* it.

Hobbes: You are both right and both wrong. Dr Clarke fails to observe the distinction that I draw between 'demonstrating' and 'explicating', and often uses the term 'showing' to mean either. The result is that our Critic takes him to be demonstrating the causal maxim, when in fact he is merely explicating causality by pointing out that what we call an effect must be something *other than* its cause. 'To be effected but by nothing' is therefore rightly pronounced a contradiction in terms, on a par with 'to be a husband but of nobody'.

Setting aside this 'explication' (or conceptual remark) on causality, I can extract from Dr Clarke's passage two distinct demonstrative arguments to the same conclusion, both relying on the causal maxim. The first is a *modus ponens*: If something begins to exist it must have as its cause something else which existed before it; something (the universe) now exists; therefore something has always existed. The second argument is a *reductio*: Whatever begins to exist must have been preceded by a cause; suppose there was empty time (with 'nothing' in it) before the universe began; then the universe must have begun without a prior cause, which yields a contradiction; therefore something has existed from all eternity.

Locke: Actually, I advanced the same two arguments in my *Essay Concerning Human Understanding*, where the *modus ponens* argument is given at IV.x.3, and the *reductio* at IV.x.8. The *reductio* form of the argument was added in order to refute any atheist who believed in the spontaneous generation of the world out of nothing.

I thought this proved the existence of an eternal Being; but as Leibniz later pointed out, my argument was a failure. That something has always existed is another way of saying that there was no time in which nothing existed; but from this it does not follow that there has always been a certain thing, an eternal Being.[25]

Clarke: I surmounted the difficulty by insisting, as you saw, that even a perpetual chain of contingent beings requires as an ultimate cause a necessary being.

Locke: I am not at all convinced. I reject the notion of a necessary being, and hold that no idea of ours guarantees the real existence of anything answering to it: 'the real existence of a God', like the real existence of anything else, 'can only be proved by the real existence of other things'.[26]

Critic: The assertion that nothing cannot be a cause certainly figures prominently in these two sections of your *Essay*; indeed Hume even reproduces your enigmatic statement (in section 3) that 'nothing can no more produce any real being than it can be equal to two right angles'. This has led to the suggestion that Hume's third argument is based on these two sections.[27]

Locke: I never pretended to prove that whatever begins to exist must have a cause—which I took to be an ultimate principle. It is true that in a letter to Stillingfleet I said that 'we *come to know*' this proposition by 'perceiving' that the idea of a beginning is necessarily connected with the idea of being caused; but this was intended to be an epistemic justification, not a proof.[28]

Critic: So by 'nothing' you meant empty time. I think I can now see the point of that 'nothing' statement of yours. It emphasises a conceptual truth; or if you like, it exposes a category-mistake. It is as nonsensical to suggest that empty time produces an object as to equate empty time with two right angles: only time-occupants count as causes, only angles can be equated with angles.

In general, I am inclined to think that since Hume omitted these arguments in the first *Enquiry*, he must by then have come to realise that he had misrepresented you all in the *Treatise*: otherwise, I can see no good reason for their wholesale omission.

Clarke: That cannot be true of me. Many years later Hume discussed my own version of the cosmological argument in his *Dialogues*; but the proponent of the argument, Demea, gets it wrong from the start.[29] Instead of treating the causal maxim as an assumed premise, Demea starts with a proof of it identical with the one which Hume attributed to me earlier in the *Treatise*.[30] In any case, why did Hume misrepresent us all in the *Treatise*?

Critic: I think two important factors have emerged from our discussion. The first is his failure to distinguish conceptual remarks from substantive claims. The second is his tendency, contrary to all just reasoning, to impose his own position upon his opponents. After all, his opponents did not all share his view that 'all causes are of the same kind',[31] nor did they all wish to confine the causal maxim to what *begins* to exist. And yet his refutations have been widely admired, while his misrepresentations have passed almost totally unnoticed for more than two hundred years.[32]

1.   *A Treatise of Human Nature*, pp. 78–82. Page references are to the Selby-Bigge edition (Oxford 1888).

2.   *The Philosophical Works of David Hume*, ed. T. H. Green and T. H. Grose (London, new edition, 1886; reprinted by Scientia, Aalen 1964) vol. I, pp. 381–2; first published in 1874–5. The references are added by the editors in square brackets to the three footnotes in which Hume names his three opponents.

3.   Charles W. Hendel *Studies in the Philosophy of David Hume*, second edition (New York: Bobbs-Merrill 1963) p. 60 n. and p. 61 n.; first published in 1925.

4.   John Laird *Hume's Philosophy of Human Nature* (London: Methuen 1932) pp. 97–8.

5.   J. W. N. Watkins *Hobbes's System of Ideas* (London: Hutchinson 1965) p. 43 n. Watkins' conjecture that Hume's first argument was actually used by Hobbes in *De Corpore* is no doubt an inadvertency. For he insists throughout his book that Hobbes regarded the causal maxim as an ultimate, and hence unprovable, principle.

6.   James P. Ferguson *The Philosophy of Dr. Samuel Clarke and Its Critics* (New York: Vantage Press 1974) p. 114. The same inadvertency occurs

in this book. The author says, on the one hand, that for Clarke 'the necessity by which a cause determines its effect' is not logical but 'physical or natural' (pp. 168–9); but, on the other hand, he concedes (p. 114) that Hume was right in attributing to Clarke an argument that purported to establish the principle to be a logically necessary truth; only, Ferguson identifies that argument as the third rather than the second of the Hume-reported arguments.

7.   *The English Works of Thomas Hobbes,* 11 volumes, ed. Sir William Molesworth (London 1839–45; reprinted by Scientia, Aalen 1962), hereafter referred to as *EW*.
8.   cf. F. Brandt *Thomas Hobbes' Mechanical Conception of Nature* (Copenhagen 1928) especially pp. 267–8.
9.   See J. L. Mackie *Problems from Locke* (Oxford 1976) pp. 217, 220.
10.   See *O.E.D.,* s.v. CONCEIVE, Sense 11*b*, with an illustration from Hobbes (1651).
11.   Hobbes adopts a subjectivist view of time saying that it is 'not in the things without us, but only in the thought of the mind'. Hence he defines time as 'the phantasm of before and after in motion'; here he is deliberately amending Aristotle's famous definition of time as 'the number of motion according to former and latter'. (*EW* i, pp. 94–5.)
12.   See *Treatise* I. ii. 3.
13.   See especially *De Corpore, EW* i, pp. 91–132.
14.   See *The Leibniz–Clarke Correspondence,* ed. H. G. Alexander (Manchester University Press 1956) pp. 20–1.
15.   Samuel Clarke *A Demonstration of the Being and Attributes of God.* References throughout are to the first edition (London 1705); facsimile reprint by Friedrich Frommann Verlag (Stuttgart-Bad Cannstatt 1964). The work is based on a course of Boyle Lectures which Clarke delivered as sermons at St Paul's Cathedral in 1704.
16.   *Demonstration,* Proposition III, p. 28.
17.   Proposition I, p. 19.
18.   Proposition III, pp. 27–8; Proposition II, p. 26, cf. Proposition X, p. 187.
19.   Proposition II, p. 25.
20.   Proposition II, *passim.*
21.   Proposition III, p. 30.
22.   Proposition III, p. 28.
23.   The view is held by both Laird and Ferguson; see notes 4 and 6 above.
24.   *Demonstration,* Proposition I, pp. 18–19. Words in square brackets have been added to spell out the argument.
25.   G. W. Leibniz *New Essays Concerning Human Understanding,* trans. A. G. Langley, third edition (Open Court 1949) pp. 500–1.
26.   For this reason Locke rejected the ontological argument in a paper entitles *Deus* written in 1696; quoted by R. I. Aaron *John Locke,* second edition (Oxford University Press 1955) p. 242.
27.   The suggestion is made by Green and Grose, Hendel, and Laird; see notes 2–4.
28.   First Letter to Stillingfleet; see *The Works of John Locke,* 10 volumes (London 1823; reprinted by Scientia, Aalen 1963) vol. IV, pp. 61–2.
29.   *Dialogues Concerning Natural Religion,* Part IX, para. 3.
30.   Demea starts by saying, 'Whatever exists must have a cause . . . of its existence, *it being absolutely impossible for anything to produce itself*'.

31. *Treatise* I. iii. 14 (p. 171). Hume considers this to be a 'corollary' of his
     own analysis of causation given in this section, yet he took it for granted
     eleven sections earlier.

32. This is an extensively revised version of a paper read by E. J. Khamara at
     the Hume Conference, held in Edinburgh on 9–14 August 1976. We are
     grateful to Professor D. D. Raphael and Mr Knud Haakonssen for many
     valuable suggestions.

Hume's Causal Scepticism

As Is Often Remarked, it is easy to find inconsistencies in Hume's philosophy by comparing one passage with another. But of the apparent inconsistencies, the most blatant occurs when Hume sums up his analysis of causation with 'a precise definition of cause and effect' (T169).[1] He says a cause is

> D1 An object precedent and contiguous to another, and where all the objects resembling the former are plac'd in like relations of precedency and contiguity to those objects, that resemble the latter (T170)

And, in addition,

> D2 A CAUSE is an object precedent and contiguous to another, and so united with it, that the idea of the one determines the mind to form the idea of the other, and the impression of the one to form a more lively idea of the other (T170)

Hume says that D1 and D2 differ only 'by their presenting a different view of the same object' (T170). This seems to imply that causation is what D1 and D2 *both* define. But D1 and D2 refer to different sets of impressions and so define different ideas. If so, what can Hume possibly mean when he says that both are 'of the same object'? And what *is* his 'precise definition of cause and effect'?

The history of commentary on Hume on causation can be viewed as a response to this problem. One tradition opts for D1 and treats Hume as a proponent of the Uniformity Thesis: to say of something, a, that it is the cause of something else, b, is to say that when a occurs, b occurs contiguous with and successive to a and whenever anything relevantly similar to a occurs, 'no matter where or when, observed or unobserved,' something relevantly similar to b occurs.[2] On this view the focus of Hume's scepticism is the problem of induction: if we cannot distinguish causal from casual regularities, how can we justify inferring unobserved events from observed ones?

The other tradition opts for D2 and commits Hume to a subjectivist thesis: to say of something, a, that it is the cause of something else, b, is to say of some subject that that subject has a propensity to conceive of or to believe in the occurrence of b or something relevantly similar to b upon the perception of a or something similar to a.[3] On this view Hume's scepticism centres not on how we can determine when we have got an objective causal relation, but on how we can even say that there could be one. Since, it is claimed, causation 'involves the *necessity* of the connexion of the existence of different things',[4] and since, for Hume, the only relevant idea of necessity is derived from a mental propensity, any causal statement is either meaningless or a remark about some subject.

I shall argue that D1 and D2 are both definitions and are of the same kind,[5] but that neither is Hume's definition of the causal relation. In the *Treatise* at least Hume was concerned not with causation, but with causal judgments,[6] and to opt for D1 or D2 as his definition is thus to respond to a question Hume was not concerned to ask. We shall see that in giving D1 and D2 Hume is making a sceptical point about causation even more devastating to human pretensions than he has been thought to be making on either alternative. Let me begin with D2.

Pivotal to the case for D2 is Hume's claim that

> An object may be contiguous and prior to another, without being consider'd as its cause. There is a NECESSARY CONNEXION to be taken into consideration. (*T*77)

What this passage proves, it is claimed, is that for Hume

> causation is more than sequence, and more also than invariable sequence. We distinguish between mere sequence and causal sequence; and what differentiates the two is that the idea of necessitation (determination or agency) enters into the latter as a quite essential element.[7]

Unfortunately, all statements of the argument are as cryptic and curious as this one. 'Surely,' one wants to say, 'it is not the *idea* of necessitation that enters into the causal relation, but necessity itself.' But the argument's overall thrust seems clear enough. Hume claims that necessary connection is essential to any causal relation. Yet if we are to have any idea what it is, we must refer to the mind's determination in D2. Therefore, it is concluded, D2 is Hume's definition of causation.

Spelled out more fully, the argument comes to this:

(i) Contiguity and succession are essential relations in any causal relation (*T*75–6).[8]

(ii) Necessary connection is an essential relation in any causal relation (*T*77).

Hume offers no other relation or feature as essential before he gives D1 and D2. He must therefore think that

(iii) Only contiguity, succession, and necessary connection are essential in any causal relation.

But given that

(iv) The only idea we have of any necessary connection is derived from the impression of the mind's determination (*T*165),

(v) Any definition acceptable to Hume must refer to the impression or impressions from which the idea or all its component ideas are derived,

(vi) D2 is a definition that refers to impressions, and

(vii) D2 is the only definition that defines the causal relation by referring to the impressions and only the impressions of contiguity, succession, and the mind's determination,

it follows that

(viii) D2 is the only definition that defines the causal relation in terms of all and only those impressions Hume considers essential,

and that therefore,

(ix) D2 is Hume's definition of causation.

This argument is powerful. (i)–(iv) and (vii) seem well supported, and (v) and (vi), which may seem problematic, are true.[9] Let me begin with them.

At the beginning of the section 'Of the idea of necessary connexion' Hume rejects 'all the vulgar definitions' in which one term is defined by another 'nearly synonimous' in favour of what we may call a philosophical definition:

> instead of searching for the idea [of cause] in these definitions [in which cause is defined in terms of power, efficacy, etc.], [we] must look for it in the impressions, from which it is originally deriv'd. If it be a compound idea, it must arise from compound impressions. If simple, from simple impressions. ($T157$)

Hume implies he is defining the *idea* of cause and says he is defining it by referring to impressions. A philosophical definition is thus a real ostensive definition. In short, (v) is true, and we should expect D2 to be a philosophical definition.

And it is. The first clause states that 'A CAUSE is an object precedent and contiguous to another.' Hume's satisfaction that these relations are 'essential to that of causation,' after stating that he is 'examining [those] primary impression[s], from which it [the idea] arises,' implies that he thinks we have impressions of those relations ($T75-76$).[10] But there is another clause in D2. A cause, a, and an effect, b, are 'so united,' Hume says, 'that the idea of the one determines the mind to form the idea of the other, and the impression of the one to form a more lively idea of the other.' Thus, a is the cause of b only if there is a determination of the mind upon the perception of a to have an idea of or belief in b.[11] Hume identifies the determination as 'an internal impression' ($T165$), and D2 thus defines the idea of cause in terms of a set of three impressions: the *succession* of a and b, the *contiguity* of a and b, and the mind's *determination* to conceive of or believe in the occurrence of b upon the perception of a.[12]

To equate the determination with an impression is to mis-identify elements of the mind's structure as its content.[13] But one can understand how Hume boxed himself into this mistake. He thinks we infer effects from causes. When he hunts for an explanation for this, he finds that he must appeal to the mind's response to the world: the mind is so structured as to develop a propensity which, when activated by the perception of a or an object similar to a, determines the mind to conceive of, or believe in, the occurrence of b or an object similar to b. That propensity is the connecting link of our inferences, and it is not within our control: the mind does not determine, it is determined. Since it is not within our control, and since Hume thinks that we have an idea of necessity and that every idea is derived from some precedent impression, it is understandable that he should say there is no 'impression, which has any relation to the present business, but that propensity . . .' (T165). Hume's philosophical discoveries have at this point outrun his classificatory machinery—and the principles of his empiricism. One may well regret Hume's failure to realize this, but since we are concerned to understand his giving two definitions of 'the same object', we ought to constrain our interpretation by his mistakes. Given his mis-identification and theory of definition, D2 is a definition.

An apparent difficulty with it is that, as Kemp Smith puts it, ' "determination" is here more or less synonymous with causation' and this

> is one of the reasons why his definition of causation, as a natural relation, does not amount to a definition in the strict logical sense. It is in the main ostensive.[14]

This is incredible. To claim that D2 is not a definition because it is 'in the main ostensive' is to miss Hume's attack on vulgar definitions. It is not the *word* 'determination' that figures in D2, but the impression. Hume thinks we know what a cause is, in sense D2, because we are acquainted with the impressions that make up that complex idea. He may be mistaken about that, but D2 *is* a definition and a non-circular one by the only standard that counts, namely Hume's. In short, premise (vi) is true.

Each premise of the textual argument for D2 is thus either true or well-supported, and the argument is valid. But there are compelling reasons for denying the conclusion. Thus Hume says that the constant conjunction of similar objects cannot by itself produce 'the idea of power,' but that

> the *observation* of this resemblance produces a new impression *in the mind*, . . . This determination is the only effect of the resemblance; . . . (T165)

This says that observation *causes* the determination in D2. But this new causal relation cannot be the relation defined in D2. A condition necessary for the existence of the causal relation cannot be the causal relation itself.

Hume might have inadvertently committed himself to the existence of another kind of causal relation in giving D2. But in fact he explicitly rejects D2. He says that 'it is impossible to give any just definition of cause, except what is drawn from something extraneous and foreign to it' (*E*75; see *T*170). What is needed for a definition not 'drawn from circumstances foreign to the cause,' Hume says, is

> that circumstance in the cause, which gives it a connexion with its effect. We have no idea of this connexion, nor even any distinct notion what it is we desire to know, when we endeavour at a conception of it. (*E*77)

The determination in D2 does provide a connection. What it connects, however, is not a cause with its effect, but a *perception* of a cause with a conception of or belief in the occurrence of its effect. It is the wrong kind of connection; it is necessary for its existence that the mind observe the relations of contiguity and succession holding between similar objects 'in a sufficient number of instances' (*T*165), and that the mind react to that observation by producing it. What is foreign in D2 is thus that natural relation. D2 makes it a condition of something causing something else that a mind observe and react to what it observes. That Hume does not accept such a condition is clear from his claiming that there are 'secret [i.e., unobserved] causes'.[15]

This leaves us with a puzzle and with D1. The puzzle is what is wrong with the textual argument for D2. No premise has been put in doubt, the argument is valid, and yet the conclusion is false. Let me begin, however, with D1. It does not suffer from one difficulty afflicting D2: Hume explicitly says of the relations in D1 that they are philosophical (*T*168).

Is D1 A PHILOSOPHICAL definition? The first clause is the same as that of D2. The second says that 'all the objects resembling the former [the cause] are plac'd in like relations of precedency and contiguity to those objects, that resemble the latter'. For those who think Hume committed to the Uniformity Thesis this is read as saying that *a* is the cause of *b* only if there is *invariable* conjunction. This reading is *prima facie* plausible, for Hume does say '*all* the objects resembling the former'. But the evidence is that he does not mean what he seems to say.

In explication of the second clause he wants, he says, to 'consider the influence of this constant conjunction' (*T*170). The implication is that he means to refer to constant conjunction in the second clause. But when he introduces 'this new-discover'd relation' he says it 'implies no more than this, that like objects *have* always *been plac'd* in like relations of contiguity and succession' (*T*87–8, my italics). This restriction to past cases is repeated at least twice (*T*89–90; see *T*93). Since Hume refers to constant conjunction in explication of D1, the natural assumption is that he means to refer only to *observed* conjunctions—despite talking of 'all objects resembling the former'.

A possible explanation for his talk lies in his theory of philosophical relations and his claim that they come into existence only if the mind compares the relata (*T*13–14; see esp. *T*46). But I think that Hume's theory is a quagmire, and although there is more solid ground in his theory of abstract ideas, it is too complex to examine here. It is enough for now to counter the plausibility of arguing merely from his choice of words, and then to offer evidence for what he does mean.

Is D1 a philosophical definition if Hume refers to constant conjunction? Each time we see objects similar to *a* and *b* conjoined, we have an impression of their conjunction. But we can remember only past conjunctions, and memories, Hume says, are ideas (*T*9). Our idea of constant conjunction is thus derived from other ideas and not from impressions alone.[16] Yet D1 does not define an idea in terms of other ideas 'nearly synonymous.' The ideas in terms of which it defines cause are components of the complex—as impressions would be; and although D1 may be thought a looser fit than D2, it is just what one would expect of a real ostensive definition in which one must define in terms of what is past. D1 is thus a philosophical definition.

Since D2 is not the definition of the causal relation, D1 must be if Hume gives any, since he gives no other. And, it is argued, there is textual evidence for D1. When Hume says at *T*77 that 'there is a NECESSARY CONNEXION to be taken into consideration,' he has just remarked that contiguity and succession are not sufficient. Constant conjunction has not been introduced; when it is introduced he says that

> Contiguity and succession are not sufficient to make us pronounce any two objects to be cause and effect, unless we perceive, that these two relations are preserv'd in several instances. We may now see the advantage of quitting the direct survey of this relation, in order to discover the nature of that *necessary connexion*, which makes so essential a part of it. (*T*87)

What this shows, it is argued, is that invariable conjunction is 'the sought-for missing condition which was needed to provide, with [contiguity and succession], a *sufficient* condition for *x* to cause *y*, and therefore to provide an analysis of the extra element of necessitation which was lacking when [contiguity and succession] alone had been adduced earlier'.[17] The claim is that premise (iv) of the textual argument for D2 is false.

But, firstly, Hume does not say that constant conjunction *is* 'that necessary connexion'. He says that constant conjunction will help us '*discover* the nature of that *necessary connexion*'. He thus goes on to show how the observation of constant conjunction produces a kind of necessary connection, namely, the determination in D2. Secondly, and more importantly, Hume is not saying that two things *are* causally related if we observe the relations 'preserv'd in several instances'. He makes the far weaker claim that the perception of the preservation 'in several instances' is 'sufficient to make us *pronounce* any two objects to be cause and effect'. The conditions for *making us assert* (*or think*) that *a* is a cause have been mistaken for the conditions for its *being a cause*. Hume is concerned here with causal judgments, not causation.

The textual argument for D1 thus fails. No argument can succeed. For *a* is a cause in sense D1 only if objects similar to *a have, as a matter of fact, been conjoined* 'in a sufficient number of instances' with objects similar to *b*. But Hume thinks it is logically possible for a cause to occur but once, and D1 thus cannot be the definition of cause. Besides, the textual difficulties that attend D2 attend D1 as well. If D1 were Hume's definition, we could not explain his saying of both that they are 'drawn from objects foreign to the cause' (*T*170) or explain why he calls for a 'circumstance in the cause, which gives it a connexion with its effect' (*E*77). There is no connection in D1.

IN GIVING D1 AND D2 Hume is distinguishing, in any situation we call causal, the objective conditions and what is added by the mind. D1 states what is objective, but gives no connection, and D2 gives a connection, but one consequent to and dependent upon the mind. Neither gives an objective necessity. One consequence is the problem of induction: without an objective connection, we cannot distinguish causal from casual regularities. Another consequence is that whenever we call one object a cause and another an effect, what we say is meaningless: we have no impression that can be the source of the idea of an objective connection.

But these sceptical points do not exhaust Hume's causal scepticism. Hume's claim that 'there is a NECESSARY CONNEXION to be taken into consideration' is not a claim that a cause and its effect are necessarily connected, but a claim about what we *suppose* whenever there are 'two objects, which we call cause and effect' (*T*75). What we suppose is a 'circumstance in the cause, which gives it a connexion with its effect' (*E*77). This is not a supposition we can give meaning to. Premise (ii) of the textual argument for D2 is thus meaningless. But Hume thinks we must make this supposition. We cannot help observing priority, contiguity, and constant conjunction in some cases as long as the world is intelligible to us, and when observed, these activate operations of the understanding. These operations are essential features of human nature ($T225$), and neither they nor their activation are within our control. It is the combination of the conditions and the operations which produces propensities, and these plus some unarticulated factors 'make us pronounce any two objects to be cause and effect'. We are thus made to suppose the existence of something of which we have no idea, and we cannot help making that supposition as long as we remain human and the world remains intelligible to us.

The sceptical issue is thus not simply how we can justify causal inferences, or how we can meaningfully say that there are objective causal relations, but how we can keep ourselves from supposing, meaninglessly, that there are such connections when we make causal inferences. Even philosophers who realize 'the falsehood of [the] vulgar sentiments, and discover that there is no known connexion among objects' are unable to prevent themselves from supposing the existence of an inconceivable connection ($T223$). They can change neither the world nor human nature. Their only recourse, Hume claims, is to turn 'back to the situation of the vulgar, and [regard] all these disquisitions with indolence and indifference ($T223$). Being human, they cannot cease making causal inferences and supposing a necessary connection, even after discovering that they have no idea what it is they are supposing. To think that they could would be to think that by doing philosophy a philosopher somehow ceases to be human, and only the vulgar have ever thought that.

1.   References to Hume have been put in the text. 'T' stands for the *Treatise* (Selby-Bigge edition), 'E' for the *Enquiry* (Selby-Bigge edition), and 'A' for *An Abstract of a Treatise of Human Nature* (Keynes and Sraffa edition, reprinted 1965, Archon Books). The letter is followed by the page number(s) so that $T169$ is to be read as *Treatise*, p. 169.

2.   J. A. Robinson 'Hume's Two Definitions of "Cause"' *Philosophical Quarterly* XII (1962); reprinted, with 'Hume's Two Definitions of "Cause" Reconsidered', in *Hume*, ed. V. C. Chappell (Garden City: Anchor Books 1966). References are to the Chappell volume. See pp. 138–9, 142–3, and 144 for quotations supporting the position I sketch. As I have sketched it, the Uniformity Thesis differs from Robinson's formulation in at least two ways. Firstly, he claims that spatial contiguity is an essential element of any causal relation. The formulation I have given does not specify whether it is spatial or temporal contiguity or both that is necessary. In fact, I do not think Hume thinks spatial contiguity is essential. When he introduces it, he says 'we may . . . *consider* [it] as essential . . .; at least . . . till we can find a more proper occasion to clear up this matter, by examining what objects are or are not susceptible of juxtaposition and conjunction' ($T75$). He then goes on in Part IV, §5 to claim

that some perceptions are not susceptible of spatial relations even though they are susceptible of causal relations. Robinson's formulation thus holds of only *some* causal relata. He has been misled in part, I assume, by Hume's having pitched his entire examination in the *Treatise* around causal relata that are susceptible of spatial relations. Secondly, Robinson formulates the Uniformity Thesis by identifying the class of 'particular occurrences $x, x', x'', \ldots$, and the class $\ldots$ of particular occurrences $y, y', y'', \ldots$, [with] the *event X* and the *event Y'* and then claiming that the events X and Y are 'universally juxtaposed' (op. cit., p. 144). This amounts to claiming, on his analysis, that one class of occurrences always follows immediately after another class in the other's immediate vicinity. And this will not do. Hume holds that only particulars exist, and invariable conjunction is clearly not a relation that holds between a particular cause, a, and its effect, b. What Robinson has done is to scrounge around for some strange particulars as relata, and these are particulars that Hume, I think, would be ill-disposed to accept.

3. See Ralph W. Church *Hume's Theory of the Understanding* (London: Allen & Unwin 1968) pp. 81, 83, and 39 for quotations supporting the position I sketch. When I use 'a' and 'b' to stand for the relata of a causal relation, I mean to imply that the relata are particulars, but not that they are particular particulars—objects, events, perceptions, or what have you. Hume's analysis of the causal relation in the *Treatise* is of causal relations between 'objects' or, as he sometimes puts it, between impressions. He means us to remember when he is done that 'the ideas of cause and effect [are] deriv'd from the impressions of reflexion as well as those of sensation' and that therefore whatever he says 'of them may also extend to the former' (*T*78). In short, he says,

    > Passions are connected with their objects and with one another; no less than external bodies are connected together. The same relation, then, which belongs to one, must be common to all of them (*T*78).

4. Kant *The Critique of Practical Reason*, ed. T. K. Abbott (London: Longmans 1959) p. 140; see also p. 141.

5. Robert MacRae is an example of someone who denies that Hume has contradicted himself in giving two definitions of 'the same object' because two different kinds of definition of the same object are conceivable ('Hume on Meaning' *Dialogue* VIII (1968) 486–91). It is worth noting that MacRae's article is one of the few in the literature that has grown up from Robinson's original article that worries at all about what Hume means to do in giving a definition of something. Yet the apparent contradiction cannot even be properly formulated without first examining Hume's theory of definition and determining in what sense(s) D1 and D2 are meant to be definitions.

6. This claim must remain an *obiter dictum* in this paper. For a detailed analysis of Hume's theory in the *Treatise* see my 'David Hume: Naturalist and Meta-sceptic' in *Hume: A Re-evaluation*, ed. D. W. Livingston and J. T. King (New York: Fordham University Press 1976) pp. 23–49.

7. Norman Kemp Smith *The Philosophy of David Hume* (London: Macmillan & Co. 1960) pp. 91–2.

8. Let me note again that the relation of contiguity in D2 (and in D1 as well) is referred to ambiguously: it may cover temporal contiguity, spatial contiguity, or both. In fact it covers both, but that is only because Hume has

chosen, consciously and carefully, to examine the causal relation as it holds between relata susceptible of spatial relations. In the *Enquiry* this restriction is dropped, and for this reason the parallels there to D1 and D2 differ. If one fails to note this point one may be misled, as, e.g., was Selby-Bigge, into thinking that Hume has changed his position in some fundamental way (*Enquiry*, pp. xv–xvi).

9. (v) has actually been ignored in the literature. Robinson says of (vi): 'Definition (2), . . . is now seen not to be a definition at all, but simply a restatement of the proposition that the (already defined) cause-effect relation is a *natural* relation, in a somewhat elliptical formulation' (op. cit., p. 139). He goes on to claim that 'it is clearly an error on Hume's part to have offered it *as a definition*', but the error, I suggest, lies on Robinson's part: Hume is well aware of what he is doing in offering D2 as a definition.

10. There is an obvious difficulty here: how can we have an impression of time when time, by Hume's theory, is a succession of perceptions? This is a problem I shall ignore for the purposes of this paper, for it is a problem Hume seems not to have worried about. He apparently thought we could have an impression of succession.

11. The determination is not between the *idea* of *a* and the *idea* of *b*, as Robinson sometimes says (op. cit., pp. 136–7). It is between the *perception* of *a* and the idea of *b*. If the perception is an impression, then the idea of *b* is intense and so is a belief; if the perception is an idea, then the idea of *b* is simply an idea. The point is important not least because Hume carefully distinguishes the questions why we conceive an effect and why we believe an effect, calling the latter 'a new question unthought of by philosophers' (*A*17). But the point is also important because one may come to think that natural beliefs hold only between ideas and are, in that way, distinguished from philosophical beliefs.

12. This analysis of D2 will not do as it stands, although its failures do not affect my argument. Its failures are of two sorts. Firstly, I may have included more in D2 than should be included. It is not clear that Hume means, in D2, to define the causal relation in terms of the contiguity and succession of *a* and *b* as well as in terms of the natural relation of determination holding between the perception of *a* and the idea of *b*. He may simply want to define it in terms of the determination, the references to succession and contiguity being made to point out how it comes about that there is a determination. A reason for thinking this is that if contiguity and succession are included then there is a mixture of philosophical and natural relations in D2, whereas Hume says that he is there defining the causal relation as a natural relation and that D2 is meant to explain how it is that we make inferences; there is no need for reference to contiguity and succession for that explanation. An additional reason is the presence, in D2, of a phrase that I have left out of the analysis, namely, 'so united'. This is the second failure of the analysis. I read that as meaning that when *a* and *b* have been perceived to be contiguous and successive, *and when similar objects have been similarly conjoined*, then the determination of the mind occurs. If this reading is correct, Hume *is* referring to the causal conditions necessary for the creation of the determination and so probably not to essential features of the causal relation in sense D2. A reason for leaving out 'so united', though not for leaving out contiguity and succession, is that if it is omitted then D2 is true of a single causal relation. For, as

I shall argue, the difficulty with constant conjunction is that it is not a relation that can hold in single instances of the causal relation. Since I think that Hume is after what is true of a single causal relation, this is an additional reason for supposing that D2 ought really to refer to the single impression.

13. See Robert Paul Wolff 'Hume's Theory of Mental Activity' *The Philosophical Review* LXIX (1960) 289–310; reprinted in Chappell, op. cit., pp. 99–128; in Chappell, see esp. p. 112.

14. op. cit., p. 401. Kemp Smith's error is not an isolated instance. See also, e.g., John Passmore *Hume's Intentions* (London: Duckworth & Co. 1968) p. 76 and A. G. N. Flew 'Hume' in D. J. O'Connor (ed.) *A Critical History of Western Philosophy* (New York: Free Press 1964) pp. 263–4.

15. See, e.g., *E*39, 58, 87 for references to secret causes. An investigation of Hume's remarks in the *Treatise* on the probability of chances and causes shows that he thinks the judgment we sometimes make that something happened by chance is really a reflection of our ignorance of 'the secret operation of contrary causes' (*T*132; see *T*403–4). What is at issue is not whether Hume is justified in saying there are secret causes, but what his intentions are in regard to D1 and D2 given that he says there are.

16. Church claims that D1 cannot be the definition of causation because we cannot have an impression of constant conjunction: that is to 'mistake a repetition of impressions and ideas for an impression of repetition' (*Hume's Theory*, p. 85).

17. Robinson, op. cit., p. 144.

Hume on Self-Identity,
Memory and Causality

IN *Treatise* I.iv.6 ('Of Personal Identity') Hume presents a theory of
self-identity, in the sense of a theory designed to explain one's thinking
of oneself as identical through change. There are many deep obscurities
in this theory. It is far from clear what problem(s) Hume intends to
solve, and as a result there are many dark places in the solution Hume
proposes to his problem(s). But the following brief account, in Hume's
own words, should permit my investigation to get underway. One's
mind is 'nothing but a bundle or collection of different perceptions,
which succeed each other with an inconceivable rapidity, and are in a
perpetual flux and movement' (p. 252). Given this, it is necessary to
explain why we have 'so great a propension to ascribe an identity to
these successive perceptions, and to suppose ourselves possest of an invariable and uninterrupted existence thro' the whole course of our
lives' (p. 253). '[I]dentity', he says, 'is nothing really belonging to
these different perceptions and uniting them together; but is merely a
quality, which we attribute to them, because of the union of their ideas
in the imagination, when we reflect upon them' (p. 260). Given this
'the only question . . . which remains, is, by what relations this uninterrupted progress of our thought is produc'd, when we consider the
successive existence of a mind or thinking person' (p. 260). Hume
answers this question by invoking the relations of resemblance and
causality.

I shall display two difficulties in this theory of self-identity, one having to do with memory and resemblance, the other with causality. I
certainly would not claim that these are the only, or the most important,
difficulties in the theory. But they have not, I believe, been noted elsewhere, and they have the virtue of drawing our attention to certain
aspects of Hume's general theory of mind that have often gone unnoticed and sometimes been denied. I have in mind certain aspects of
his views about introspective awareness and about the relations between
mind and body.

Hume's explanation of mental identity in terms of resemblance
appears in a single paragraph devoted largely to the case of other minds:

To begin with *resemblance*; suppose we cou'd see clearly into the
breast of another, and observe that succession of perceptions, which
constitutes his mind or thinking principle, and suppose that he

always preserves the memory of a considerable part of past perceptions; 'tis evident that nothing cou'd more contribute to the
bestowing a relation on this succession amidst all its variations.
For what is the memory but a faculty, by which we raise up the
images of past perceptions? And as an image necessarily resembles
its object, must not the frequent placing of these resembling perceptions in the chain of thought, convey the imagination more
easily from one link to another, and make the whole seem like the
continuance of one object? In this particular, then, the memory
not only discovers the identity, but also contributes to its production, by producing the relation of resemblance among the perceptions. (pp. 260–1)

Having said this, Hume remarks, simply: 'The case is the same whether
we consider ourselves or others' (p. 261). His point seems to be that
what goes on when one thinks of one's own identity parallels what
would occur in thinking about the identity of another person if one
were able to 'see into his breast'. To be sure, this is a very curious way
to proceed. One can only conjecture that Hume thought his explanation
would be somehow more perspicuous if worked out first for a third-
person case.

I shall overlook the obvious difficulties with Hume's procedure and
with the supposition on which it rests. What is important for my present
purpose is that we get clear about the picture that controls Hume's
discussion. For the third-person case the picture is this. One person
(call him the *observer*) notices a resemblance between certain past and
present perceptions had by another person (call him the *subject*). The
resemblance in question is specifically that between the subject's
present recollection and the past perception the subject recalls. Upon
noticing this resemblance the observer comes to view the subject's
perceptions as 'the continuance of one object', comes to view the subject
as identical through change. This, of course, requires both that the
observer be aware of the subject's present recollection and that the
observer himself recall the subject's past perception. For the simplest
case, then, four perceptions are involved: two belong to the subject (his
past perception; his present recollection of that past perception); two
are the observer's (his awareness of the subject's present recollection;
his recollection of the subject's past perception).

Distinguishing between the subject's and the observer's recollection
of the subject's past perception does, I think, help us to understand
Hume's somewhat obscure remark that 'memory not only discovers the
identity, but also contributes to its production' (p. 261). Hume says
that memory 'contributes to its [the identity's] production, by producing the relation of resemblance among the perceptions' (p. 261). I take

this to mean that since a memory resembles the perception recalled, memory provides the resemblance, the noticing of which gives rise to the thought of the identity. He explains the meaning of 'memory . . . discovers the identity' when he discusses self-identity based on causality: 'In this view, therefore, memory does not so much *produce* as *discover* personal identity, by shewing us the relation of cause and effect among our different perceptions' (p. 262). I take this to mean that only if one recalls a past perception can one notice its causal connection with present perceptions, and thus be in a position to think of the successive perceptions as one object.[1] If this is Hume's meaning, however, it is clear that memory must play its discovering role *whatever* relation between successive perceptions is in question, and thus for the case of resemblance as well as for that of causality. But if this is so it can be only the *subject's* memory which 'produces' personal identity, and the *observer's* memory which 'discovers' it. For it is the subject's memory that provides the necessary resemblance, the observer's memory that enables the observer to note the resemblance.

Now, if this picture is applied to the case of *self*-identity (and if it is not, of course, Hume has offered no explanation of self-identity), the consequences are fairly obvious. Basically, a distinction must be drawn between the self as subject and the self as (self-)observer. More precisely, a distinction must be drawn between those resembling perceptions that provide the basis for one's judgment of self-identity and those perceptions that in some way constitute one's awareness of the former perceptions and of their resemblance to one another. Once again four perceptions are needed. As subject one must both have had a past perception and (now) recall that past perception; as self-observer one must (now) be aware of the subject's present recollection of some past perception *and* one must (now) recall that past perception. It is one's perceptions as subject that 'produce' the thought of one's identity by providing the resemblance upon which this thought is based. It is one's perceptions as self-observer that constitute the awareness of these resembling perceptions. As self-observer one comes to view oneself as a subject identical through change.

This, I take it, is Hume's uncompromisingly third-person picture of one's awareness of one's own identity through change. It must be admitted that Hume does not draw out the implications of his picture in this explicit way. His whole discussion of the topic is much too cursory for that. Despite John Laird, however, Hume does make it fairly plain that he accepts the central distinction between having a perception and being aware of that perception.[2] (The distinction between the subject's recalling a past perception and the self-observer's awareness of this recollection would be a special case of this distinction.)

He asks 'whether it [identity] be something that really binds *our several perceptions* together, or only associates *their ideas* in the imagination' (p. 259, my italics) and adopts the latter alternative. He says that identity 'is merely a quality which we attribute to *them* ['these different perceptions'], because of the union of *their ideas* in the imagination, *when we reflect upon them*' (p. 260, my italics). And in the 'Appendix' discussion of personal identity he cites with apparent approval the view of 'most philosophers' that 'personal identity *arises* from consciousness; and *consciousness is nothing but a reflected thought or perception*' (p. 635, my italics, save for 'arises').

Once Hume's theory of self-identity based on resemblances is spelled out in detail, a great many objections spring to mind. One may well doubt the intelligibility of Hume's whole enterprise. There are problems concerning the veridical or non-veridical character of the memories involved. And it may be urged that Hume has surreptitiously smuggled in the self he rejected at the start. The objection I wish to press, however, concerns the possibility of distinguishing, as the theory requires, the subject's and the self-observer's recollection of the subject's past perception. Given my earlier argument, this amounts to questioning the possibility of distinguishing the productive and discovering roles for memory in the first-person case.

The difficulty is this. If Hume's third-person picture is to have application to the case of self-identity, it must be possible for a given person to have, at a given time, two numerically distinct recollections with the same content. Two numerically distinct recollections are necessary; failing this the subject-observer distinction is lost, and there is no way of introducing both the *resemblance* between present recollection and past perception and the *awareness* of this resemblance. The two recollections must be had by a single person, for otherwise we do not have a case of self-identity. The recollections must occur at the same time (or at least must overlap for a stretch of time). For if the subject's recollection ceases before the self-observer's begins, the self-observer cannot link the subject's past and present perceptions.[3] And if the temporal ordering is reversed, the self-observer will no longer recall the subject's past perception when he is alleged to notice its resemblance to the subject's present recollection. Finally, the two recollections must have the same content; they must be of the same perception. Failing this the whole point of an explanation in terms of resemblance is lost. Unfortunately, however, these several conditions cannot be satisfied for the case of self-identity, for there can be no way of individuating two numerically distinct memories in the circumstances envisaged. It follows that Hume has failed to explain self-identity in terms of memory and resemblance.

Two ways of defending Hume must be briefly considered. It may be said that there is clearly a sense in which a given person can have, at a given time, two numerically distinct memories of the same event. If we individuate memories by their content, a given person could, at a given time, have two memories (different contents) of what was in fact, though he did not remember it as such, the same event. It should be obvious, however, that this cannot help Hume, for his theory requires the memories to have the *same* content. Otherwise, as we have seen, resemblance could not do its job.

Rather differently, it may be argued that a person can remember what he recognizes as a single event in two different ways at once. It is possible for one's recollection of what is recognized as a single event to alter with time, so perhaps it is possible to have such partially resembling memories at the same time. Now, it is not clear to me that this is possible; to determine its possibility would require a detailed examination of the possible criteria for individuating perceptions. Even if the possibility be granted, however, we are left with no intelligible explanation of self-identity based on resemblance for what I take to be the normal case, that is, the case where one does not, at a given time, have differing memories of what one takes to be the same event.

There is no need to spell out the details of Hume's explanation of self-identity in terms of *causal* connections between one's perceptions, for the explanation simply parallels that in terms of resemblance. And for obvious reasons the explanation in terms of causality is not subject to the objection just developed (save for the special case of causal connections between recollections and perceptions recalled). But there is a difficulty of a very different kind in Hume's explanation based on causality, to which I now turn.

Hume holds that a cause and its effect are temporally contiguous; if a purported cause and its effect are not contiguous they must, if causally connected, be linked by a continuous series of contiguous causes and effects:

> [W]hatever objects are consider'd as causes or effects, are *contiguous*; and . . . nothing can operate in a time or place, which is ever so little remov'd from those of its existence. Tho' distant objects may sometimes seem productive of each other, they are commonly found upon examination to be link'd by a chain of causes, which are contiguous among themselves, and to the distant objects; and when in any particular instance we cannot discover this connexion, we still presume it to exist. We may therefore consider the relation of CONTIGUITY as essential to that of causation . . . . (p. 75)[4]

The requirement of contiguity reappears, as well, in the two definitions of causality that Hume offers toward the end of *Treatise* I, iii.14 (p. 170).

Hume also holds that minds are discontinuous entities, in the sense that during the period of their existence there are periods when they are unconscious and have no perceptions. In terms of his own theory minds are bundles of perceptions, but they are not temporally continuous ones. He holds that this is an important element in one's ordinary conception of minds, as opposed to bodies, and even undertakes to explain what it is in our experience that leads us to think that minds do not 'require a continu'd existence' as do physical objects, which would 'otherwise lose, in a great measure, the regularity of their operation' (pp. 195–6). And the point is stressed in the course of his discussion of personal identity: 'When my perceptions are remov'd for any time, as by sound sleep; so long am I insensible of *myself*, and may truly be said not to exist' (p. 252). His position here echoes Locke's remark that 'every drowsy nod shakes their doctrine, who teach that the soul is always thinking'.[5]

Putting the two points together we can see a difficulty in his account of self-identity based on causality, which seems to have been noticed by neither Hume nor his commentators. If minds are discontinuous entities in the sense indicated, then the perceptions before and after a given gap in consciousness cannot be causally linked unless there are items other than perceptions to link them. Failing such non-perceptual links, self-identity based on causality can extend only as far as the first perceptions one has had since one's last period of unconsciousness. Every drowsy nod would, as far as causality goes, systematically debar one from thinking of oneself, before dozing, as the same as oneself, now awake. If the account of self-identity in terms of causality is to work it requires supplementation from some source other than one's perceptions. Hume cannot, of course, invoke a substantial (sometimes dozing) self. What other remedy is available to him?

I suggest that one remedy open to Hume is the obvious one of viewing persons as psychophysical substances, whose intervening physical states serve to fill up the gaps in consciousness. Given such physical states it is possible, at least in theory, to effect the required causal continuity between one's present and all of one's past perceptions. (By hypothesis, of course, a person could not be aware of, that is, conscious of, these physical states while remaining unconscious—but that is another matter.)

Adopting this remedy is, I submit, perfectly consistent with Hume's views about substance and causality. A psychophysical substance could be construed as a bundle of suitably related 'perceptions' and 'sensible qualities' (Hume's terminology), perhaps even displaying the features of 'reciprocal causality', 'sympathy of parts' and 'common purpose' that Hume mentions when discussing physical substances (p. 257). And Hume explicitly argues that there can be no *a priori* objection to causal interaction between mind and matter (pp. 247–8). More importantly, perhaps, the remedy is simply an application of a position he adopts frequently in the course of the *Treatise* but which has not received sufficient attention, namely, that mental and physical events are, as a matter of fact, causally connected. ''Tis certain,' he says, that we experience causal connections of this kind: '[E]very one may perceive, that the different dispositions of his body change his thoughts and sentiments', and 'we may certainly conclude . . . [that] motion . . . is the cause of thought and perception' (p. 248).[6]

Some think that Hume is a subjective idealist, and would object that, given his considered views about the external world, he could not adopt the remedy I am suggesting. Unfortunately a reply to this fundamental objection is far beyond the scope of this paper. One point must, however, be noted. If Hume *were* a subjective idealist he could not provide a satisfactory account of self-identity based on causality. At least, he could not do so without giving up fundamental elements in his theories of causality and of the mind. For the crux of my present objection is Hume's need to provide for causal continuity. I do not see how, if he were a subjective idealist, Hume could manage this.[7]

1. Hume, in fact, indicates two dimensions to memory's discovering role. Because of its connection with our general ability to make causal judgments we are enabled to 'extend the same chain of causes, and consequently the identity of our persons beyond our memory, and can comprehend times, and circumstances, and actions, which we have entirely forgot, but suppose in general to have existed' (p. 262).

2. Laird asserts, apparently without argument, that Hume 'never supposed that one part of the mental bundle was engaged in inspecting either itself or some other part of the bundle'. John Laird *Hume's Philosophy of Human Nature* (London: Methuen 1932) pp. 190–1.

3. Interestingly enough, there is one passage in which Hume writes as though in thinking of oneself as identical through change one is thinking only of one's *past* perceptions: 'It follows, therefore, that the thought alone finds personal identity, when reflecting on the train of *past* perceptions, that compose a mind, the ideas of them are felt to be connected together, and naturally introduce each other' (*Treatise*, p. 635, my italics). If this were his considered view he would escape my present objection only to run into others.

4. The passage continues: 'at least may suppose it such, according to the general opinion, till we can find a more proper occasion to clear up this matter, by examining what objects are or are not susceptible of juxtaposition and conjunction' (*Treatise*, p. 75), and in a footnote refers ahead

to *Treatise* I. iv. 5. The reference makes clear, however, that Hume's hesitation concerns spatial, not temporal, contiguity, for he is concerned to admit causal connections between two non-spatial items, or between spatial and non-spatial items.

5.   John Locke *An Essay Concerning Human Understanding*, II. 1. 13.

6.   cf. *Treatise*, pp. 60, 123, 185, 192–3, 211, 230, 237, 250, 267, 275–6, 287. At *Treatise* II. iii. 1 (as elsewhere) Hume commits himself to the mental causation of physical events.

7.   I am indebted to Páll S. Árdal for his very helpful comments on an earlier version of this paper. The research on which this paper is based has been supported by The American Council of Learned Societies, The Institute for Advanced Studies in the Humanities (University of Edinburgh), and the University of Kansas.

Hume on Qualitative Content

THE DISTINCTION between the primary and the secondary qualities
has often been drawn either by saying that the primary qualities are
those which physicists use to describe the world or by using Locke's list.
The result in either case is that primary qualities are those and only
those qualities that are objective, publicly measurable and independent
of the observer. The secondary qualities are those lacking these public
properties.

Philosophers as diverse as Berkeley, Hume, Kant, Whitehead, Arm-
strong, and Sellars have maintained that a physical object cannot be
coherently individuated, described, or re-identified without the use of
some qualitative content. I will call this 'the S-Q thesis'. It is the claim
that at least one secondary quality is required for description of a macroscopic, middle-sized object in physical space. After some preliminary
remarks, I will use as my test Hume's account in 'Of The Modern
Philosophy' (pp. 225–51).[1]

There are two tests that philosophers have employed to decide
whether a quality is to be called primary: these I shall call 'the measurability test' and the 'perceptual relativity test'. The measurability test
is historically the important test; it was the real basis of the mathematiz-
ing of nature undertaken by the philosopher-scientists of the seventeenth
century. To be measurable (in the strong sense required) a property
(a) must be an extensive magnitude with a true zero point, and (b)
must be a fundamental and not a derived measurement, that is, it must
not require prior measurement. The perceptual relativity test contends
that the primary qualities are those qualities that can be known by
more than one sense, and are consequently more objective or less subject
to perceptual relativity.

Descartes, it will be recalled, maintained that the principal attribute
of matter is extension. For him the logically necessary and sufficient
condition for a physical object is occupancy of space. Occupancy of space,
however, is a necessary but not a sufficient condition for the individuation of a physical object. The kinematical and geometrical properties of
matter that Descartes recognizes are insufficient to differentiate or pick
out a chunk of matter from empty space or a vacuum.

Locke adds solidity or impenetrability to his list of primary qualities,
but still fails to solve the problem of individuation. The origin of the
idea of solidity is described by Locke as follows:

The *idea* of *solidity* we receive by our touch; and it arises from the resistance we find in body to the entrance of any other body into the place it possesses, till it is left it.[2]

Solidity is defined as that 'which hinders the approach of two bodies, when they are moving one towards one another'.[3] The Newtonian term for solidity is 'impenetrability' and Locke is willing to see these terms treated as synonymous. His reason for choosing the term 'solidity' over 'impenetrability', he tells us, is that the former 'carries something more of positive in it than *impenetrability*; which is negative'.[4]

The most important thing in Locke's account of solidity is the attempt to distinguish solidity from hardness. Hardness is defined by Locke as 'a firm cohesion of the parts of matter making up masses of a sensible bulk, so that the whole does not easily change its figure'.[5] Hardness is thus to be contrasted with softness, which does change its shape. I press the butter and it squishes. It is clear that Locke treats hardness as a secondary quality.

> Indeed, hard and soft are names that we give to things only in relation to the constitutions of our own bodies: that being generally called hard by us which will put us to pain sooner than change figure by the pressure of any part of our bodies; and that, on the contrary, soft, which changes the situations of its parts upon an easy and unpainful touch.[6]

Impenetrability is distinguished from hardness by Locke by its 'utter exclusion of other bodies out of the space it possesses'.[7] The hard only physically excludes other bodies from occupying a space whereas the impenetrable logically excludes them. The distinction Locke is making here may seem somewhat unreal unless one recalls that Locke is connecting solidity or impenetrability with the atomic theory of the seventeenth century. Solidity is an intrinsic characteristic of matter; when the atoms are pushed together there will come a time when they are incompressible. In Locke's terminology the characteristic property of solidity is that it is 'utterly inseparable from the body, in what state so ever it be'.

But a little reflection shows us that solidity fails to pass either of the two standard tests. Like density, solidity is a derived measurement. It cannot, as a consequence, negotiate condition (*b*) for measurability. It fails the perceptual relativity test even more obviously since it is known only by the sense of touch.

The fundamental principle of what Hume calls 'the modern philosophy' is the Lockean doctrine that the secondary qualities are 'nothing but impressions in the mind', that is, sensations (pp. 226). Hume's list of the secondary qualities is the usual one comprising colours, sounds, tastes, smells, heat and cold. Again, not surprisingly, the argument that Hume finds decisive for the subjectivity of the secondary qualities is the relativity of sense perception. There are, he says, 'variations of those impressions, even while the external object, to all appearances, continues the same' (p. 226). These variations, Hume finds, depend on three factors: differences in health or bodily condition, different bodily constitutions, and differences of external situation and position.

Hume argues, as Locke had before him, that although different impressions of the same sense 'arise from any object, every one of these impressions has not a resembling quality existent in the object' (p. 227). The consequence is that 'we are reduc'd merely to what are called primary qualities, as the only *real* ones, of which we have any adequate notion' (p. 227). The resultant list of primary qualities is: 'extension and solidity, with their different mixtures and modifications; figure, motion, gravity and cohesion' (p. 227). But Hume draws a devastating conclusion from this Lockean position. He writes:

> Instead of explaining the operations of external objects by its means [Locke's primary-secondary distinction], we utterly annihilate all these objects, and reduce ourselves to the opinions of the most extravagant scepticism concerning them. (pp. 227–8)

In analyzing Hume's argument a systematic definition of primary and secondary qualities is needed. A primary quality—and this is my definition—is a non-relational, monadic, determinable property alleged to be intrinsic to a physical object in a determinate form.[8] Those qualities that are not primary are secondary. The intuition I am appealing to in this definition is that in speaking of a quality as primary we mean that it adheres literally in the physical object as a monadic predicate and not merely relationally. A relational property is the referent of a relation. Relational properties are properties whose essential characteristics involve references to some other thing. They are dyadic predicates which assume that the physical object is already individuated. There is, of course, a trivial sense in which a primary quality is indeed dyadic since it is related to the physical object whose property it is, but in this case the field of the relation is still confined within the physical object. We do not need to consider predicates of any degree other than monadic and dyadic since by the well-known Wiener-Kuratowski result n-adic predicates of degrees higher than two can be reduced to dyadic predicates, that is, a triadic relation among relations y, z, and w can be construed as a dyadic relation borne by y to z; w.[9]

Hume's argument that Locke's version of the primary-secondary quality distinction annihilates body can be stated in three steps. Hume argued, in the first place, that motion reduces to extension since motion is 'a quality altogether inconceivable alone and without reference to some other object. The idea of motion necessarily supposes that of a body moving' (p. 228). Hume is contending that motion is a relational property and thus a dyadic predicate.

The second step in Hume's argument is that extension cannot be conceived except as composed of colour or solidity. But colour is a secondary quality; extension thus reduces to solidity. There is one doubtful point in Hume's account that needs to be noted. Hume contends, although the argument is only alluded to in this section, that extension is composed of sensible minima, a view that had curious consequences in his account of space and time and that led him into finitist views on mathematics, which, if not actually inconsistent, are certainly very strange. But the contemporary Humean need not accept such exotica. The central point to note is that the physical object—what Hume calls the 'extension'—can be coherently described only if it has colour (a quality) or solidity.

The third and final step in Hume's argument is that solidity cannot be the property that differentiates a physical object from its environment, any more than motion can, because it too is a relational property.

> Solidity . . . is perfectly incomprehensible alone, and without the conception of some bodies, which are solid, and maintain this separate and distinct existence. (pp. 228–9)

This central thesis is buttressed by two characteristic Humean arguments. Hume thinks of solidity as a logical impenetrability and recognizes that it depends upon the atomic theory. In his own terminology he says that 'the idea of solidity is that of two objects, which being impell'd by the utmost force, cannot penetrate each other' (p. 228). When Hume tests this idea by his empirical criterion of meaning he has two arguments to show that the idea of solidity cannot be derived from the sense of touch. His first argument shows in effect that solidity must be distinguished from hardness. He writes: 'A man, who has the palsey in one hand, has as perfect an idea of impenetrability, when he observes that hand to be supported by the table, as when he feels the same table with the other hand' (p. 230).

His second argument is that impressions of touch are simple, and thus cannot adequately represent solidity, which is a complex idea. Hume asks us to consider the following two cases: (1) pressing a stone or other solid body with the hand, and (2) pressing two stones together. Since there is a sensation in the former case which does not occur in the latter, no one would be inclined to argue that these cases are identical. To make them identical would require removing some part of the impression in (1), namely, that of the sensation in the hand. But it is impossible to remove part of the simple impression. Thus the sense of touch is complex.

In summary, Hume's essential point is that the primary qualities as Descartes and Locke conceive them are relational predicates and not monadic predicates. The trouble with using relational predicates exclusively to describe primary qualities is that such predicates assume that the relata are already known, that is, that a physical object is already capable of being individuated and re-identified. Hume exploited this point to reach his sceptical conclusion about what he called 'the modern philosophy'.

Since Hume's time modern particle theory has suggested several candidates that could be used to differentiate a macroscopic physical object from the environment. Mass, electrical charge, spin, and isospin are obvious examples. Yet clearly these properties are relational properties that bodies or particles hold to one another. Consequently a defender of the S-Q thesis can argue that these advances in science do not tell against his case. Hume's argument is a very powerful one, and I know of no arguments that would strengthen his case.

Nevertheless the S-Q thesis has been widely rejected. Contemporary scientific realists, for whom the world is exactly the way science describes it, reject the S-Q thesis as an unnecessary excrescence. I want to suggest a way in which this controversy can be mediated by showing that the dispute is conducted on two levels.

Let me borrow a useful piece of terminology from Sellars and say that the properties science uses to describe the world make up the scientific image, and that the secondary qualities are part of the manifest image of the world. Consider the following example. At the level of analysis at which the S-Q thesis operates an argument such as the following can be furnished. Motion is simply a change in the relative position of a body. Motion thus requires body for its definition, and is consequently derivative. At the macroscopic level I think the argument is valid. But in a bodiless universe containing force fields of astronomical dimensions through which disturbances are propagated, the case in which maximum value of some field-parameter (the point of maximum value) changes its position in a continuous fashion is a case of *motion without bodies*. The same thing could even be said of light rays.[10] But such arguments as these, and indeed Locke's argument for solidity, are at a level other than the macroscopic level at which the manifest image operates.

I suspect that the differences between the defender of the manifest image on the one hand and of the scientific image on the other are ultimately irreconcilable. The manifest image is supported not only by philosophical arguments but also by language, culture, and philosophical tradition. *Pace* Sellars, the history of philosophy is in fact the history of the vicissitudes of the manifest image. The defender of the manifest image will always ask, with Diderot, how many snowballs it takes to heat an oven. To ask him to deny qualitative content as ultimate is to ask him to believe his world is illusory, indeed that he himself must be crazy. On the other side the scientific image is supported by the powerful tradition of scientific objectivity. In some of our moments, at least, all of us expect the secondary qualities either to yield to measurement or to be abolished as part of the furniture of the world. Hume, whom we honour at this gathering, presented in a few short pages the most powerful defence the S-Q thesis has ever received.

1.   Page references in brackets are to Hume's *Treatise*.
2.   *Essay Concering Human Understanding* II. iv, 1.
3.   ibid.
4.   ibid.
5.   op. cit., II. iv. 4.
6.   ibid.
7.   ibid.
8.   I have modified a definition of C. D. Broad's.
9.   Details to show that all relations can be treated as dyadic relations can be found in W. V. Quine *Mathematical Logic*, revised edition (Harvard University Press 1955) pp. 201, 202.
10.   I owe the example to a commentator on another version of this paper.

Durationless Moments in Hume's Treatise

HUME GIVES AN argument against endless divisibility of the parts of time. The argument in question is well known. It is the so-called 'additional' argument peculiar to time:

'Tis a property inseparable from time, and which in a manner constitutes its essence, that each of its parts succeeds another, and that none of them, however contiguous, can ever be co-existent . . . 'Tis certain then, that time, as it exists, must be compos'd of indivisible moments. For if in time we could never arrive at an end of division, and if each moment, as it succeeds another, were not perfectly single and indivisible, there would be an infinite number of co-existent moments, or parts of time; which I believe will be allow'd to be an arrant contradiction.[1]

Conceding divisibility of a temporal part, as he appears to do ('For if in time we could never arrive at an end of division'), Hume cannot terminate the process of division short of postulating 'minimum durationless moments'. Yet, it is objected, minimum durationless moments are what the argument is supposed to prove:

Any sub-division of one of his postulated minimum durationless moments could only be into moments which were at the same time both different and simultaneous; which is indeed absurd. But . . . this reconstruction presupposes the conclusion it is supposed to prove.[2]

Having conceded divisibility of a temporal part, Hume proceeds to take it back in the same sentence: 'each moment, as it succeeds another', he states, must be 'perfectly single and indivisible'.

It might be thought that Hume is not really taking it back. 'Perfectly single and indivisible moment' refers not to any moment, regardless of its size, but rather to that moment which terminates the process of division. It refers to a minimum moment. If so, the objection to Hume's argument stands: it presupposes what it is supposed to prove.

Nevertheless, Hume does not assert that each *minimum* moment must be perfectly single and indivisible. Rather, he asserts that each moment, regardless of its size, is perfectly single and indivisible. In fact, throughout his discussion of time Hume, as we shall see, says nothing about the measurement or, therefore, about the size of a moment. But even if Hume *is* thinking of a 'minimum' moment (whatever that might mean), his argument against its divisibility appeals, not to its size, but to the nature, or essence, of time. In that case, indivisibility of *any* moment, not just a minimum moment, is allegedly precluded by the nature, or essence, of time.

Hume is concerned with the essence of time because of its bearing on the indivisibility of an existent part, or moment, of time. Such topics as the direction of time, simultaneity, tense, and the measurement of time do not belong to the essence of time. Accordingly, Hume does not discuss these topics.

However, these topics are among those usually thought to be central to an account of time. What, according to Hume, belongs to the essence of time? In order to answer this question and thereafter to assess the indivisibility claim, let us turn to Hume's account of time.

Existents, none coexisting one with another, constitute an order (pp. 39–40). This order is succession, that is, time. 'Since it [time] appears not as any primary distinct impression, [it] can plainly be nothing but different ideas, or impressions, or objects dispos'd in a certain manner, that is, succeeding each other' (p. 37).

'Time' and 'succession', then, are synonyms. Still another is 'duration'. Hume, when using 'duration' synonymously with 'time', calls it 'duration proper' (p. 37). Proper duration contrasts with fictive duration. Hume's example of five notes sounded by a flute (p. 37) illustrates this contrast. If presented as continuous sound, the notes sounded are qualitatively different. Each note may run insensibly into another. Yet, their qualitative difference and succession are discernible. They constitute a proper duration. In contrast, a single (monotonous) note, in the interval between its inception and cessation, is unchanging. None the less, it must have duration in some sense, since we can and do inquire about its length: we can and do ask how long it endured. The sense in which it has duration, however, is not the literal sense of proper duration. Its duration, according to Hume, is fictive. It is fictive because the change implied in the question, 'How long did it endure?', is not intrinsic to it but conferred on it from the outside, by comparison with a duration proper—with something that changes (pp. 37, 65). We may compare it to another and suitably changing thing, for example, to a blinking light. Using this device, we can ask and answer the question, 'How long does the sound endure?' We can speak intelligibly of the sound's temporal parts and, by summing them, say that it endured for such a length of time. It lasted, we might say, two blinks of the light. Notice, however, that the sound's division is not something intrinsic to it. It does not literally consist of light blinks. The reason for this is clear: the sound's duration is improper, that is, it is a fiction effected through comparison.

Even though Hume characterizes temporal order (succession) as perceivable (p. 35), he is aware that it is unlike the ordinary, 'primary distinct', impressions (p. 37) that constitute it. It is not, he states, an impression presented to a single sense:

> Five notes play'd on a flute give us the impression and idea of time; tho' time be not a sixth impression, which presents itself to the hearing or any other of the senses. Nor is it a sixth impression, which the mind by reflection finds in itself. (p. 36)

Elements in succession could be: a sound, a flash of light, a taste, an odour. Each of these is perceived by a single sense. Their succession is not. Time is an impression, and thus perceivable because its parts are impressions and time is nothing without parts. It is an idea—as we shall see the idea is abstract—because it has its parts by their manner of appearance, by their succession, not by their being impressions. Hume has it both ways: time is impression *and* idea.

Not long after characterizing succession as 'perceivable' (p. 35) and as an 'impression' (p. 36), Hume switches to 'The mind takes notice of the manner in which objects appear'.

> But here it only takes notice of the *manner*, in which the different sounds make their appearance; and that it may afterwards consider without considering these particular sounds, but may conjoin it with any other objects. (p. 37, Hume's italics)

It is one thing to think that sounds alone are successive and another to think that other things, too, are successive. Either way, things are distinct from their succession. The latter is abstracted from the former, and, as in all abstractions, resemblance is involved. The resemblance, however, does not lie between, say, five sounds and five flashes of light in respect of their being identically successive. The resemblance in question is a recurrent contrast: existent versus nonexistent. Thus, even if one sensed nothing but sounds, one could abstract the sounds from their manner of appearance—from that certain order called their succession. The abstraction at bottom is one of a sound versus its existence. For one makes this abstraction, first, by contrast with nonexistence, and, second, by recurrence of this contrast. Yet, just this recurrent contrast is the abstract idea of temporal order. As he repeatedly states, time is 'the manner or order, in which objects *exist*' (p. 40). Again, 'Time is nothing but the manner, in which some real objects *exist*' (p. 64). Or, time is 'changeable *existence*' (p. 65, my italics).

It is worth noting that time is identical with this order of concreta (ideas, impressions, objects). The abstract idea of time is identical with this order abstracted from any and all concreta. Further, this abstraction is consistent with Hume's alleged extreme nominalism. Neither 'existent' nor 'nonexistent', according to Hume, refers to a property (see pp. 66–8).

More needs to be said about what counts as an element and about the minimum number of elements sufficient for the order. Hume uses several terms to designate an element, among them, 'moment', and 'part of time'. A part of time is a tenseless existent. As for the claim that it is tenseless: it may be present to one person and past to another person. For example, the odour of burned gunpowder at the Battle of Gettysburg is present to General Meade and past to me. As for the claim that it is an existent: a temporal part is not a part of a spatial whole. In fact, in no literal sense is succession identical with time describable as a whole. 'Part', therefore, is being used in this context in a nonliteral sense—in a sense correlated with a nonliteral sense of 'whole'. The whole in question is what Hume calls changeable existence. Where 'E!' abbreviates 'existent', it is represented as follows: $[\sim\!E!/E!/\sim\!E!]$. This is what Hume means by 'changeable existence'. 'Part', or 'moment', refers to the component designated by 'E!' and without which 'changeable existence' makes no sense. (The recurrent contrast between existent and nonexistent, with which changeable existence, that is, time, is identified, probably should be expanded to two occurrences of 'E!', as follows: $[\sim\!E!/E!/\sim\!E!/E!]$.)

Given that the essence of time is the order of concreta, set forth above, and given the distinction between proper and fictive duration, we have at hand the premisses sufficient to prove that there must be durationless moments. The argument is as follows: the E!'s in a proper duration cannot themselves have proper duration. The sense of 'cannot' is logical. No element in an order is identical with that order. It follows that all E!'s—all moments or parts of time—are devoid of real, or proper, duration.

Let 'E!' designate a monotonous sound. Although it lacks real, or proper, duration, by reason of being monotonous, it may have fictive duration. This was demonstrated earlier by the device of a blinking light. Now, however, more needs to be said about fictive duration, and, in particular, about the sense, if any, in which the blinking light 'divides' the monotonous sound.

An E! counts as one, as opposed to many, by being surrounded, as it were, by $\sim\!E!$'s. Thus, (1) $[\sim\!E!/E!/\sim\!E!]$ counts as one E! and (2) $[\sim\!E!/E!/\sim\!E!/E!/\sim\!E!]$ counts as two E!'s. Given this count criterion for an E!—and there is no other if time is changeable existence—and simultaneity, one can imagine the two E!'s of (2) replacing the one E! of (1), such that one of the E!'s of (2) is shorter than the E! of (1). But let us be clear *what* we are imagining: we are not imagining the E! of (1) as, absurdly, being one and many. Nothing is both one and many. Failure to observe this logical truth, or, more fundamentally, failure to get clear about, and then abide by, the count criterion for an

E!, leads to the absurdity, remarked by Hume and Flew, of moments being simultaneous and different. Notice, however, that this absurdity obtains, as alleged at the outset, for any moment.

There is no puzzle about what we are doing when we imagine two E!'s in the place of one E!. Among other things, we are imagining that one of the former is shorter than the latter.

Imagining a moment shorter than a given moment divides no moment into shorter moments. Imagining a moment divided into shorter constituent moments violates the count criterion for a moment. It cannot be imagined. Hume is right to defend indivisibility by insisting on the absurdity of divisibility.

It is worth noting that Hume argues that division of space must end in visible and tangible minima (pp. 26–31). The structure of his argument is as follows: (1) Our ideas, if just, adequately represent objects and their relations. (2) Our ideas must be composed of a finite number of parts, because our capacities are finite. Therefore, (3), objects must be composed of a finite number of parts—ultimately, of visible and tangible minima.

This argument is extended to time (p. 31) and, so extended, it commits Hume to the view that one moment is divisible into many shorter constituent moments—a view which, if I am right, cannot be made intelligible. This proves, perhaps, that Hume, himself, was not, at the beginning of his account of time, immune to the forces to which Flew in particular and the sceptical tradition in general succumbed. However, Hume did not succumb to them. His account of time is remarkably free from their influence.

1.   *Treatise*, p. 31. Subsequent references to the *Treatise* are inserted in parentheses in the text.
2.   Antony Flew 'Infinite Divisibility in Hume's *Treatise*' *Rivista Critica di Storia della Filosofia* (1967) Fasc. IV, 466.

The Textual and Philosophical
Significance of Hume's MS Alterations
to Treatise III

TWO WORKS BY HUME, a copy of the first edition of volume three of the *Treatise* and a copy of the *Abstract*, each bearing MS alterations, have recently turned up in the British Library.[1] That such annotations could have gone unnoticed for over one hundred and thirty years in a library to which scholars have relative ease of access calls for an explanation.[2] Briefly, what seems to have happened is that in 1841 two copies of volume three, both bearing nearly identical MS comments, one set in Hume's hand, the other not, came into the possession of the British Museum. Owing, presumably, to a cataloguing oversight only one copy was recorded in the *British Museum General Catalogue*. The other—as it happened the copy bearing Hume's autograph comments—was thereby effectively removed from circulation and laid to rest in some dark corner of the British Museum stacks where (we may reasonably assume) it remained until 1971.

Its existence was never suspected until 1951 when Professor Raymond Klibansky published a note on the MS comments in the catalogued copy. Professor Klibansky concluded that while the handwriting in the catalogued copy did not appear to be Hume's 'the character of the notes makes it most improbable that they go back to anyone but the author himself'.[3]

As a result of a curious chain of events the 'Hume-copy' of volume three, the existence of which Professor Klibansky could only infer, actually came into my hands in July 1974. It seems that in 1971 the three volumes of the first edition were removed for rebinding, and the copy of volume three bearing Hume's autograph was erroneously bound in place of the catalogued copy and given the same shelf mark. This meant that the originally catalogued copy, the one that Professor Klibansky saw in 1951, was now out of circulation and the other catalogued copy was available (presumably for the first time) to readers in the British Library. Fortunately this error has led to the confirmation of Professor Klibansky's original conclusion concerning the textual authority for the alterations.

THE APPEARANCE of Hume's alterations on a copy of volume three of the *Treatise* raises two important questions for Hume scholarship:

(1) the question of the textual significance of the alterations—now that we have this information, how might we set about constructing a 'copy-text' for the purpose of preparing a new critical edition of the *Treatise*?; and (2) the question of the philosophical significance of the alterations—do they necessitate any reappraisals of Hume's philosophical positions? Although I intend to concentrate on the second of these ''twill, perhaps, be found in the end, that the same answer will serve for both questions'.

Presumably the first question to consider is a question about Hume's intentions. In simple terms: why did he make these alterations on this copy? We cannot of course answer this question with absolute certainty, but of the various possibilities the most likely, in view of the available bibliographical evidence, is that Hume intended the alterations to be incorporated as corrections to the first edition but for one reason or another they were not all included.[4]

I turn now to the second question, the question of the philosophical significance of the alterations. For this purpose I have listed seven of the alterations which appear on the 'Hume Copy'. These seven seem to make important emendations to the text. I have also included a series of alterations Hume made to his *Enquiry concerning the Principles of Morals*,[5] alterations that, I believe, also have a thematic connection with the alterations to the *Treatise*. For the moment I shall not attempt to explain why I have selected these particular alterations beyond saying that all of the alterations listed are such that they appear to have some bearing on the question of the nature of the motive to virtue or justice.

THE FOLLOWING are a series of alterations which Hume made to his own works over a period of some thirty-six years. The first alteration (A) is one that Hume made on a MS of the 'Conclusion' of volume three of the *Treatise* and submitted as an enclosure with his letter of 4 March 1740, to Francis Hutcheson.[6] It will be noticed that Hume has scored out the words 'both our Selfishness and Pride'. The passage corresponds to page 620 of the 1888 Selby-Bigge edition and pages 669–70 of the 1969 Mossner edition, in both of which it appears in its emended form.

<blockquote>
(A)   The same System may help us to form a just Notion of the <u>Happiness</u>, as well as of the <u>Dignity</u> of Virtue, and may interest every Principle of our Nature, ~~both our Selfishness and Pride,~~ in the embracing and cherishing that noble Quality.
</blockquote>

'I have sent you the *conclusion,* as I have alter'd it, that you may see I
desire to keep on good terms with the strictest and most rigid' (Hume
to Hutcheson, 4 March 1740, MS in R.S.E.) See also Ernest C. Mossner
Notes and Queries, 194 (1949) p. 521.

Hume's Alterations to Treatise III

Alterations (B) through (H) are alterations occurring on the 'Hume-
copy' of volume three. (B) alters *But private benevolence is, and ought to
be* to read *But private benevolence towards the proprietor is, and ought to
be.* The next alteration (C) adds two sentences. The first sentence,
asserting self-interest to be the original motive to the establishment of
justice, appears in some copies of the first edition on a cancel. In (D),
Hume changes the word *interest* to read *self-interest.* Alteration (E)
withdraws a qualified assertion regarding *public interest* and substitutes
another qualified assertion regarding our *own Interest.* Alterations (F)
and (G) change the phrase *public interest* to read *interest* unqualified.
(F) and (G), incidentally, depart from the revised errata (the cancel at
A4.^{v}) which has *common interest* in both cases. With (H) Hume adds the
assertion that the scheme of law and justice is advantageous not only
to the society but to every *individual.*

Page references corresponding respectively to the first edition, the
Selby-Bigge edition and the Mossner edition appear in square brackets
below each passage quoted.

(B)

towards the proprietor ∧

But private benevolence∧is, and ought
to be, weaker in some persons, than
in others: And in many, or indeed in
most persons, must absolutely fail.
Private benevolence, therefore, is
not the original motive of justice.
[47, 483, 535, cf. Letters, I.47-8]

(C)

*Thus Self-interest is
the original Motive to
the Establishment of
Justice: But a Sympathy
with public Interest is
the Source of the moral
Approbation, which attends
that Virtue. This latter
Principle of Sympathy
is too weak to controul
our Passions; but has
sufficient Force to in-
fluence our Taste, &
give us the Sentiments
of Approbation or Blame.*   ∧

The *general rule* reaches beyond those
instances, from which it arose; while
at the same time we naturally *sym-
pathize* with others in the sentiments
they entertain of us.∧

   THO' this progress of the sentiments be *natural,* and even necessary,
'tis certain, that it is here for-
warded by the artifice of politicians,
who, in order to govern men more
easily, and preserve peace in human
society, have endeavour'd to produce
an esteem for justice, and an abhorrence of injustice.
[76, 499-500, 551]

(D)

Self ∧

to be common to all
mankind.   ∧

UPON the whole, then, we are to
consider this distinction betwixt
justice and injustice, as having
two different foundations, *viz.* that
of∤*interest*, when men observe, that
'tis impossible to live in society
without restraining themselves by
certain rules; and that of *morality*,
when this interest is once observ'd,∧
and men receive a pleasure from the
view of such actions as tend to the
peace of society, and an uneasiness
from such as are contrary to it.
[131, 533, 585]

(E)

our own Interest, or at
least to that of the
public which we partake
of by Sympathy.

But tho' a present interest may thus
blind us with regard to our own
actions, it takes not place with regard to those of others; nor hinders
them from appearing in their true
colours, as highly prejudicial to
~~public interest, and to our own in~~
~~particular.~~
[152, 545, 597]

(F) and (G)

If the sense of ~~public~~ interest were
not our original motive to obedience,
I wou'd fain ask, what other principle
is there in human nature capable of
subduing the natural ambition of men,
and forcing them to such a submission?
Imitation and custom are not sufficient. For the question still recurs,
what motive first produces those instances of submission, which we imitate, and that train of actions, which
produces the custom? There evidently
is no other principle than ~~public~~ interest; and if interest first produces
obedience to government, the obligation to obedience must cease, whenever
the interest ceases, in any great
degree, and in a considerable number
of instances.
[165, 553 (follows revised errata)]

(H)
& to every individual∧

The whole scheme, however, of law and
justice is advantageous to the society;
and 'twas with a view to this advantage, that men, by their voluntary
conventions, establish'd it.
[211, 579, 630]

Hume's Alterations to the Enquiry

Hume made several alterations in successive editions of his *Enquiry concerning the Principles of Morals*. Of these, only two, referred to below under (K) and (L), are among the variations mentioned in the Green and Grose edition of Hume's *Philosophical Works*.[7] I reproduce, under (I), a passage from the 1751 edition, which was to undergo a series of changes in later editions. Note the first sentence asserting the existence of a *disinterested benevolence*. This first sentence appears in this form in the editions of 1753–56 also, and again in the edition of 1758 (*Essays and Treatises*). Under (J) I give the first sentence as it occurs in the 1764 edition of *Essays and Treatises*; the word *disinterested* has been deleted from the text. (K) is from the letter of 30th July 1776, in which Hume directed Strahan, his printer/publisher, to make two alterations to the (posthumous) edition of 1777. He specified that the opening passage of the section entitled 'Of Benevolence' should be transferred to the end of the text, where it should become a second appendix. He further specified that the passage should not appear under the original title 'Of Benevolence' but should be given the new title 'Of Self-Love'. The final alteration to the *Enquiry concerning the Principles of Morals* was to delete from the passage, quoted under (I), the phrase 'that there is such a sentiment in human nature as benevolence'.[8] Under (L) I reproduce the amended passage from the posthumous edition.

(I)   UPON the Whole, then, it seems undeniable, *that*
        there is such a Sentiment in human Nature as disin-
        terested Benevolence; *that* nothing can bestow more
        Merit on any human Creature than the Possession of it
        in an eminent Degree; and *that* a Part, at least, of
        its Merit arises from its Tendency to promote the In-
        terests of our Species, and bestow Happiness on human
        Society. *[p.31, 1751 edition (corresponding to p.181
        of P.Nidditch's revised version of the Selby-Bigge
        edition). The passage also appears in this form in
        the editions of 1753-6 and 1758]*

(J)   Upon the whole, then, it seems undeniable, *that*
        there is such a sentiment in human nature as benevo-
        lence; *that* nothing can bestow...
        [Essays and Treatises, 1764, vol.2, p.246]

(K)   'That whole Passage from Page 231 till Page 239 line
        3 must be thrown into an appendix under the Title
        Of Self-love; It must be the second Appendix...'
        *[Letter from Hume to Strahan, 30 July 1776 (see
        Letters, II.330); cf. T.H.Green's note regarding the
        'Hutchesonian' character of this passage (Philo-
        sophical Works, vol.IV, p.52n)]*

(L)   Upon the whole, then, it seems undeniable, *that*
        nothing can bestow more merit on any human creature
        than the sentiment of benevolence in an eminent de-
        gree; and *that* a *part*, at least, of its merit arises
        from its tendency to promote the interests of our
        species, and bestow happiness on human society.
        [Essays and Treatises, 1777, vol.2, p.229]

I shall try to offer an explanation for this series of alterations. Before I begin, however, I must introduce a distinction which, though obvious enough, is of crucial importance for my argument.

While it is a universal truth that anyone, on any occasion, thinks what he or she thinks, it is by no means universally true that anyone, on any occasion, *writes* what she or he thinks. Certainly there is abundant evidence to suggest that Hume did not always write what he thought.[9] The lack of relevant source material for deciding such questions is, no doubt, one reason why Hume scholars have generally avoided raising questions about Hume's more esoteric opinions concerning such matters as human nature, religion and morality.[10]

On one of the most fundamental, and certainly one of the most controversial, questions to be debated in the eighteenth century, the question of the nature of the motive to virtue, Hume has left us, in effect, two mutually incompatible assertions.[11] On one occasion he has written that there *is*, and on another that there *is not*, a sentiment of disinterested benevolence. Now each of the alterations I have mentioned is, at least potentially, an important clue to Hume's real opinion on this question. Behind each lies a deliberate decision on Hume's part to alter what he has written. If we can understand why Hume was led to make these alterations—and this is a question that must occupy Hume's editors no less than his philosophical critics—we may be able to draw some conclusions concerning his real opinions on this important matter.

If we turn to the alterations occurring on volume three of the *Treatise*, (B) *through* (H), we see first of all that some of the alterations, namely (B), (C), (D), (E) and (H), reveal a tendency on Hume's part to a greater explicitness on the question of the motive to justice. With other alterations, such as (F) and (G), we find him actually withdrawing an assertion that appeared in the text of the original and substituting another, quite different assertion. For example, in both (F) and (G) we find him withdrawing the assertion that *public interest* is the motive to obedience, and asserting instead that *interest* unqualified is the motive to our obedience to the laws of justice. With alteration (C) he adds the assertion that self-interest is the original motive to justice.

These alterations to volume three, although not in themselves re-markable, do, I think, take on a certain significance when we consider

Hume's second major publication in the area of moral theory, his *Enquiry concerning the Principles of Morals*, published in 1751. One possible explanation of Hume's alterations is that he made them in the course of preparing the second *Enquiry*. In this case we might expect to find that the alterations made to the earlier work show Hume to be revising certain passages in the direction of the later work. In other words, we might very well expect the alterations to indicate some mid-way position between the *Treatise* and the *Enquiry*. Short of this we might at least expect to find the alterations on the earlier work to be compatible with the later. However, what in fact we find, if we compare certain passages in the 1751 *Enquiry* with some of the alterations in the *Treatise*, is that Hume has altered the *Treatise* in a direction that is opposed, broadly speaking, to the direction taken in the 1751 *Enquiry*.

It is generally agreed that at least one of the differences between the *Treatise* and the *Enquiry* consists in the greater overall importance given to the sentiment of benevolence in the *Enquiry*. There seems in the later work to be a greater emphasis placed upon the altruistic motives—benevolence and fellow-feeling—and a correspondingly diminished emphasis on self-interest or self-love as the motive to virtue. In the *Treatise* (p.481) Hume writes: 'In general, it may be affirm'd, that there is no such passion in human minds, as the love of mankind, merely as such, independent of personal qualities, of services, or of relation to ourself.' This statement appears to conflict with the position he adopts in the 1751 edition of the *Enquiry*, where (in passage (1) above) he asserts the existence of a *disinterested benevolence*. Since the alterations we have been considering appear to be a revision of the *Treatise* in the direction (so to speak) of self-interest and (in the case of such alterations as (G) and (H)) away from 'other-regarding' motives, they cannot be regarded as anticipating the 1751 edition of the *Enquiry*.

Two of Hume's nineteenth-century editors, T.H.Green and L.A. Selby-Bigge, have drawn attention to important theoretical differences between Book III of the *Treatise* and the *Enquiry concerning . . . Morals*.[12] Green, for example, points out that on the question of the motive to virtue Hume seems to have moved from a tendency to reduce all desire to a desire for pleasure to (in the *Enquiry*) a polemic *against* such reductions. Green mentions in particular the passage in the *Enquiry* that appeared in the early editions as the first part of the section 'Of Benevolence', which he calls 'the lovely representation of human nature'. The phrase is borrowed from Francis Hutcheson.

I mention Green and Selby-Bigge only as a reminder that the common practice of quoting more or less indiscriminately from both works (in order to arrive at one comprehensive philosophical position, Hume's 'theory of morals') has not always prevailed. In the present case there is one very good reason why we should avoid it: it obliges us to regard the tension that exists between the two works over the question of egoism versus benevolence as of relatively minor theoretical importance. It is, however, precisely this tension that I believe to be the important clue to the significance of the alterations to volume three.

A second clue to the puzzle posed by the alterations is again provided by Hume's nineteenth-century editors. It is significant that, following upon their observation of an important theoretical difference between the *Treatise* and the *Enquiry*, both Green and Selby-Bigge remark that the *Enquiry* exhibits, far more conspicuously than does the *Treatise*, certain affinities with the position of Francis Hutcheson.[13] It will be recalled that Selby-Bigge, at about the time he wrote this, was engaged in the preparation of his edition of several of Hutcheson's main works on morals[14] and so would have been in a good position to make this kind of comparison.

The thesis of Professor Norman Kemp Smith, that there is an important affinity between Hume and Hutcheson, is, of course, well known.[15] Kemp Smith argued that it was Hume's early reading of Hutcheson's *Inquiry*[16] and *Essay on the Passions*[17] that provided him with the important point of departure for his attack on rationalism. For several reasons I am unhappy with this thesis, and I tend to agree with Professor Mossner that Kemp Smith has somewhat overstated his case for Hume's indebtedness to Hutcheson.[18] Since Kemp Smith's book was written we have been given a far more detailed picture of Hume's background and early reading. The painstaking research of Mossner and others has had the effect of making Kemp Smith's early thesis about Hutcheson's unique influence on Hume far less compelling, resting as it does on a somewhat unhistorical treatment of the external evidence.

The view that morality is based upon feeling, the principal theoretical affinity alleged to exist between Hume and Hutcheson, in fact appears in works by several writers of the seventeenth and eighteenth centuries. It is powerfully expressed in Bayle, a writer whom Hume studied very carefully in his youth.[19] Of perhaps even greater importance with respect to the question of Hume's relationship to Hutcheson is another work that we may be reasonably sure Hume consulted in his early period, prior to the composition of the *Treatise*,[20] namely John Gay's *Preliminary Dissertation Concerning Virtue and Vice*.[21] This work contains not only an attack on rationalist theories of ethics,[22] which is very similar to Hume's in the *Treatise*,[23] but also a criticism of Hutcheson's theory of morals as set out in his *Inquiry*.[24] I believe there are good grounds for supposing it was Hume's reading of this work that primarily determined his attitude (implicit in the *Treatise*) to Hutcheson's moral philosophy.

I have also argued elsewhere against the view of Kemp Smith that Hume constructed his theory of morals upon a Hutchesonian base.[25] I suggest instead that the Hutchesonian echoes, unmistakably present in certain sections of the *Treatise*, are to be accounted for, not in terms of an important theoretical indebtedness, but by a probable hypothesis concerning the peculiar nature of Hutcheson's involvement in the publication of volume three. This in turn will suggest an explanation for the alterations I have listed.

Although I shall have to by-pass any detailed discussion of the connection between Hume and Hutcheson, I suggest that a systematic theoretical difference between the two writers becomes most apparent when we examine their different use of the doctrine of the association of ideas. Not only do they adopt different theories of association,[26] but they differ importantly in the manner in which they apply their theories. Of relatively minor importance for Hutcheson,[27] the association of ideas was for Hume his most important theoretical innovation.[28] It is largely by means of this principle that Hume sought to exhibit various moral and psychological phenomena as merely instances of uniform psychological principles. Whereas Hutcheson postulated original principles in order to account for the phenomena of moral approbation,[29] Hume offered, for essentially the same phenomena, a different sort of explanation. Hume was no less willing than Hutcheson to admit that men can tell the difference between virtue and vice. But unlike Hutcheson, for whom this ability was an irreducible fact of man's nature, and the endpoint of his theory,[30] Hume evidently regarded this 'sense of morals' as being susceptible of further reduction.[31] Hume thought he could reveal such postulates as a moral sense, to be theoretically unnecessary and therefore unscientific.[32] In the *Treatise* (though, again, not as clearly in the *Enquiry*) Hume takes what Hutcheson regards as an irreducible faculty (namely, the moral sense) and explains it in terms of his principle of sympathy—an instance of the principle of the association of ideas operating over particular pleasures and pains.

Of Hume's early relationship with Hutcheson we know very little beyond what can be inferred from their surviving correspondence (four letters from Hume to Hutcheson between 1739 and 1743, and a letter from Hutcheson to Henry Home).[33] I shall not discuss their relationship as indicated in the correspondence beyond saying that the latter reveals four important pieces of information. We learn firstly that Hume submitted volume three in M S for Hutcheson's criticism,[34] secondly that Hume sought Hutcheson's asistance in securing a publisher for the work,[35] thirdly that Hume undertook to revise his work in certain particulars, apparently so as not to cause any embarrassment to Hutcheson over its publication on his [i.e. Hutcheson's] recommendation,[36] and fourthly, that Hutcheson eventually consented to recommend Hume to his own publisher, Thomas Longman.[37]

Now it seems to have been widely assumed that the text Hutcheson saw in MS was substantially the text that appeared in print. However, I believe that a close examination of the evidence—and here all we have is the Hume/Hutcheson correspondence—does not strictly warrant such a conclusion. We know from certain of the remarks made in the letters that Hutcheson was familiar with at least some of the themes from volume three, such as Hume's important assertion that justice is an 'artificial virtue' (one, incidentally, to which Hutcheson appears to have objected[38]), but we cannot necessarily conclude that Hutcheson saw Hume's manuscript *in the form in which it went to print.*

We know from the letters that, after some initial reluctance, Hume offered to make some alterations to his work[39] in order, presumably, to overcome reservations that Hutcheson had expressed about recommending the work to his publisher. Hume explicitly mentions the case of certain passages that might give offence to the religious[40] and gives Hutcheson to understand that he will remove them.[41] What has not been remarked in the correspondence, however, is that several passages seem calculated to give Hutcheson the impression that Hume was also revising his work in a more generally *Hutchesonian* direction.

There is, for example, in the letter of 16th March 1740, Hume's request for advice from Hutcheson on what he calls a 'Point of Prudence'. Hume quotes the passage in which he compares virtue and vice to sounds and colours, and asks Hutcheson whether he ought to include it.[42] There may well have been a point of prudence at stake; on the other hand, it would be difficult to find any more characteristically Hutchesonian passage in the whole of the *Treatise.*[43] It is in this light, I believe, that we ought to consider the first alteration, (A), which I have listed. In the letter which accompanies the MS 'Conclusion' Hume assures Hutcheson that 'The Book is pretty much alter'd since you saw it'.[44] As an earnest of this, he writes 'I have sent you the *Conclusion,* as I have alter'd it, that you may see I desire to keep on good Terms even with the strictest & most rigid.'[45] In scoring out the words 'both our Selfishness and Pride', which occur in apposition to the phrase 'every Principle of our Nature', Hume may appear to be repudiating (and most certainly would have been taken by Hutcheson as repudiating) a certain sort of basis for morality, namely selfishness and pride, a position popularly associated with Dr Bernard Mandeville and other writers who came to be called 'the selfish school'. Hutcheson was vehemently opposed to such theories and his main work on morals, the

Inquiry, was (he tells us in the title page) directed against the 'Author of the *Fable of the Bees*'.[46]

While Hume and Hutcheson were on the same side of one contemporary debate, the question of whether morality was based on reason or sentiment, they seem to have been on opposite sides with respect to another: the question of the origin of the 'peculiar' feelings specifically associated with morality (Hume makes interesting allusion to this debate on two occasions in Book II).[47] Unlike Hutcheson, Hume maintained that the particular feelings associated with virtue, in particular the virtue of justice, were not 'original' and 'implanted' (as Hutcheson believed[48]) but were rather the result of 'interest' and 'education'. Again, this is most evident from a consideration of the way Hume employs the psychological principle of the association of ideas.[49] The clearest evidence for this is to be found in certain sections of Book III, sections, I suggest, that Hutcheson may not have seen in MS.[50]

It is against this background that the alterations I have cited may be understood. It is evident from his correspondence with Hutcheson that Hume felt obliged to make some alterations to his work simply in order to satisfy Hutcheson. Having succeeded in this, however, Hume could not resist making some last minute alterations to the text. At least part of his reason for doing this was to make more explicit his real position on the question of the motive to justice, and, thereby, to dissociate his own theory from Hutcheson's moral sense and benevolence theory. This is also consistent with the bibliographical evidence, which tends to suggest that Hume was making fairly substantial alterations during the final stages of printing.[51]

If the preceding hypothesis is correct, the alterations to volume three have a rather peculiar significance in the metamorphosis of the work. It may be inferred from Hume's correspondence with Hutcheson on the one hand, and Hume's MS alterations on the other, that over two different periods Hume revised his work in two somewhat diverging directions, the first to overcome Hutcheson's moral and religious scruples, and the second to emphasize a certain point about human nature that the first revision may have partially concealed. The MS alterations, then, are important for the light they shed upon this latter line of development.

Whether Hutcheson actually received the impression that Hume was trying to convey in his letters, namely, that he was developing an essentially Hutchesonian theory, is, perhaps, a moot point. It is clear, however, that after initially voicing certain scruples Hutcheson did finally consent to the request that he use his influence on Hume's behalf to find him a publisher (his own as it happened).[52]

I now wish to suggest, as briefly as I can, the way in which Hume may have been able to give Hutcheson (and, therefore, a good many Hume scholars) the false impression that his theory of morals was a development of Hutcheson's own position without actually having to commit himself to Hutcheson's theory.

Anyone well acquainted with the *Treatise* will be aware of Hume's tendency to use a term of ordinary discourse in an unfamiliar and quite technical sense,[53] an almost unavoidable practice of a reductionist theory. If terms such as 'sympathy'[54] and 'natural'[55] were used ambiguously by Hume in such a way as to conceal the fact that he *was* using them in a quite specific technical sense, he could easily have succeeded in creating on Hutcheson's part a somewhat mistaken impression about the tendency of his theory. Thus, like Hutcheson, Hume could insist on the importance of having a 'virtuous motive' but mean by this expression something quite different from what Hutcheson would have understood by the phrase. Hume seems to use 'virtuous motive' to refer indifferently to anything which could successfully prompt us to perform a virtuous act. In other words he seems to use the phrase 'virtuous motive' as if it were equivalent in meaning to 'motive to virtue'.[56] When we recall that Hutcheson would have been acquainted with Hume's theory of morals in MS instalments only, and, possibly, only *selected* MS instalments, it is not difficult to see how Hutcheson could have been left with the impression that Hume's position had greater affinities with his own than it really had.

Many of Hume's commentators have expressed puzzlement at Hume's apparent admission of a moral sense in section ii of part I.[57] It seems to be inconsistent with the reductionist tendency of the *Treatise*. Indeed, this admission is perhaps the strongest *prima facie* evidence for Hume's connection with Hutcheson. Yet, appearances to the contrary notwithstanding, it is surely a mistake to ascribe a moral sense theory to Hume. It is significant that, apart from one isolated instance, Hume does not use the phrase 'moral sense' in the section in which he is supposed to maintain the theory of the moral sense. He speaks instead of a 'sense of virtue'[58] (which, since it denotes no more than the phenomena of moral approbation and disapprobation, Hume believed he could reduce after the manner I indicated on page 214 above). The isolated instance is in the section title, 'Moral distinctions derived from a moral sense', and its appearance here certainly does create the impression, which, if I am right, Hume wanted Hutcheson to have, that he accepted the moral sense theory.[59] It is most likely that Hutcheson would have been shown Hume's early draft of this section, with its extraordinary concession to revealed religion (in the form of an italicized sentence implying Hume's belief in the 'miracles, on which our religion is founded')[60] as well as its rather uncharacteristic panegyric on the beauty of noble and generous actions.[61] This section contains also some of the most perplexing passages in the *Treatise*, as anyone who has tried to make sense of the passage on page 471 (intended it would seem to clarify the connection between pleasure and moral approbation) will surely agree.

As for those sections of the *Treatise* that, in all likelihood, Hutcheson did *not* see, I suggest, as one obvious candidate, the section entitled 'Some farther reflections concerning justice and injustice'. In this section Hume announces that he will 'open up a little more distinctly' his sentiments on the subject of the origin of justice.[62] Here Hume explicitly denies that there is any need to postulate the existence of any 'peculiar original principles' in human nature beyond self-interested passions.[63] Repudiating the view (which, elsewhere, he ascribes to Hutcheson[64]) that men have been endowed with a strong regard for moral good, Hume maintains that, on the contrary, ''tis self-love which is their real origin' (sc. the laws of justice).[65]

I hope I have said enough to show at least the *possibility* of a connection between Hume's negotiations with Hutcheson on the question of a new publisher and some of the alterations made by Hume on a copy of volume three. As to the question of the textual significance of the alterations, I think that we are entitled to draw at least one general conclusion. Any new edition of the *Treatise* making use of these alterations should incorporate them in such a way as to make it clear to the reader that he is reading a passage Hume altered. Moreover, it would be preferable if this were done in such a way as to indicate the original reading, so enabling the reader to form his own conclusions regarding the significance of the alterations.

In conclusion, I would like to apologize for adding yet another exegetical complication to the study of a work which is already difficult enough. There may be a few benefits, however. The traditional constraint placed upon any interpretation of Hume on morals, that it be consistent with his admission of a moral sense, has tended to conceal other, positive, features of Hume's thought in the *Treatise*. The emphasis upon self-interest suggests, perhaps, a more immediate connection between the *Treatise* and his essays on Political economy in the *Political Discourses*, between his critique of certain tenets of so-called merchant capitalism or mercantilism and Adam Smith's classic theory.[66] The assumption that a close theoretical connection existed between Hume and Hutcheson has similarly tended to obscure for us Hume's very real affinities with those writers, such as Hobbes, Bayle and Mandeville, from whom Hume inherited, most importantly, his view of human nature.[67] It was in works by Hobbes that Hume's most important theoretical tool, his doctrine of the association of ideas, was forged.[68] We may find in Bayle Hume's thesis that reason cannot prompt us to any action,[69] and, in all three writers, the common belief concerning human nature that man almost always follows the ruling passion of his soul.[70]

This view of human nature, so carefully concealed in his later works, Hume never abandoned. It is significant that, shortly before his death, Hume should have described the love of literary fame as his own particular 'ruling passion'.[71] Some have been puzzled that Hume should have left us with a statement that seems to invite cynical speculation about his philosophical integrity. The statement, however, merely highlights Hume's sincerely held belief about human nature. I believe it can be taken as the final autobiographical statement of a man who, looking back upon his life, refused to do so in bad faith.

However, if Hume did turn his back on philosophy, it may equally be said that philosophy had done no less to him. After his major contribution to philosophy 'failed even to excite a murmur among the zealots' Hume's choice was either to abandon writing for a philosophical audience altogether, or to bury his real philosophical sentiments so deeply in his more accessible works as to render them all but impossible to detect.

It is, perhaps, in this light that we should interpret his final alteration to the *Enquiry*, and his real position on the question of self-love versus benevolence. The final alteration to his *Enquiry*, to my knowledge the last alteration Hume made to any of his works, is one he made two hundred years ago. On 12th August 1776 Hume penned the following letter to Strahan, his printer/publisher:

Dear Sir

Please to make with your Pen the following Correction. In the second Volume of my philosophical Pieces, p. 245, l.1, and 2, eraze these words, *that there is such a sentiment in human nature as benevolence.*

This, Dear Sir, is the last Correction I shall probably trouble you with. . . .[72]

Shortly before directing Strahan to remove the only assertion in the text of the *Enquiry* that explicitly committed him to the existence of an original principle of benevolence, Hume had asked Strahan to transfer the opening passage of his first section, 'Of Benevolence' (the Hutchessonian 'lovely representation of human nature'), to the end of the book, where, Hume directs, it should become a second appendix under a new title, 'Of Self-love'.[73] The philosophical significance of the dying author's last literary act has not yet been fully appreciated. Rather than rewrite the passage that condemns any attempt to reduce benevolence to self-love, Hume sets the record straight by a simple change of title.

As Ernest C. Mossner has justly remarked 'Never was the philosopher more ironical than in making his preparations for dying',[74] to which he might have added 'and, ironically, never was he more of a philosopher'.

1.   See R. W. Connon 'Some MS Corrections by Hume in the Third Volume of his *Treatise of Human Nature' Long Room* 11 (1975) 14–22. The discovery was first announced in a letter in the *TLS* (4 April 1975) 376. MS alterations to the *Abstract* are listed in R. W. Connon 'Some Hume MS Alterations on a Copy of the *Abstract' Journal of the History of Philosophy* 14 (1976) 353–6.

2.   For a more detailed discussion see 'Corrections . . . in the Third Volume . . .', 14–15.

3.   Professor Klibansky's note appeared in *Hume; Theory of Politics*, ed. F. Watkins (Edinburgh 1951) pp. 245–6.

4.   Other possible explanations are (i) Hume made the alterations in the hope of interesting a publisher in bringing out a second edition of the *Treatise*, (ii) Hume made the alterations in the course of preparing a new work on 'morals'. (His *Enquiry concerning the Principles of Morals* was published in 1751.) (iii) Hume made the alterations on a particular copy for private circulation. On the basis solely of the textual and bibliographical evidence there is, I believe, some slight reason for supposing that the alterations were intended for the first edition of the work. A comparison with other copies suggests that the 'Hume Copy' is probably an early copy of the edition since it exhibits fewer corrections, i.e. corrections made by the printer, than other copies. Moreover, the alterations made on the copy, in addition to conforming to eighteenth-century proof correction conventions, appear to have been made on the printed sheets before the book was bound. There is the additional fact that some of the MS alterations were incorporated in the text of some copies by means of cancelled leaves. This would be consistent with the hypothesis that they may all have been intended as proof corrections to be incorporated into the first edition. The principal variants within the edition, and certainly all the major ones that I have come across have been given by William Todd in his recent bibliographical description of the *Treatise* ('David Hume. A Preliminary Bibliography' in W. B. Todd (ed.) *Hume and the Enlightenment. Essays presented to Ernest Campbell Mossner* (Edinburgh and Austin 1974) pp. 189–205, esp. p. 190.

5.   The first edition of this work was published in London in 1751.

6.   *Letters*, i. 37.

7.   P. H. Nidditch is preparing a new critical edition of the *Enquiries* with an apparatus of variant readings. See his notes to his revised version of the Selby-Bigge edition of *Enquiries Concerning the Human Understanding and Concerning the Principles of Morals by David Hume*, 3rd edition, ed. L. A. Selby-Bigge, with text revised and notes by P. H. Nidditch (Oxford 1975) pp. 348n–9n.

8.   *Letters*, ii. 331–2.

9.   See *Letters*, i. 25, 36–7, and cf. D'Alembert's response to Voltaire's criticism of several articles on theology and metaphysics, which had appeared in the French *Encyclopédie*: 'No doubt we have bad articles in

theology and metaphysics, but since we publish by favour, and have theologians for censors, I defy you to make them any better. There are other articles that are far less exposed to the daylight, and in them all is repaired. Time will enable people to *distinguish what we have thought from what we have said.*' (Quoted in Kingsley Martin *French Liberal Thought in the Eighteenth Century* (London 1954) p. 97, italics mine.)

10. See in this regard Selby-Bigge's excellent discussion of the relationship between the *Treatise* and the *Enquiries* in his 'Introduction' to the *Enquiries*, esp. pp. xxiii–xxxi.

11. See p. 212, below.

12. See Selby-Bigge's 'Introduction' p. xxiii and T. H. Green's note (*The Philosophical Works of David Hume*, ed. T. H. Green and T. H. Grose, 4 vols. (London, 1874–75) vol. IV, p. 52n.) See also Ernest Albee 'Hume's Ethical System' *The Philosophical Review* 6 (1897) 337–55.

13. *Philosophical Works*, vol. IV, p. 52n and Selby-Bigge's 'Introduction', p. xxiv.

14. *British Moralists*, ed. L. A. Selby-Bigge (Oxford 1897).

15. Norman Kemp Smith *The Philosophy of David Hume* (London 1941); see, for example, the preface, p. vi.

16. Francis Hutcheson *Inquiry Concerning the Original of our Ideas of Virtue and Moral Good* (Dublin 1725). All references to Hutcheson's *Inquiry* are to the second edition reprinted in *British Moralists*, ed. L. A. Selby-Bigge.

17. Francis Hutcheson *Essay on the Nature and the Conduct of the Passions and Illustrations on the Moral Sense* (London 1728).

18. E. C. Mossner *The Life of David Hume* (Edinburgh and Austin 1954) p. 76n.

19. Evidence concerning Hume's reading of Bayle may be found in Professor Mossner's edition of Hume's MS notebook 'Hume's Early Memoranda, 1729–40: The Complete Text' *Journal of the History of Ideas* IX (1948) 492–518.

20. 'Hume's Early Memoranda . . .', p. 498.

21. John Gay *Preliminary Dissertation Concerning the Fundamental Principles of Virtue or Morality*, included in the 1731 edition of William King *An Essay on the Origin of Evil*, trans. from the Latin by Edmund Law (London 1731) pp. xi–xxxiii.

22. Gay, pp. xi–xiii.

23. See esp. Section 1 of pt. III, bk. III, pp. 466–67. All references to the *Treatise* are to the Selby-Bigge edition.

24. Gay, pp. xiiiff.

25. I have argued this at length in my unpublished Doctoral Thesis to be submitted at the University of Oxford, esp. chapters V, VI and VIII.

26. For a recent discussion of the differing origins of Hume's and Hutcheson's doctrines of the association of ideas see Martin Kallich *The Association of Ideas and Critical Theory in Eighteenth-Century England* (The Hague 1970), esp. pp. 56–65, 68, 70, 73–95. Kallich argues that the doctrine of the association of ideas took two more or less distinct forms in the eighteenth century, one deriving from Locke and the other from Hobbes. Kallich maintains that in Hume's case the form of associationism adopted was the Hobbesian version whereas Hutcheson adopted the Lockean version. In another study of associationism Luigi Ferri makes the same point concerning the form of Hutcheson's associationism, *La*

Psychologie de l'Association depuis Hobbes jusqu'à nos jours (*histoire et critique*) (Paris 1883) p. 12.

27. cf. James McCosh *The Scottish Philosophy* (London 1875) pp. 77–8.

28. See Hume's own remarks concerning his use of the doctrine of the association of ideas in *An Abstract of a Treatise of Human Nature* (London 1740) p. 31.

29. cf. *Inquiry*, sec. iv, para. 144, p. 127.

30. cf. *Inquiry*, sec. ii, para. 94, p. 87. See also Sir James MacIntosh 'Dissertation on the Progress of Ethical Philosophy' *The Miscellaneous Works of Sir James MacIntosh*, 3 vols. (1846) vol. I, p. 126.

31. On Hume's account the 'sense of virtue' is not regarded as an 'original instinct' of the human mind but is instead accounted for in terms of the more general doctrine of sympathy; see, for example, *Treatise*, p. 619.

32. To postulate an original moral sense to explain the phenomenon of moral discrimination (where the latter could be accounted for in terms of a principle of greater generality such as the principle of the association of ideas) might be seen as a violation of Newton's first 'Rule of Reasoning in Philosophy' (viz. 'We are to admit no more causes of natural things than such as are both true and sufficient to explain their appearances', Sir Isaac Newton *Philosophiae Naturalis Principia Mathematica*, 2 vols (London 1686) vol. II, 202). This is implied by Gay's remarks on p. xiv, (see note 21, above); cf. note 50, below.

33. Ian Ross 'Hutcheson on Hume's *Treatise*: An Unnoticed Letter' *Journal of the History of Philosophy* IV (1966) 69–72.

34. *Letters*, i.32.

35. *Letters*, i.36–7.

36. *Letters*, i. 37.

37. *Letters*, i. 38.

38. *Letters*, i. 33; cf. also 46–8.

39. cf. *Letters*, i. 33, 34, 36, 37.

40. *Letters*, i. 34, 37.

41. *Letters*, i. 34.

42. *Letters*, i. 39–40. The corresponding passage in the *Treatise* occurs in Book III, Part I, Section I, p. 469. This may perhaps be taken as an indication that the first section and possibly the entire first part of Book III may have been among the last sections which Hume composed.

43. cf., for example, Hutcheson's passage in sec. i, art. xvi, in his *An Inquiry Concerning Beauty, Order, Harmony, Design* (London 1725), edited in a modern reprint by Peter Kivy (The Hague 1973) pp. 38–39. (The text is based on the fourth edition.)

44. *Letters*, i. 37.

45. ibid.

46. Bernard Mandeville *The Fable of the Bees, or Private vices publick benefits. Containing several discourses to demonstrate that human frailties . . . may be turned to the advantage of civil society* (London 1714). In the Advertisement that Hutcheson added to the fourth edition of his *Reflections upon Laughter* he again mentions Mandeville's *Fable*, describing it as 'that pernicious book', 4th. edition (London). Kaye, the editor of the standard edition of Mandeville's *Fable* describes Hutcheson as Mandeville's 'most persistent opponent': Mandeville was an obsession with Hutcheson according to Kaye 'He could hardly write a book without devoting much

of it to attacking the *Fable*'. (*The Fable* . . . , ed. F. B. Kaye, 2 vols. (Oxford 1924) vols. I, cxli and II, 345n–346n.

47. cf. *Treatise*, pp. 295–6, and esp. p. 310.
48. See *Inquiry*, sec. ii, para., 87, p. 83; cf. Sir James MacIntosh, I, p. 126.
49. Hume's frequent appeals to the influence of 'general rules' on human nature testify to his awareness of the familiar psychological phenomenon of the conditioned response.
50. See p. 217, below.
51. See note 4, above.
52. The *Treatise*, Book III, *Of Morals*, was published for Thomas Longman at the Ship in Pater-noster-Row. Longman was Hutcheson's London publisher and bookseller.
53. cf. Hume's remark on p. 124 concerning a writer's right to use 'his terms in what sense he pleases'.
54. cf. *Treatise*, pp. 317, 369, 384–6, 427. Hume's concept of sympathy has some affinities with that of Mandeville as expressed in his *Fable*, see remark (N), pp. 163, 165 (Harmondsworth: Penguin Books 1970); cf. also pp. 100 and 192. James Noxon has also suggested a connection with Mandeville via Hume's concept of sympathy, in *Hume's Philosophical Development; A Study of his Methods* (Oxford 1973) p. 23.
55. cf., for example, Hume's use of the phrase 'natural sentiments' on p. 500. For more information concerning Hume's original MS alterations to this passage (which are partially incorporated in the Selby-Bigge edition) see Connon, 'Corrections . . . in the Third Volume . . . ' p. 15, the alteration to p. 76 of the first edition.
56. Hume seems to use the phrase 'virtuous motive' in a rather loose sense simply to mean 'the motive to virtue' (which turns out, for Hume, to be pleasure in some qualified sense). This use of the phrase amounts to something of a departure from 'ordinary language' where the word 'virtuous' would be understood as modifying the word 'motive'.
57. cf. John Hill Burton *Life and Correspondence of David Hume* (Edinburgh 1846) vol. I, p. 121.
58. cf. *Treatise*, pp. 471, 475, 484, 500. Hume, on a number of occasions, also uses the phrase 'sense of morals'; see pp. 483, 499 and 619 (this last reference is to a passage which Hutcheson would have seen in the MS 'Conclusion'). Hume sometimes also refers to a 'sense of morality', p. 479.
59. The only other occasion I have found where Hume uses the phrase the 'moral sense' is on p. 588. Here it is even more clear that Hume did not accept the doctrine of an original moral sense, for he refers to his own 'explication of the moral sense' in terms of sympathy. The passage also contains an interesting allusion to Newton's 'Rules of Reasoning in Philosophy'; cf. note 32 above.
60. *Treatise*, p. 474.
61. *Treatise*, p. 470. Hume expresses a similar enthusiasm for virtue and the generosity of human nature (altered by Hume to read 'our nature', see Connon, p. 21) in his 'Conclusion', p. 619. This we know (see above p. 207) was submitted to Hutcheson in MS.
62. *Treatise*, p. 527.
63. *Treatise*, p. 526.
64. *Letters*, i. 46–7.

65. *Treatise*, p. 529.
66. Many of the entries in the surviving memoranda notebook (see note 29) bear witness to Hume's interest in political economy. See Mossner 'Hume's Early Memoranda . . . ', pp. 497–9. See also my doctoral thesis, chapter VIII.
67. For a succinct statement of this view of human nature see Mandeville *The Fable* . . ., Kaye edition, vol. I, p. 39.
68. I have argued this at length in my doctoral thesis, chapter IV. See also Kallich, pp. 14, 93; Ferri, pp. 1–2; Gabriel Compayré *La Philosophie de David Hume* (Paris 1873) pp. 60–1; Thomas Reid 'Train of Thought in the Mind' in *Essays on the Intellectual Powers of Man* (London 1969) ch. 4, Essay 4, p. 455; Dugald Stewart *Collected Works*, 11 vols. (Edinburgh 1854–60) vol. I, p. 81.
69. See, for example, Pierre Bayle *Miscellaneous Reflections Occasion'd by the Comet Which appear'd in December 1680. Chiefly tending to explode Popular Superstitions (trans) to which is added the author's Life*, 2 vols. (London 1708) vol. II, pp. 374, 363, 546. In my thesis I present external evidence for Hume's having read this particular work by Bayle.
70. Bayle, I, pp. 272, 279. Also cf. Mandeville *The Fable* . . . (Penguin) pp. 200, 143; Thomas Hobbes *Leviathan* (Harmondsworth: Penguin Books 1968) pp. 127–8.
71. *Letters*, i. 7.
72. *Letters*, ii. 331–2.
73. *Letters*, ii. 329–30.
74. Mossner *Life*, p. 591.

Hume on some Non-Natural Distinctions

IN HIS *Enquiry concerning the Principles of Morals*, (III.ii), Hume compares distinctions of property with distinctions made by superstition. Of course, the point of the argument is to show how unlike they are—the one so useful and the other so useless, burdensome and frivolous. But Hume considers one fundamental respect in which they resemble each other. What is my property is determined by customary symbolic acts, and is marked by some object that serves as a reminder or proof that this symbolic action has been performed. In a parallel way, land or building that is sacred is determined by a symbolic act—the act of consecration; and it is commonly marked by some holy sign or object that indicates what has been done. In each case we have a difference *established* by the carrying out of a ritual action, and *marked* (very often) by a permanent sign: initials on a boundary-stone, crosses in a wall, a name added to a record. Of course, the ritual action is sufficient to make the distinction. But actions may later be forgotten or denied. 'The faintest ink is better than the strongest memory'. So say the Welsh, and they should know.

The difference between my land and yours cannot be observed. A division of *territory* occurs where a river flows or the hills begin. These are essentially observable: they are natural distinctions. A division of *property* is non-natural and therefore is marked by walls or landmarks.

What is needed, then, to make and to mark the distinctions, are symbols correctly made. In any ritual, only certain kinds of mistake matter at all. In a deed of conveyance a spelling mistake would be disregarded; nobody worries if an oath of allegiance is uttered in bad Latin and bad Latin has conferred many an Honorary Degree.

An oath of allegiance is an example of a kind of symbolic act that seems to me very important. It establishes a distinction not of property but of status; it makes a division not of land or of things but of persons. Hume takes it for granted that all such distinctions are non-natural. The difference between a lord and his liegeman is essentially unobservable and is therefore marked by differences of dress and address. There are differences between distinctions of property and distinctions of status: persons are not quite as simple as lands or goods.

The non-natural distinctions of religion relate to lands and goods and persons. Hume considers the consecration of a building or territory.

What *difference* could the muttering of certain words make to the building? Is not this a non-event?

A Syrian would have starved rather than taste pigeon; an Egyptian would not have approached bacon.[1]

But there is no observable difference between the uneatable pigeons of Syria and the wholesome pigeons of Scotland. Still more striking, how can chicken on Thursdays be good food and chicken on Fridays abominable? There is no natural kind called chicken-on-thursday or chicken-on-friday: there is just chicken.

But Hume does not dismiss these superstitious distinctions because they are non-natural. On the contrary, he uses them to explain in what way the distinctions of property are non-natural:

> Had I worn this apparel an hour ago, I had merited the severest punishment; but a man, by pronouncing a few magical syllables, has now rendered it fit for my use and service.[2]

Hume's total rejection of religious distinctions is not made on the grounds that they are meaningless or derive from non-events. He rejects them because of what he takes to be their meaning. If there were a realm of supernatural beings actually existing—if indeed the supernatural were natural—these distinctions would be extremely useful. If there were gods, we should do well to offer prayers and sacrifices and the whole apparatus of religion might be very well worth while.

I wish to make the following three comments and to support them:

(1) Distinctions of persons are often valued for themselves and not (or not only) on account of the natural advantages they bring. We see this where the symbol which marks out a certain status is itself richly valued—as, for example, a family name.

(2) Friendship may be regarded as a kind of status marked by symbols which have to be respected if the friendship is to hold. Other distinctions of persons bestow a temporary status, as *the bride*. In such cases the status is marked chiefly by the way we behave to its possessor. It is the deference shown to the bride that makes her brief status worth having.

(3) Religious distinctions are better understood by comparing them with distinctions of status rather than with distinctions of property.

(1) It is no doubt useful in many ways to be a wife or a husband, an Elder of the Kirk, a Peer of the Realm or a BA. But there is also something attaching to the status itself: the symbols that mark out the status are themselves enjoyed. Of course, this always means within a given society, against the more or less permanent background of an organised society. It is something that has to do with the being of the society rather than its doing; and with the being of those who enjoy the status

rather than with what they may do or get. What is there to being a
lord? I am told it has advantages: you can get your credit extended because even a bank feels it a privilege to lend you money. But I suspect
there is one outstanding benefit and this is being addressed as 'Lord
So-and-so', or 'Your Lordship', or 'My Lord'. The symbol itself com-
mands regard, it is poetic, imaginative. And this especially attaches to a
title that has been not earned but inherited. An earned title is a sign of
achievements; one might be proud of these and think of the title as
marking out for other people a *natural* distinction (which they might
otherwise fail to notice) between big You and little Them. This seems
to be Aristotle's account of honour. It is the inherited title that is the
purer commodity. One can enjoy the title with no benefits but the
honourable status: the address, the uniform, the symbols. One can
enjoy heraldic achievements without having any other achievements
to one's credit. By contrast, the symbols that mark out landed property
and other possessions are not valued on their own account. We do not
buy suits in order to collect receipts, and even title-deeds do not themselves add anything to life. I believe that symbols of status often do
precisely that: they add something to life; not any of the 'things to be
met with in space'—not natural goods but non-natural goods. This
unfashionable view derives from Coleridge.

(2) We use symbols in order to express to others our feelings towards
them. We send messages of sympathy and flowers and grapes and good
wishes, and none of these is intended to be useful to the person who
receives them. In this way we may express the feeling of the moment.
But our lives are not entirely consumed in the spontaneous overflow of
powerful feelings. Our likes and dislikes, affections and sympathies
settle down into long-term attitudes to people and places. The structure
we settle for makes distinctions between persons—some of whom
acquire with us a certain status. There are, one might say, formalities
to be observed between friends. The structure we settle for, in fact, is
demarcated by certain symbols, and some of these are all but essential
to any sort of friendship. A friend acquires rights. What might be called
basic to any friendship are 'friendly gestures' and immunity from un-
friendly gestures. If my friend announces his forthcoming marriage
and I find myself considering the omens with despair, what am I to do?
If I am to preserve the existing relationship then I must send him my
congratulations and good wishes. My silence would be taken as deliberately damaging. I have good reason for a symbolic action; and he, to
expect it.

In a somewhat similar way there are people who, while not our
permanent friends, may acquire a temporary status: someone who acts
as my host or guest, the bride, the bereaved, the new graduate. One

does not write congratulations or condolences every day or year by year, but the structure of our lives requires us to send one or other on occasion. We write to the bereaved to acknowledge for whom the bell has tolled. It may be that this is absolutely all that we can do. The symbolic, expressive character of these actions comes out most clearly in the case of someone who has to face a great trial in the near future. We send him our good wishes now. It is understood that this cannot affect the issue of the ordeal. If a dentist, about to extract a tooth, were to offer you his best wishes that would be cause for alarm. It is as symbols that our messages of good will matter. Again there are cases where not to send such a message would be to upset an existing order. Even those who are not welcome may be entitled to a welcome. (The host who omitted this was rebuked by Jesus: 'Thou gavest me no kiss'.)

The formality of these symbols serves to moderate the expression of feelings and to exclude the expression of contrary feelings. And certainly the control of the expression tends to be also a control of the feelings themselves. The use of formal modes may either inhibit or stimulate the feelings. It makes a difference to the way we feel about cousins of the opposite sex if the customary greeting is a kiss.

(3) The symbolic actions and objects of religion express what believers (and others) feel or what in some sense they ought to feel. It is possible to think of prayers as a kind of good wishes, albeit wishes that invoke a power. This is very much Hume's view. Prayers for deliverance help because they support us now, not because they bring deliverance. No prayers are answered except by chance, and the power invoked only seems to be external. In so far as there is any operative power it must lie in the feelings of the well-wisher or supplicant and of the person prayed for. The whole thing is subjective, but the minds and hearts of those involved are more strongly affected if they believe that a prayer is something more than a wish. A blessing is a special form of prayer and may be quite strictly formalised. It matters what formula is used and who utters it. It is a symbolic act: an expression of good will and something else as well. The formula marks out a boundary between the natural and the supernatural. This is, of course, not an observable distinction. The symbol that makes it is the blessing itself.

The hopes and fears that give rise to symbols are the same that lead us to imagine powers that help or defend us. The powers of love or fear prompt the imagination to shape ideas of powers external to us, and in this way, according to Hume, we are carried 'beyond the present course of things'. The passions involved must be the common primitive passions:

> the ordinary affections of human life; the anxious concern for happiness, the dread of future misery, the terror of death, the thirst of revenge, the appetite for food and other necessaries.[3]

To these Hume elsewhere adds the need for children—still, all over the world, the aim of votive offerings. Such needs (of which we may not be conscious) and such desires stir the imagination, and in this way we come to view with astonishment 'the first obscure traces of divinity'.[4] The important word in Hume's account is 'astonished'. There must be something that goes on below the level of conscious scrutiny. We ourselves imagine supernatural powers and we view them with astonishment. The need or desire, the external power and the symbol are necessarily connected. The power must have a name, and to cause the power to operate, some symbolic action is also needed. Hence passion (internal and projected), symbolic object and symbolic action.

1. *Enquiries*, p. 198.
2. *Enquiries*, p. 199.
3. 'The Natural History of Religion' in *The Philosophical Works of David Hume*, ed. T. H. Green and T. H. Grose (London 1874–5) vol. IV, p. 316.
4. ibid.

Hume's Law, Hume's Way

As You May Recall, when Hume was on his deathbed, Boswell journeyed to Edinburgh to ask the Great Atheist if he thought it was possible that his soul might survive. Hume responded that it was possible that a piece of coal, thrown on the fire, would not burn. Just in case that piece of coal did not burn and Hume is still with us, I think he would appreciate it if we got straight what *he* was saying, instead of using him for our own purposes. For this reason I would like to re-open the question of the now famous 'is-ought' passage in the *Treatise of Human Nature*. Hume has usually been taken to be saying, in this passage, that moral statements can never be derived from statements that do not contain moral terms, so that morality becomes an autonomous branch of knowledge or of discourse, depending on the sophistication of one's position. This interpretation of the passage is not merely quoted but approved of by many disparate groups, each anxious to show that factual premises cannot lead to moral conclusions, and has entered the lexicon as 'Hume's Law'.

It is my contention that this is not what Hume is talking about, and that the Hume's Law passage is at best only peripherally relevant to the meta-ethical disputes of the twentieth century. For the clue to the correct interpretation of the passage, we must remember that it does not stand alone, but is part of a chapter in which Hume has been arguing that reason can not be the basis[1] of morals. He claims that he can establish this by showing that reason alone can never make the distinction between right and wrong, and that even if it could, it could do nothing to make us act accordingly. As Hume puts it: ''Tis one thing to know virtue, and another to conform the will to it.' (*Treatise*, p. 465). The Hume's Law passage is an explication of this point.

The approach, then, will be oblique. I intend to look at the argument of Book III, Part i, section 1 of the *Treatise*; from this we shall be able to see what Hume is doing in the Hume's Law paragraph.

The intention of the entire section is to show, as against the Rationalists, that reason can not be the sole basis (in any sense) of morality. In the second half, Hume sets and discusses two problems for the Rationalists. (A) They must be able to show the relations on which a distinction between right and wrong is founded, in such a way as to exclude anything which has nothing to do with morality. (B) They must be able to show that, if there were such perceivable moral relations, they would

in fact be binding on us. Problem A is not the issue here; problem B is
what I shall concentrate on. This is a discussion, then, of an argument
which runs from page 464 to page 470 of the *Treatise*. My claim will
be that it is immediately relevant to the interpretation of the Hume's
Law passage, which is its final step.

Hume's challenge to the Rationalist is issued, and the impossibility
of his meeting it is argued for, in a paragraph much-ignored until
recently:

> But it will be still more difficult to fulfil the *second* condition,
> requisite to justify this system. According to the principles of those
> who maintain an abstract rational difference betwixt moral good
> and evil, and a natural fitness and unfitness of things, 'tis not only
> supposed, that these relations, being eternal and immutable, are
> the same, when consider'd by every rational creature, but their
> *effects* are also suppos'd to be necessarily the same; and 'tis concluded
> they have no less, or rather a greater, influence in directing the
> will of the deity, than in governing the rational and virtuous of
> our own species. These two particulars are evidently distinct. 'Tis
> one thing to know virtue, and another to conform the will to it.
> In order, therefore, to prove, that the measures of right and wrong
> are eternal laws, *obligatory* on every rational mind, 'tis not
> sufficient to shew the relations upon which they are founded: We
> must also point out the connexion betwixt the relation and the
> will; and must prove that this connexion is so necessary, that in
> every well-disposed mind, it must take place and have its influ-
> ence; tho' the difference betwixt these minds be in other respects
> immense and infinite. Now besides what I have already prov'd,
> that even in human nature no relation can ever alone produce any
> action; besides this, I say, it has been shewn, in treating of the
> understanding, that there is no connexion of cause and effect, such
> as this is suppos'd to be, which is discoverable otherwise than by
> experience, and of which we can pretend to have any security by
> the simple consideration of the objects. All beings in the universe,
> consider'd in themselves, appear entirely loose and independent of
> each other. 'Tis only by experience we learn their influence and
> connexion; and this influence we ought never to extend beyond
> experience.

> Thus it will be impossible to fulfil the *first* condition required
> to the system of eternal rational measures of right and wrong;
> because it is impossible to shew those relations, upon which such a
> distinction may be founded: And 'tis as impossible to fulfil the
> *second* condition; because we cannot prove *a priori*, that these
> relations, if they really existed and were perceiv'd, would be

universally forcible and obligatory.

(*Treatise*, pp. 465–6)

The general direction of the passage is to point out that there is a distinction between the relation of rightness and the motivation to act. A psychological motive is taken to be the same as a physical motive: a push/pull which forces us to move in a certain way. This is Hume's standard psychological mechanism, and is what he means when he subtitles the *Treatise* 'An attempt to Introduce the Experimental [i.e. Newtonian] method of Reasoning into Moral Subjects'. The passage then becomes a challenge to the Rationalists in terms of Books I and II of the *Treatise*. Even if we could see rightness *a priori* by means of certain relations, this does not mean we should be moved to do right acts (cf. Bk. II, esp. iii, 3). And in fact we cannot know *a priori* that we should be so moved, for this is a causal relationship, and we can know nothing about causal relationships *a priori* (Bk. I). So the Rationalist has come up against another insoluble problem, and this even after we have granted him what he can not show (problem A), that there is a way in which vice and virtue can be based on relations.

The point that everyone has overlooked is that when Hume uses— and italicizes—the word 'obligatory', he is talking about this Newtonian kind of motivation. This is a common way of using the words 'obligatory' and 'obligation' (and 'ought') in the moral writings of that part of the eighteenth century. Thus Berkeley in *Alciphron* (1732) says that previous moralists of whom he approves 'took great pains to strengthen the obligation to virtue' (Bk. I, sect. 13), and Hutcheson defines 'obligation' as 'a motivation . . . sufficient to determine . . . a certain course of action' (*An Inquiry concerning Moral Good and Evil*, 1725, Bk. VII, sect 1).[2] To speak of something as obligatory, then, is to say that there is some motive for doing it, some psychological mechanism which provides the force for it to move us.

Hume begins the passage by saying that the effects of these relations (of rightness, etc.) are supposed to be necessarily the same, and he italicizes 'effects'. That is, they must move all rational creatures to act; this is the whole point of moral judgments. Then come the key sentences: ' 'Tis one thing to know virtue, and another to conform the will to it. In order, therefore, to prove that the measures of right and wrong are eternal laws, obligatory on every rational mind, 'tis not sufficient to show the relations upon which they are founded: We must also point out the connexion betwixt the relation and the will.' We have already seen how Hume uses one part of this as a challenge to the Rationalist to show how morality becomes obligatory, how it acquires the force by which it moves us to act. Hume can answer the challenge in terms of a push/pull which can only be a passion (reason being powerless in this respect—II, iii, 3), so that men end up being *prima facie*, though not necessarily finally, moved to do what they are obliged to do. But it is important that we keep in mind the other part of what Hume is saying here as well: that there is therefore a distinction between 'right and wrong' on one hand and 'obligation' on the other. It is hard for us to accept this because we tend to identify a right act with one which is obligatory, perhaps by definition. But in Hume's sense, where obligation includes motivation, it is always possible to ask 'Why ought I (why am I obliged to) do what's right?', and the answer has to be something that moves us. For Hume, a first-person moral judgment is promoted by a passion, which creates a *prima facie* motivation in fact, not merely in principle. Hence it is theoretically possible for something to be right but not obligatory, and Hume is careful to keep these terms distinct. In fact, if the Rationalists are right about morality being a matter of relations, then right and obligation would be separate in fact as well as in principle, unless they can show how 'these relations [of rightness, etc.], if they really existed and were perceiv'd, would be universally forcible and obligatory'.

Hume then goes on to 'make these general reflections more clear and convincing' (*Treatise*, p. 466) by illustrating them with particular instances. These are the arguments that are meant to prove that morality can not be based on relations, by showing that non-human objects are capable of entering into all the relations that humans are capable of. This is an expansion of Hume's challenge A to the Rationalists. And it seems that nothing more gets said about challenge B, as set out in the long paragraph I quoted.

This would leave Hume's argument incomplete, and would be odd in another way, since it is just after stating B that he says he intends to make these reflections more clear. And it turns out that B is not dropped completely after all. Hume has pointed out a distinction between making any kind of judgment—even a moral judgment—and acting on it, and has asked how it is that we are moved to act by these judgments. He does not say that it can not be done; he says that no relation alone can do it. Nor does he say that we could not know of such a relation, but only that we cannot know of it otherwise than by experience. The Rationalists, he says, cannot cope with this. But Hume can, and does, although the placement of his answer—in a paragraph about reason not discovering any matter of fact which can be the basis of morality—makes it seem that he is still talking about A. For in the last sentence of the penultimate paragraph of the section, just after saying that 'when you pronounce any action . . . vicious, you mean . . . you have a feeling or sentiment of blame from the contemplation of it', he goes on to say:

Nothing can be more real, or concern us more, than our own

sentiments of pleasure and uneasiness; and if these be favourable
to virtue, and unfavourable to vice, no more can be requisite to
the regulation of our conduct and behaviour.
(*Treatise*, p. 469)

That is Hume's answer to the challenge B, which he expands elsewhere. No judgments necessarily move us to action. Judgments of pure
reason can never do so. But moral judgments are not 'relations alone';
they are connected with our feelings of pleasure and pain, which *do*
move us. This is how the 'obligation' comes into morality. If virtue is
(a name for) pleasurable sensation, we simply will be moved to do
virtuous acts—at least, those that we ourselves judge to be virtuous.
(The 'can' in 'Nothing can be more real, or concern us more . . .' must,
I take it, be a matter-of-fact 'can' for Hume, not a logical 'can'. That's
the way human nature is; it has nothing to do with a point of logic.
Indeed, Hume's whole point is to say that nothing about human nature
can be settled by pure logic; it must be studied experimentally.)

We can now return to the Hume's Law passage, which we left some
time ago, but there is still one general point to keep in mind. On a
broad view of the *Treatise*, it seems that Hume was more concerned
with explaining why we have certain mental phenomena than he was
in providing justifications for our having them. Given this, it may be
that, in saying that the sudden appearance of an 'ought' in any system
of morality must be 'observed and explained' and that 'a reason should
be given' how this 'ought' suddenly makes its appearance amidst a
series of factual propositions, Hume means not that we must justify the
jump from 'is' to 'ought', but that we must recognize that the jump
does happen and explain how it happens.

As to the Hume's Law passage itself, its interpretation now becomes
simple. *Hume's statement of Hume's Law has to do with obligation-and-
motivation in the sense we have discussed, and not with right (or value).*
He has just finished carefully distinguishing judgments of right from
judgments of obligation, and nowhere in the Hume's Law passage does
he say anything about judgments of right. The 'ought' statements he
does talk about here are just the judgments of obligation which he has
distinguished from any statement of fact that could not by itself move
us. Once again, from the passage containing B:

> These two particulars are evidently distinct. 'Tis one thing to know
> virtue, and another to conform the will to it. In order, therefore,
> to prove, that the measures of right and wrong are . . . *obligatory*
> on every rational mind, 'tis not sufficient to shew the relations
> upon which they are founded: We must also point out the con-
> nexion betwixt the relation and the will . . .
> (Hume's italics)

The 'is' statements which the Hume's Law passage says are not enough
to let us deduce these 'oughts' can include value judgments—right is
not the same as obligatory, although for morality to make sense judgments of right have somehow to be obligatory, that is, to be motivating. The passage says nothing about not being able to derive value
judgments from factual premises. It says that there is nothing that pure
reason can do to get us from any 'is' statements, including 'is' statements of value ('*x* is good', '*x* is right', '*x* is worthwhile'), to any
'ought' statements, which, in the first person at least, influence the will.
It is this influencing the will that is the 'new relation or affirmation'
that Hume says needs observing and explaining, and it is what he has
been saying all along with regard to obligation, or 'oughts'. There is
nothing in the Hume's Law passage about a 'quantum jump' into
talking about right and wrong, which he has carefully distinguished
from obligatory; there is nothing in the passage about right and wrong
at all. Reading the central part of the passage, then:

> . . . of a sudden I am surpriz'd to find, that instead of the usual
> copulations of propositions, *is*, and *is not*, I meet with no proposi-
> tion that is not connected with an *ought*, or an *ought not*. This
> change is imperceptible; but is, however, of the last consequence.
> For as this *ought*, or *ought not*, expresses some new relation or
> affirmation, 'tis necessary that it should be observ'd and explain'd;
> and at the same time that a reason should be given, for what seems
> altogether inconceivable, how this new relation can be a deduction
> from others, which are entirely different from it.'
>
> (*Treatise*, p. 469)

The 'new relation' is that of influencing the will, and this can not be a
deduction from others that are different from it, so the Rationalist
loses. But Hume has observed the new relation and has explained how
it can come from these relations plus the passions, in an absolutely
standard Humean way. Vice and virtue by themselves, like colours,
are 'perceptions in the mind', which makes them passions. The new
relation of obligation, of motivating force, comes from an impression of
reflection, in this case pleasure or uneasiness. And no more can be requisite to the regulation of our conduct.[3]

This ends the argument for this interpretation from content. From
context, the Hume's Law passage comes just two pages after he has
criticized the Rationalists for not seeing that reason, even if it appre-
hends a relation which makes acts right, can not make acts obligatory.
Hume says that he will give considerations for this and show that
reason alone can not discover the relations which make acts right (A).
He does the latter in the intervening pages. He shows that *he* can
answer the question of the relation between value judgments and

action (B), in the last sentence of the penultimate paragraph ('Nothing can concern us more, than our own sentiments of pleasure and un-easiness . . . no more can be requisite to the regulation of our conduct and behaviour.') What we do not yet have is anything making point B against the Rationalist 'more clear and convincing'. And the very next sentence begins the Hume's Law passage, which is to be taken as saying more specifically that the Rationalists, ignoring the passions, cannot answer the question.

It is also significant that the passage ends with the statement that attention to this point would 'let us see, that the distinction of vice and virtue is not founded merely on the relations of objects, nor is per-ceiv'd by reason.' This is the sentence that nearly everyone leaves out when quoting the passage, and it is the one that shows that the passage is still a part of Hume's general anti-Rationalist argument. Vice and virtue are not founded on relations of objects (A); if they were founded on reason, this would not explain how they force us to act (B). (He does not say that this proves that they are not founded on reason because B is not a proof at all, but merely a challenge to the Rationalist, which we see that he can not meet.) So the passage, which concludes Section 1, ends with a statement showing that it is an integral part of Hume's argument throughout the section.

A further consideration in favour of this reading comes from the *Enquiry concerning the Principles of Morals*. There is nothing in the *Enquiry* resembling the Hume's Law passage. Nor is there any chal-lenge to the Rationalists to show how value judgments lead us to act. The anti-Rationalist arguments, in Section 1 and Appendix I, are all aimed at showing that reason alone can not make moral distinctions (A). There is nothing saying that even if it could do this it could not make us act (B); and there is no (supporting) statement of Hume's Law.

This interpretation of the passage, of course, save's Hume's con-sistency. For there is nothing wrong with deriving an 'ought' from an 'is' in a way dependent on human nature, and then saying that the Rationalist can not do it by reason alone. In this way we can even placate those who insist that '*deduce*' means deduce, not infer by taking 'deduce' to mean just that, since the Rationalist is going to have to deduce this new relation—being obligatory, that is, being motiva-ting—from others that are entirely different from it, even if one of those others happens to be a relation of virtue.

Where does all this leave Hume in respect of current controversy over factual statements and normative ones? Well, nowhere—at least as far as the Hume's Law passage is concerned. Given the right / value-*vs*-obligation / motivation interpretation of his distinction between 'is' and 'ought', the passage has nothing to say on the question of defining moral terms; for Hume is allowing that we may know what is right, or what 'right' is (although this is the province of Grammarians, not Philosophers), may know this from merely factual considerations, and then, oddly enough to the modern moral ear, saying that this knowledge still is not shown to be obligatory, that knowing this will not necessarily move us. That is, he interprets the judgment of right as an 'is' statement ('x is right') from which an 'ought', which includes a motivation to act, cannot follow—not at least if we try to do it by pure reason. And this is not at all connected with the current meta-ethical dispute.

So Hume's Law, *Hume's* way, stands firmly in the eighteenth century, not the twentieth. Reading it as a part of his argument against the Rationalists, with specific regard to the motivating force of 'oughts', both makes Hume's position consistent and gives his argument a symmetrical finish. Some other reading of the passage might still be right; but then, that piece of coal might still not be burning.

1. In *any* sense of 'basis' (or, as Hume often puts it, 'foundation' or 'origin'), whether logical or causal or psychological. The seventeenth and eighteenth centuries were unclear on this, just as they were on whether 'morals' meant 'moral systems' or 'moral judgments'. For the purposes of this paper I will continue to use the word in the general way that Hume used it.

2. As late as 1785 we find the same use in Paley: 'A man is obliged when he is urged by a violent motive . . .' (*Principles of Moral and Political Philosophy*, ch. 2). See also Defoe *Journal of the Plague Year* (1725): 'Self preservation obliged the people to these severities'. And note on the Berkeley quote that if 'obligation' here were to mean something other than 'motivating force', then he would be speaking of strengthening the moral tie to being moral.

3. To forestall the possible objection that 'ought' and 'obligatory' are separate words: in the 18th century, they generally are not so. Thus Price, responding specifically to Hume's challenge B: 'It is not indeed plainer, that figure implies something figured . . . than it is that *rightness* implies *oughtness* (if I may be allowed this word) or *obligatoriness*.' (*A Review of the Principal Questions in Morals*, 1758, ch. VI.) But the word is almost never used—only three times each in the *Treatise* and *Enquiry*, and no entry in Johnson's Dictionary. 'Obligatory' is the word that is met with regularly; Hume is using 'ought' as an active verb equivalent.

Hume and the Concept of Pleasure

IN HUME'S philosophical writing there is a number of puzzles about pleasure. As on other topics, he writes at times in an infuriatingly imprecise manner, and from the text of the *Treatise* alone one may unearth a variety of *prima facie* incompatible claims, about, or involving pleasure. A standard response, on this and other points in Hume scholarship, is to stress the 'carelessness' of Hume's writing, and to combine this with what has come to be for many the accepted account of Hume on virtually everything. It is assumed that, for Hume, pleasure and pain are in the end private experiences of some sort (simple impressions), which are identified introspectively, and named without essential reference to any public criteria or form of expression. Although Hume does much to encourage such a view of the nature of the passions and of the moral sentiments there are, nonetheless, residual difficulties in it that are of particular significance for Hume's account of pleasure. Granted the fundamental importance of the concept of pleasure for Hume's moral theory it is surprising that comparatively little attention has been paid by his interpreters both to elucidating the significance of the passages that do not fit the standard account, and indeed to formulating a general account of Hume on pleasure. This paper will attempt to press the case for a rather fuller discussion of Hume on pleasure than is normally offered.

That there is such a standard view of Hume on the passions and moral sentiments should not require much in the way of substantiation, and I have already expounded and attacked the view elsewhere.[1] However, it will be of some value to attribute its propagation to specific sources, and, in addition to its exposition in Kenny and Broiles,[2] it is sufficiently widely established to be referred to in passing in a variety of otherwise admirable works not concerned primarily with Hume, one of which I shall quote by way of illustration:

> I an not saying that there are two sorts of objects, objects of sense and objects of reason, and that murder and vice belong to the latter category. I am not arguing over the inventory of the universe. It was G.E.Moore's solution in a similar predicament to increase the number of objects in the universe by one, and then call it 'good'. Hume's solution was to turn somewhere else ('into his own breast') where he could perceive or introspect something, because he thought that this was the sort of thing knowledge was or ought to be.[3]

The limitations of such an account are easier to establish than to interpret. The strategy of this paper will be to contest the general thesis as applied to pleasure, by arguing that in Hume's alleged moments of carelessness he is making substantial philosophical points. In what follows I shall not comment on those pleasures and pains which Hume classifies as bodily sensations:[4] rather, the discussion will focus upon those aspects of his treatment of pleasure and pain that have the most direct bearing on his account of moral approval.

Kemp Smith reminds us that Hume does not treat the concepts of pleasure and pain systematically, but 'only very cursorily, and only in their bearing on this or that special topic'.[5] Even then, however, his remarks seem to be rather disparate, perhaps even inconsistent. In fairly general terms Hume stresses the intimate involvement between pleasure and pain on the one hand, and virtue and vice on the other. 'Moral distinctions', he tells us, 'depend entirely on certain peculiar sentiments of pain and pleasure' (T 574). This is set in the context of the wider claim that pleasure or pain is 'the chief spring or actuating principle of the human mind'. In such a context it does seem initially to support the first of the four obvious possible interpretations of the sense of the 'dependence' of moral distinctions upon 'certain peculiar sentiments of pleasure and pain': these four interpretations are,

(i) that the moral distinctions are distinctions between different sorts of feelings, approval and disapproval, and that these feelings have as efficient causes respectively, pleasure and pain;

(ii) that the distinctions drawn between feelings of approval and disapproval *are* distinctions between feelings of pleasure and pain;

(iii) that to draw moral distinctions is to have particular sorts of feelings, and that one criterion to be used in denominating them feelings of *moral* approval and disapproval is the presence or absence of *particular sorts of* pleasure or pain;

(iv) that the object or end of moral action is the pursuit of pleasure and the avoidance of pain. This fourth interpretation raises issues rather different from the other three and I shall not consider it further in this paper.

Each of these interpretations can find some support in the writings of Hume, and each has been canvassed by one or other of the Hume commentators. Yet there is a *prima facie* implausibility in the expectation of finding all or even some of them compatible. How, it might be asked, can pleasure be both the *cause* of a feeling of approval and a *criterion* that helps us decide that it is approval? Or again, how can it be either of these, and also *be* the feeling of moral approval? My argument will be that interpretations (i), (ii) and (iii) can each be stated in a fashion that renders them compatible with one another, and that a refusal to see this can be traced largely to the application of what I have called the standard[6] view of Hume to his concept of pleasure, that is, to an account of Hume's concept of pleasure as an inner 'sensation' recognized by introspection, but otherwise defying characterization. A corollary of this is that the approach to Hume's account of pleasure *via* Book III of the *Treatise* rather than *via* Book I may well result in establishing a rather different emphasis in interpretation.

(i) In addition to the general comments already quoted from Book III, other passages offer clear evidence that Hume was prepared to see pleasure and pain as causes of the moral sentiments. In *Treatise* II, i, 7, in the course of a discussion designed to substantiate the view that pride and humility have dual roots in the manner described in his account of 'the double relation of impressions and ideas', Hume entertains as one possible view of the relation between virtue and pleasure the view that 'the pain and pleasure . . . [are] the primary causes of vice and virtue' (*T*296). But he also makes the important point that, as in the case of pride and humility, there are other causal factors at work. A further possibility envisaged in this crucial passage is that 'the very essence of virtue . . . is to produce pleasure, and that of vice to give pain'. Pleasure may on this view be the effect of virtue.

(ii) There are several passages in which Hume seems to equate sentiments of vice and virtue with pleasure and pain. The most unambiguous is his passing comment in *Treatise* II, iii, 9 (*T*439), 'beside good and evil, or in other words pain and pleasure . . .', but earlier in Book II he states explicitly, 'The uneasiness and satisfaction are not only inseparable from vice and virtue, but constitute their very nature and essence' (*T*296). In Book III we find a similar identification: 'To have the sense of virtue, is nothing but to *feel* a satisfaction of a particular kind from the contemplation of a character. The very *feeling* constitutes our praise or admiration' (*T*471). The puzzle, here, of resolving Hume's disparate suggestions that pleasure can be a cause of the moral sentiments as well as their effect, and also that it can in some sense *be* the sentiment of virtue, requires that we remind ourselves that, for Hume, there were many different kind of pleasure.

The question of the discrimination between different sorts of pleasure will be considered in due course. At this stage of the argument, however, the various hypotheses offered about the role of pleasure as cause, effect and constituent part of virtue are each compatible with the 'standard' view that pleasure is a private feeling identified by introspection. The grounds for challenging this view will be offered following discussion of the third interpretation of the sense of the 'dependence' of moral distinctions upon 'certain peculiar sentiments of pleasure and pain'.

(iii) The central textual support for viewing the presence of pleasure as a criterion in moral evaluation is to be found in Book III: 'The distinguishing impressions, by which moral good or evil is known, are nothing but *particular* pains or pleasures' ($T471$). Two points require to be noticed: firstly, the stress on the word 'particular', and secondly, Hume's insistence, several sentences later in the same paragraph, that 'We do not infer a character to be virtuous, because it pleases'. Hume is not re-introducing reason (cf. 'infer') as the arbiter of morality but he does wish to avoid saying what the 'standard' view seems to impute to him, namely, that moral approval is a simple sentiment of pleasure which, when experienced, is immediately known. Such a view ignores the variety to which Hume testifies in the section quoted above. '. . . 'tis evident, that under the term *pleasure*, we comprehend sensations, which are very different from each other, and which have only such a distant resemblance, as is requisite to make them be express'd by the same abstract term.' ($T472$)[7]

The variety of pains and pleasures should, and does, pose a problem for Hume, the problem of how we may discriminate between different pleasures and between different pains. Significantly, Hume does not at any point suggest that it is a simple matter of introspective discrimination as Kovesi and numerous others have implied. It should be emphasized, however, that the appeal to criteria is not to settle what ought to be morally approved, but is to settle when we are having the 'particular' sentiment which *is* moral approval.

My proposal for reconciling interpretations (i), (ii) and (iii) is this. There is a causal story to be told about the arousal of moral approval. One of the causal conditions, and perhaps, though not necessarily, the efficient cause, is the presence of pleasure. This pleasure is not, of itself, however, moral approval. It may be undifferentiated pleasure, or it may, in some cases, be the pleasure involved in liking someone or some state of affairs. In the former case, moral approval presupposes that this undifferentiated pleasure becomes more specific—a 'particular' pleasure. In the latter case, two presuppositions make possible the transformation of liking into approval: (1) Hume's theory of association, and (2) his view that the many different types of pleasure do, in their variety, *resemble* one another. That there is such a precise difference between liking and approving is important for Hume's moral theory, and Hume indicates as much in his clear characterization of the distinction:

> Nor is every sentiment of pleasure or pain, which arises from characters and actions, of that *peculiar* kind, which makes us praise or condemn. The good qualities of an enemy are hurtful to us; but may still command our esteem and respect. ($T472$)

It is only the pleasure that 'makes us praise' is that both part of moral approval and is a *criterion* of whether or not what we feel is moral approval.

As we see then, Hume can offer a causal account of the role of pleasure in moral approval that is compatible with the appeal to pleasure as a criterion, but that does not pre-suppose that pleasure is to be treated as a private sensation available only to introspection. Indeed, quite the reverse is true since Hume deals with the question of the discrimination between pleasures without mentioning introspection.

In Book III Hume confronts explicitly a fear that is bound to arise concerning any attempt to give a causal account of moral approval that traces the latter back to particular sentiments; such an account seems to imply a contingent relation between moral approval and its objects.

> Now it may . . . be objected to the present system, that if virtue and vice be determin'd by pleasure and pain, these qualities must, in every case, arise from the sensations; and consequently any object, whether animate, or inanimate, rational or irrational, might become morally good or evil provided it can excite a satisfaction or uneasiness. (*T*471)

Hume's solution to the problem is to specify three conditions that are necessary for the correct application of the term 'moral approval' to the sentiment in question:

(i) that the sentiment in question is pleasurable rather than painful;

(ii) that the object of our sentiment is a person;[8]

(iii) that the pleasure is one which could be felt by a disinterested person contemplating the same situation.

Ipso facto these conditions specify the 'particular pleasure' in question: it is one that has as its object a person; and it is one that is had by a person whose relation to the situation in question is one of disinterestedness. These conditions specify criteria, not discoverable through introspection, for determining whether the pleasure in question is the pleasure of moral approval. They show, *inter alia*, that Hume was worried by the epistemological question of how we may know which sentiments are being experienced, and that *ipso facto* in working out his moral theory he rejected any tendency in Books I and II of the *Treatise* that would answer this question in terms of the immediacy of introspection.

Undoubtedly, there were influences at work in the composition of Book III of the *Treatise* that might lead Hume to regard pleasure as a private and introspectable experience. His inheritance of Locke's 'way of ideas' and his modified version of it in Book I both point strongly in this direction. That he saw in general, but limited, terms the inadequacy of Locke's terminology and theory is clear from his footnote explicitly correcting Locke's use of the term 'idea' (T_2).

But beyond this, his treatment of philosophical questions, as well as his sensitivity to the human experiences that gave them form, stretched to breaking point this particular philosophical tradition. Hume attempted to deal with these ruptures in his development of a 'science of man', but what never seemed clear to him, as it became clear to Kant, was the need to jettison the terminology, and the conceptual implications, of the whole 'way of ideas'. At points, however—and his treatment of pleasure in the context of his moral theory is one of them— Hume did step beyond 'the way of ideas'.

Certainly pleasure and moral approval are both classified as sentiments, and thereby both are easily accommodated on the 'impressions' side of the impression-ideas division, but both, as we have seen, are individuated in a fashion quite independent of procedures derivable from 'the way of ideas'. Certainly also, for Hume, pleasure is an experience, and thereby episodic, but equally certainly what makes a pleasure the particular pleasure indicative of moral approval has to do not with some fine inner quality or *timbre* of the experience, but rather with the object of the experience, and also with the beliefs which are at least partly constitutive of it: beliefs, that is, about one's real or sympathetically imagined relationship to the person who is the object of the approval.

Whether or not one accepts these views it cannot be disputed that they involve substantial philosophical claims. They were also, as far as Hume was concerned, expressions of general truths about human beings. Whether claims of a conceptual or an empirical nature, they certainly cannot be regarded, as the 'standard' view seems to imply, as minor inconsistencies of no great significance for the interpretation of Hume on pleasure, or indeed on other aspects of experience.

1.   'Hume on Morality and the Emotions' *Philosophical Quarterly* (January 1976).
2.   cf. A. Kenny *Action, Emotion and Will* (London: Routledge and Kegan Paul 1963) and R. D. Broiles *The Moral Philosophy of David Hume* (The Hague: Nijhoff 1964).
3.   J. Kovesi *Moral Notions* (London: Routledge and Kegan Paul 1967) p. 19.
4.   cf. *Treatise*, p. 192. All other quotations from the *Treatise* will be noted as ' *T* ' plus page number, e.g. 'T 192'.
5.   cf. *The Philosophy of David Hume* (London: Macmillan & Co. 1941) p. 162.
6.   I apologise for this barbarous shorthand. My hope is that the view in question is sufficiently common to be recognized even under this contentious name.

7.   From the context it is clear that the word 'sensations' is here used in a much wider sense than the earlier classification of *some* pains and pleasures as 'impressions conveyed by the senses' (*T* 192).

8.   Since this aspect of Hume's moral theory has had less attention than it deserves I quote the following

      'Now virtue and vice are attended with these circumstances.

      They must necessarily be plac'd either in ourselves or others . . .' (*T* 473).

Other papers presented at the Conference

A Dilemma in Hume's Account of Force and Vivacity
   Robert F. Anderson, University of Nebraska

A Short Note on the so-called 'Probabilism' of Hume as reflected in the so-called 'Analytical Index' of Selby-Bigge
   Oruc Aruoba, Hacettepe University

Hume's Conception of Hope and Fear
   Sidney Axinn, Temple University

Hume's Theory of Justice in the *Treatise* and *Of the Original Contract*
   Luigi Bagolini, University of Bologna

Causality without Association in Hume
   Lewis W. Beck, University of Rochester

Custom, Cause and Cohesion in Hume
   Christopher J. Berry, University of Glasgow

Hume on Self-Identity and Memory
   John I. Biro, University of Oklahoma

Body Ex-Humed
   Ronald J. Butler, University of Kent

Self and Substance in Hume's Ontology
   Nicholas Capaldi, City University of New York

David Hume's Leviathan
   John R. Carnes, University of Colorado

Hume's Scepticism
   Houghton B. Dalrymple, University of Texas

Hume on Virtues and Natural Abilities
   N. J. H. Dent, University of York

Hume on Is and Ought
   W. D. Falk, University of North Carolina

In Defence of David Hume
   Ronald J. Glossop, Southern Illinois University

Hume's Nominalism Reconsidered
   Donald Gotterbarn, University of Southern California

Hume's Idea of Necessary Connexion
   O. Hanfling, the Open University

Hume's Labyrinth
   W. Dean Hazelton, Wheaton College

Moral Attitudes in Hume's *Treatise*
  Thomas K. Hearn Jr, University of Alabama
Hume on Belief
  Michael Hodges and John Lachs, Vanderbilt University
Virtuous Motives in the *Treatise*
  Vincent M. Hope, University of Edinburgh
In Sympathy with Hume
  John Iorns, Victoria University of Wellington
Hume's 'True' Scepticism
  Oliver A. Johnson, University of California
Hume's Conception of Knowledge and of Philosophy
  Peter Jones, University of Edinburgh
Hume's Historical Empiricism
  Donald W. Livingston, Northern Illinois University
Is Hume a Meta-Ethical Non-Cognitivist?
  Robert J. McShea, Boston University
Hume, Whitehead and Philosophic Method
  Kenneth R. Merrill, University of Oklahoma
Hume and Peirce on Habit
  David L. Miller, University of Texas
On Hume's Doctrine of Simple Resemblance
  Jerome Neu, University of California
Facts, Values and the Artificial
  Eileen O'Keefe, Polytechnic of North London
Hume on the Function of Tragedy
  Margaret M. Paton, University of Edinburgh
Hume's Problem about the Self
  Roland Puccetti, Dalhousie University
Reflection, Reflexion and Introspection
  J. Douglas Rabb, Lakehead University
Time, Space and Impressions
  Bernard E. Rollin, Colorado State University
On Hume's Is–Ought thesis
  David C. Stove, University of Sidney
The Critique of Causality in Malebranche and Hume
  Jean Theau, University of Ottawa
The Articulate Voice and God
  Stanley Tweyman, York University, Ontario
Hume and Inductive Rationality
  Bernt Vestre, University of Oslo

Hume's Attack on Abstract Ideas
  Gerald Vision, Temple University
Determinism and an Open Future
  Charles G. Werner, University of Miami
Some Humean Distinctions Reconsidered
  Ian R. Wilson, University of Stirling
Hume's View of 'Is–Ought'
  D. C. Yalden-Thomson, University of Virginia

reason, 10, 24, 33–4, 38n20, 47, 93–4,
 104, 108, 124, 128
 distinctions of, 73, 74
Reid, T., 23, 24, 25, 69, 70–1, 75, 105,
 121
religion
 as a social phenomenon, 2, 15
 distinctions of, 205–6, 208–9
 empiricism and, 9–10, 14
 erected on philosophical scepticism, 5,
 17
 Hume's view of, 2, 13–14, 15, 16,
 77, 103, 104, 107–8
 morality and, 9, 15, 16
 natural, 1, 14–19, 107, 130–1, 133,
 140
 orthodoxy, 7. 9, 132
 philosophical, 2, 15, 17–18, 107
 Pietist, 100–1
 politics and, 43, 44–5, 48–9
 rational, 15, 17–18, 107
 revealed, 1, 15, 17–19, 107, 131,
 132–3, 197
 'vulgar', 15, 18,
'religious hypothesis', 16, 18, 44–5,
 48–9, 111
rhetoric, 20n4, 42
Rousseau, J-J., 15, 42, 105, 144
rule of law, 41, 70
Russell, Bertrand, 61, 112

scepticism
 ambivalence in, 3, 5, 12, 14
 anti-rationalists' use of Hume's, 101–
 2, 105, 111–13
 causal, 156–63
 dialectic of, 118, 124–5
 dialogue form and, 3, 5
 in politics, 41–2
 mitigated, 3, 5, 17–18, 19, 20n5, 83
 philosophical, 15, 17
 Pyrrhonian, 20n5, 83–4, 87, 89
science(s)
 applied, 94
 imagination in, 27–9, 30, 35–7
 natural, 93–4, 98, 103, 110, 113
 Newtonian, see Newtonian
 reductionism and, 75
 theory of, 28–9, 35–6, 71–2
Scott, Sir Walter, 42
Scottish Enlightenment, 40, 42, 49–50,
 71–6, 104, 112
Selby-Bigge, L. A., 192–3
self
 -identity, 109–10, 111, 124, 167–72
 -interest, 188, 191–3, 198
 -love, 190, 192, 197, 199

Sextus Empiricus, 19, 125
Smith, Adam
 and the *Dialogues*, 1, 5, 16, 22n35
 contribution to social science, 40–1
 Essays, 25, 26
 estimate of Hume, 24, 29, 69, 70
 'History of Astronomy', 25–6, 28, 36,
 70
 influence of Hume on, 23–37, 44, 71–2
 on imagination, 27–30, 35–7
 on Natural Law, 43–4
 on political science, 40–2, 45
 Theory of Moral Sentiments, 29, 40
 Wealth of Nations, 30, 40, 42, 43, 45, 70
Smith, N. Kemp, 1, 24–5, 51, 76, 103,
 105, 106, 117, 131, 139–40, 159,
 193, 194, 219
social
 change, 40–1
 contract, 45
 science, 40–1, 70
Socrates, 13, 104, 105, 120
space, 124, 178, 185
Spinoza, B., 104, 109, 110, 112
S-Q thesis, 175, 179–80
state of nature, 45, 46, 48
Steuart, Sir James, 42
Stoics, 78
Strahan, W., 1, 190, 199
supernatural, the, 16, 17, 18, 19, 206,
 208, 209
superstition, 15, 90, 103, 119, 130,
 132–3, 205, 206
symbolic act, 205–9
sympathy, 25, 44, 141, 143, 194, 196
Swift, J., 2, 132

theism, 2, 3, 12, 14, 16, 131
theology, 8, 44, 77–8, 107
time
 causation and, 149–50, 171
 Hume's account of, 178, 181–5
 points of, 146, 147, 148–9
Treatise, 1, 23–4, 27, 28, 37, 51, 69–
 76, 100, 110, 119–20, 139–44
truth, 94, 97, 98, 109, 110, 140, 146–7

utilitarianism, 96, 112, 141
utility, 24, 29–30, 46, 140–1

value judgments, 215–16
virtue
 and vice, 212, 216, 220, 222
 artificial, see artificial
 motive to, 187, 188, 190, 191, 192, 197
 pleasure and, 214, 219, 220, 222

Williams, B., 77, 78, 79, 81